Economic Change in Modern Indonesia

Indonesia is often viewed as a country with substantial natural resources, which has achieved solid economic growth since the 1960s, but which still faces serious economic challenges. In 2010, its per capita GDP was only 19 per cent of that of the Netherlands, and 22 per cent of that of Japan. In recent decades, per capita GDP has fallen behind neighbouring countries such as Malaysia and Thailand and behind China. In this accessible but thorough new study, Anne Booth explains the long-term factors that have influenced Indonesian economic performance, taking into account the Dutch colonial legacy and the reaction to it after the transfer of power in 1949. The first part of the book offers a chronological study of economic development from the late nineteenth to the early twenty-first century, while the second part explores topics including the persistence of economic nationalism and the ongoing tensions between Indonesia's diverse regions.

Anne Booth is Emeritus Professor of Economics in the Department of Economics at SOAS, University of London. Her chief area of interest has been Southeast Asia with a particular interest in Indonesian economic history in the twentieth century.

Economic Change in Modern Indonesia

Colonial and Post-colonial Comparisons

Anne Booth

SOAS, University of London

CAMBRIDGE
UNIVERSITY PRESS

University Printing House, Cambridge CB2 8BS, United Kingdom

Cambridge University Press is part of the University of Cambridge.

It furthers the University's mission by disseminating knowledge in the pursuit of education, learning and research at the highest international levels of excellence.

www.cambridge.org
Information on this title: www.cambridge.org/9781107109223

First published 2016.

Printed in the United Kingdom by Clays, St Ives plc

A catalogue record for this publication is available from the British Library

Library of Congress Cataloguing in Publication data
Booth, Anne, 1946– author.
Economic change in modern Indonesia : colonial and post-colonial comparisons / Anne Booth.
Cambridge, United Kingdom : Cambridge University Press, 2016. | Includes bibliographical references and index.
LCCN 2015041801| ISBN 9781107109223 (hardback) | ISBN 9781107521391 (paperback)
LCSH: Indonesia – Economic conditions. | Indonesia – Economic policy.
LCC HC447 .B6747 2016 | DDC 330.9598–dc23
LC record available at http://lccn.loc.gov/2015041801

ISBN 978-1-107-10922-3 Hardback
ISBN 978-1-107-52139-1 Paperback

Contents

Tables

Acknowledgements

In the 1960s, the literature on the Indonesian economy was sparse and pessimistic in tone. Despite the improvement in economic performance after 1965, the economic future of the largest country in Southeast Asia was, for at least two decades, still considered uncertain, and very dependent on a few key commodities, especially oil. Much has changed since the 1980s, and anyone, in the early twenty-first century, attempting a survey of Indonesian economic performance in both the colonial and post-colonial eras must deal with a large body of literature from a range of sources. At the very least such a survey should try to convey both the achievements and the failures of successive governments from the early 1900s until the fall of Suharto in 1998. It should also try to engage with the more recent literature which examines the implications for the Indonesian economy of the post-Suharto political changes, most of which came as a considerable surprise to economists, both Indonesian and foreign, who had worked in the country over the decades from the late 1960s to the late 1990s.

In writing this book, I have drawn on my own work in Indonesia, which began when I first went to Indonesia as a student in the early 1970s. Since then I have benefited enormously from interaction with many scholars from various parts of the world including Australia, the Netherlands, the United States and Japan, all of whom find Indonesia as fascinating as I do. I am most grateful for their willingness to share their research with me. In particular I am especially grateful to Thomas Lindblad and his colleagues at Leiden University who have invited me to several important seminars over the years, especially the one held in Leiden in October 2008 on the Indonesian economy in the 1950s, which resulted in a special issue of the journal *Itinerario* in 2010. The editors have allowed me to draw on an article originally published in this journal in Chapter 3 of this book.

I have also benefited from teaching courses on the economic development of Southeast Asia at the School of Oriental and African Studies in London since the early 1990s, as well as giving lectures and seminars on Indonesia and Southeast Asia in various locations around the world, from the United States, Australia and Germany to Tokyo and Beijing. Different audiences raise different questions about Indonesian economic development, but in all cases they have forced me to rethink some cherished opinions and re-examine my ideas on the achievements and failures of Indonesian economic development, both in the colonial era and subsequently.

I also owe an enormous debt to the many Indonesians who over the years have helped me come to a better understanding of their remarkable country. I am especially grateful to those institutions which have invited me to give lectures and participate in seminars, including the Indonesian Institute of Sciences (LIPI) and the Centre for Strategic and International Studies (CSIS) in Jakarta, the Bogor Agricultural Institute and Gadjah Mada University in Yogyakarta. I must also thank the Central Board of Statistics in Jakarta, who over the years have helped me, along with many other scholars, to access and evaluate a range of statistical data. Their invaluable website has allowed me to complete this book over the last year without having to leave my study in London. Such are the marvels of modern technology! I am also grateful to the Indonesian Regional Science Association (IRSA), which invited me to give a keynote lecture to their conference in Makassar in 2014, and to interact with many scholars both Indonesian and foreign who have been working on aspects of regional policy in Indonesia in recent years. I do not expect that all Indonesians will agree with the views expressed in this book, but I hope that my ideas will serve to stimulate further discussion about the economic future of this important country.

1 Introduction

Indonesia's three watersheds

Indonesia's three watersheds

Many countries have had, at some point in their history, watershed moments when the opportunity seems to arise to wipe the slate clean and make a new beginning. Such moments often arise after wars or after revolutions or some other political upheaval which lead to a regime change, and the chance to start afresh. Typically at such times, new policies are introduced which seek to bring about political, economic, constitutional, administrative or social change, or some combination of all these. Not infrequently, reforms which most observers would have thought impossible under the old regime are implemented with surprising rapidity and apparently with little opposition. In many parts of Asia and Africa, such a watershed moment occurred with the granting of political independence. Beginning with the decision by the American government to grant the Philippines full independence in 1946, all the major states of Asia had achieved either self-government or full political independence by 1960.

The Indonesian struggle for independence began in the immediate aftermath of the Japanese capitulation to the Allied powers in August 1945. Two key leaders of the independence struggle, Sukarno and Hatta, under considerable pressure from younger, more radical activists, declared Indonesia's independence on 17 August 1945, a date that has been enshrined as Indonesia's national independence day ever since.[1] But in the aftermath of this declaration, the transfer of power to an independent government in Indonesia did not take place smoothly. The Dutch officials who had fled to Australia when the Japanese armed forces swept through the archipelago in 1942 returned in the wake of the British army in the latter part of 1945.[2] Even the more progressive among them were

---

[1] There are many studies of this period in Indonesian history; a good overview of the literature can be found in Ricklefs (2001: 247–86).

[2] Accounts of the British occupation and the return of the Dutch can be found in van der Post (1996), McMillan (2005) and Bayly and Harper (2007: 158–89).

determined to re-establish Dutch control over the entire archipelago and regarded the leaders of the independence movement, especially Sukarno and Hatta, as little more than lackeys of the Japanese who had no support among the Indonesian masses. These opinions were supported by almost the entire population of the Netherlands who feared that 'the loss of the Indies' would spell ruin for the Dutch economy, already severely weakened by the German occupation. It took more than four years of armed struggle and negotiations brokered by foreign powers and the infant United Nations before the Dutch finally recognised that they could no longer withstand the winds of change sweeping across Asia.

The final transfer of power to the Republic of the United States of Indonesia took place on 27 December 1949. This is not a date that Indonesians celebrate, but it should be regarded as the first of the great watersheds in Indonesia's post-independence history. At last Indonesia was an independent nation, taking its place among other sovereign powers in the international community. In international forums such as the United Nations and the Non-Aligned Movement (which Indonesia helped to create) the new republic played a prominent role. But at home, economic and social problems mounted, and the next two decades were far from easy for the infant republic. Many of these problems had been inherited from the Dutch era, but after 1949 they had to be tackled by successive governments which often appeared weak and divided. Debates between what might be termed the economic rationalists and the economic nationalists erupted shortly after independence. These debates reflected deeper divisions about what to do with the remaining Dutch presence in plantations, mining, industry, banking and commerce, and about how to deal with the Chinese minority which dominated domestic private business and the professions.

To most Indonesians who had participated in the struggle for independence, it was taken for granted that in the colonial era the profits from exploiting the country's natural wealth had accrued either to the colonial government or to foreign-owned companies. In neither case, it was argued, did indigenous Indonesians benefit much, if at all. In common with many newly independent nations, the leaders of the Indonesian struggle for independence envisaged a major role for government in implementing an economic development strategy which would use the country's resource wealth to improve the living standards of the Indonesian people. But in the years after 1949, this proved an elusive goal.

In real per capita terms, government expenditures fell from the mid-1950s onwards, and increasingly they were diverted to military goals including the liberation of West New Guinea, which had remained under Dutch control after 1949, and the confrontation with Malaysia, a federation formed in 1963 from the territories in Southeast Asia controlled by the British. Accelerating inflation in Indonesia was accompanied by economic stagnation and mass poverty. As the economy deteriorated, the political situation became more fraught. An attempted coup in September 1965, during which six senior generals were killed, triggered mass killings of people affiliated to the Indonesian Communist Party. By early 1966 it was clear that power now lay with the army.

The struggle between Sukarno and the army, which was backed by urban student groups and some leading non-communist civilians, including the Sultan of Yogyakarta and Adam Malik, came to a head in March 1966.[3] On March 11, Sukarno and his cabinet fled from Jakarta to the presidential palace in Bogor. They were pursued by a trio of senior army officers who forced a reluctant Sukarno to hand over power to a group led by a little-known officer, Suharto. Although it was probably not obvious at the time, 11 March 1966 turned out to be the second great watershed in Indonesia's post-independence history. Suharto had escaped the slaughter of senior generals on 30 September 1965 and was not at first seen as much more than a transitional figure, likely to be shunted aside in further power struggles within the military. But matters turned out otherwise. The New Order initiated by Suharto, together with his military and civilian supporters, was to last until his resignation in May 1998.

During his thirty-two years in power, Suharto presided over a transformation of the Indonesian economy. Per capita GDP, which in 1960 was lower than in many other Asian and African economies, had risen more than fourfold by 1997 (Table 1.1). Indonesia also made considerable progress in human development. Educational enrolments increased at all levels, and there were sharp falls in infant and child mortality from the very high levels which prevailed in the early 1960s. Increasingly Indonesia was viewed internationally as a leading Asian success story. Along with Taiwan, South Korea, Thailand, Singapore and Malaysia, Indonesia was included in the 'Asian Miracle' report which the World Bank published in 1993. According to this report, it was an example of a high-performing economy, which in the words of one World Bank official seemed to have done almost everything right (Bruno 1994: 10).

---

[3] The Sultan of Yogyakarta had inherited his position as traditional leader of Yogyakarta from his father just before the Japanese occupation. After 1945, he supported the nationalist movement, and Yogyakarta became the capital of the new republic during the struggle against the Dutch. He remained a highly respected figure in independent Indonesia, and served for a term as vice president under Suharto. Adam Malik, a Sumatran, was foreign minister under Sukarno, but was considered to be anti-communist and served in several posts under Suharto.

Table 1.1 *Per capita GDP in 1960, 1997, 2004 and 2010: ASEAN countries and selected Asian and African countries (2005 international dollars)*

Country	1960	1997	2004	2010
ASEAN countries				
Singapore	4,398	34,900	39,879	55,839
Brunei	NA	49,386	50,713	44,543
Malaysia	1,453	9,477	10,173	11,962
Thailand	962	6,066	6,734	8,066
Indonesia	665	3,143	3,079	3,966
Philippines	1,466	2,561	2,715	3,194
Vietnam	NA	1,371	1,912	2,779
Laos	NA	1,290	1,605	2,620
Cambodia	NA	859	1,338	1,890
Other Asian and African countries				
Korea	1,670	17,365	21,807	26,614
China (V.1)	772	2,276	3,915	7,746
India	724	1,679	2,317	3,477
Ghana	1,289	1,348	1,592	2,093
Nigeria	1,558	1,126	1,559	1,693
Ivory Coast	959	1,481	1,297	1,283
DR Congo	691	242	196	240

Note: Data refer to per capita GDP, at 2005 prices, derived from growth rates of c, g and i. No data are available for Myanmar (Burma).
Source: Heston, Summers and Aten (2012).

When the Thai authorities were forced to float the baht in early July 1997, few observers expected that there would be much impact on neighbouring economies where economic fundamentals were thought to be sound. But it soon became clear that Indonesia was more vulnerable to the regional turbulence than had been anticipated. By early 1998, capital outflow was accelerating and the rupiah had plunged to a low of around 17,000 to the dollar, compared to 2,500 in June 1997. Debates continue about how to apportion the blame for the economic turmoil of late 1997 and early 1998, but by May 1998, the political consequences were clear. After serious riots broke out in Jakarta and several other cities, Suharto lost the confidence of his cabinet, let alone the wider nation, and on 21 May he resigned in favour of his vice president, B.J. Habibie. He went into retirement and died a decade later, in January 2008.

It was immediately clear that 21 May 1998 represented a further watershed in Indonesia's post-independence history. Not only did the country's second and longest-serving president leave office, but there was a wave of demands from many civil society organisations for radical political, economic and constitutional change. Economic collapse and mounting inflation in 1998 were accompanied by increasingly sweeping demands for reform. The new president was well aware of the shifts which had occurred in public opinion and tried to accommodate them with a series of legislative changes. But he too was swept from office a year later, in the wake of the violence in East Timor and in other parts of the country. The president who took office following elections in 1999, Abdurrahman Wahid, was a widely respected politician who had come to prominence through his leadership of *Nahdlatul Ulama*, one of the largest Islamic organisations in Indonesia.

But Wahid, who was in poor health, had difficulty controlling an increasingly restive parliament and a country which seemed at times determined to fulfil the dire predictions of many external observers that Indonesia was on the verge of breaking up. In July 2001, he was replaced by the leader of the party which had won the largest number of seats in the 1999 elections, Megawati Sukarnoputri, the daughter of the first president. But she also was a rather weak and indecisive leader who seemed to be increasingly under the influence of elements within the armed forces. When Indonesia held its first direct vote for a president in 2004, she was defeated by Susilo Bambang Yudhoyono, a retired military officer who had risen through the ranks under Suharto, but who presented himself, with considerable success, as a reforming candidate who would set Indonesia on a new economic and political trajectory.

Yudhoyono's first five years in power did achieve some progress on both the political and economic fronts. Regional violence was brought under control and economic growth accelerated. He was re-elected to office for a further term in 2009, at least partly as a result of his apparent success in protecting the economy from the global economic crisis which had erupted in 2008. Unlike several neighbouring economies in Southeast Asia, let alone the United States and Western Europe, Indonesia recorded positive economic growth in 2009, and after sixty years of independent nationhood, seemed once again to be on a stable growth trajectory. Official poverty estimates showed a decline in numbers below the poverty line. Demographic and social indicators were improving. Indonesia's membership of the G-20, along with India and China, appeared to accord the country recognition as an important rising power in the global economy.

In spite of the achievements in the years after 2004, there was still discontent with Indonesia's economic performance at the end of the first decade of the twenty-first century. Much of this discontent was fuelled by growing evidence that the pace of economic change in

Indonesia was slower than in countries such as China, India and Vietnam which twenty years previously had been well behind Indonesia. In terms of both per capita GDP and non-economic indicators such as life expectancy, educational enrolments and maternal mortality rates, Indonesia's progress seemed disappointing. Per capita GDP only returned to the 1997 level in 2004, by which time China had surged well ahead (Table 1.1). In addition the government seemed unable to deal with chronic bottlenecks in infrastructure. In Java, roads and railways built in the colonial era needed modernisation. A trans-Java highway was mooted in the 1970s, but progress was slow, and it remained uncompleted in 2014. Logistics experts argued that the country needed several new container ports to ease the chronic congestion in existing facilities. Outside Java, the road network was still undeveloped, and many people in rural areas were still not connected to markets and other facilities. Fifteen years after Suharto's departure from office, there were many critics of government performance.

What is this book about?

While it might, with the wisdom of hindsight, be easy to detect the principal watersheds in Indonesia's post-independence history, it is much more difficult to determine the extent to which the slate really was wiped clean, and the new regimes able to strike out in new directions. Can any society, especially one as large and complex as Indonesia, really jettison the past and start afresh? The main purpose of this book is to argue that, in spite of the progress which has occurred in Indonesia since 1950, a number of economic problems still persist. These problems can be viewed as legacies from the Dutch colonial era, but successive governments have not been able to resolve them, and at times have exacerbated them.

To develop this argument, it is essential to examine the economic legacy of the Dutch colonial era, and especially the legacy of the first four decades of the twentieth century, often called the 'ethical' era. As in many other former colonies, the view that the Dutch colonial state was exploitative and predatory, and prevented the economic advance of the indigenous population, was widely held among many Indonesians who participated in the struggle for national independence, and who assumed senior positions in the government after 1949. In Indonesia, as in many other former colonies, it became part of the ideology of post-independence nationalism, on which most of the key political leaders based their legitimacy, that colonialism was the main reason for the country's economic backwardness and widespread poverty. But was this really the case?

The economic legacy that the Dutch bequeathed to an independent Indonesia was, and remains, a contested issue. On the one hand, many nationalists stressed the negative aspects, including the exploitation of the country's national resources and the remittance of its profits abroad and the failure to invest in the education and health of the indigenous populations. The harsh terms of the economic and financial agreement reached before the Dutch finally conceded sovereignty in 1949 have also been stressed. But, on the other hand, the Dutch could point to an impressive amount of infrastructure, especially in Java, which was handed over to the new nation. In addition by 1942 the Dutch had created an integrated national economy stretching across much of the vast archipelago. Per capita GDP was around 22 per cent of that in the Netherlands in 1900, and there was little change over the next four decades, in spite of the impact of the global depression (Table 1.2). Chapter 2 of this study will try to assess both the benefits and costs of the Dutch legacy for the new republic.

It is often taken as self-evident that, in the years between 1949 and 1966, independent Indonesia failed to build on the positive legacies of the Dutch or remedy the negative aspects of the colonial legacy. Indeed most economists have tended to view these years as characterised by increasing economic turmoil, culminating in hyperinflation and mass poverty in the mid-1960s. In Chapter 3, it is argued that, while the conventional view is broadly correct, there were achievements which have often been overlooked, especially in sectors such as health and education. These early

Table 1.2 *Per capita GDP in Indonesia as a percentage of Netherlands, China, Japan and the United States, 1900–2010*

Year	Netherlands	China	Japan	USA
1900	22	135	62	18
1920	21	na	53	16
1930	19	191	59	17
1938	20	188	43	17
1950	14	182	43	9
1960	12	153	25	9
1970	10	158	13	8
1980	13	179	14	10
1990	15	134	13	11
2000	15	94	16	11
2010	19	59	22	15

Source: The Maddison Project data, downloaded from http://www.ggdc/maddison/maddison-project/home.htm, 2013 version.

post-independence years were also important in bridging divisions within Indonesian society between urban and rural areas and between regions and ethnic groups. Slowly the idea of Indonesia as a unified nation spread among the rapidly growing population, both in Java and elsewhere, even as rebellions erupted over issues such as the role of Islam in the new republic and the economic and constitutional relations between the central government and the regions.

The story of the Indonesian 'growth miracle' of the Suharto years is well known and has been much analysed. However, in spite of the broadly favourable assessments of most outside observers, including international agencies such as the World Bank, many Indonesians were by the early 1990s increasingly critical of Suharto's achievements. To them, it was far from obvious that the government led by an ageing and increasingly autocratic president was 'getting everything right'. Per capita GDP had certainly grown quite rapidly from the late 1960s onwards, but by 1990 it was still only 15 per cent of the Netherlands, 13 per cent of Japan, and 11 per cent of the United States (Table 1.2). There was also increasing concern about economic management. The technocrats who had played a key role in drafting and implementing policies from 1966 onwards had, by 1993, left the cabinet. To an increasing extent, they were replaced by people whose main attribute seemed to be a willingness to support the whims of the president, his family and their business cronies. The widespread perception that corruption and nepotism were increasing fuelled public discontent, especially among the educated young. But until late 1997 it was far from clear that those unhappy with Suharto's government had the power to bring about a regime change.

The increasing power of the presidential family and their business associates was not the only reason for public anger. In addition there was a growing perception that the economic growth which had occurred had not trickled down to many Indonesians. Although the official data claimed that poverty had declined sharply since 1970, the poverty line being used was very low. Many activists were outraged that government officials with lavish lifestyles considered that rural Indonesians in 1996 could live adequately on as little as 28,000 rupiah (under thirteen dollars at the prevailing exchange rate) per month. There was much critical discussion about the rise of large conglomerates, owned either by Indonesians of Chinese descent with close links to Suharto, or by members of the Suharto family. Many indigenous business people felt that small- and medium-scale businesses were being crowded out by larger and better-connected groups. Some of the largest conglomerates had taken advantage of the financial deregulation of the late 1980s to establish their own banks which lent mainly to firms connected with the conglomerates on very favourable terms. The problems of environmental degradation and deforestation also began to attract attention, especially from the growing number of non-government organisations. Underpinning much of this criticism was the growing influence and authority of Islam. Chapter 4 attempts to draw up a balance sheet of the Suharto years, looking at both the achievements and the failures.

In spite of the growing criticism of aspects of Suharto's economic policies, few predicted the severity of the economic collapse of 1997/98 or its economic and political consequences. The literature on what has become known as the Asian Financial Crisis is now enormous, and Chapter 5 presents a summary of this from an Indonesian viewpoint. Because the crisis of 1998 brought in its wake sweeping changes in Indonesia's political system, the six years between the resignation of Suharto and the election of Yudhoyono have often been viewed as lost years for economic reform. Chapter 5 assesses both the achievements and the failures of these years. Chapter 6 presents an evaluation of the Yudhoyono decade, in the light of the high expectations which followed his election in 2004. It will be argued that both the achievements and failures of the SBY decade have to be viewed in the context not just of the legacy from the Suharto era but also of Indonesia's earlier economic history.

Chapters 2 to 6 present a broadly chronological survey of Indonesian economic history from the early years of the twentieth century to 2014. The next three chapters are thematic. They examine a group of problems which can be viewed as legacies of the colonial era but which successive post-independent governments have found very difficult to tackle, let alone resolve. By 1999, Indonesia had been effectively independent for fifty years. By then, few observers, either within Indonesia or abroad, were inclined to blame the problems facing the country on the Dutch colonial legacy, or on policies adopted in the immediate post-colonial era. Surely over five decades, successive post-colonial governments had had ample time to build on the positive legacies of the colonial era, and to remedy the negative legacies? If they had not done this, and if by 2010 the economic gap between Indonesia and the developed world was still large, and indeed wider than it had been in the late colonial era, that must reflect deficiencies of policy-making in the post-independence era.

It was hardly surprising that the immediate post-independence years in Indonesia triggered demands for fundamental changes in both the political and the economic system, as was the case in many other former colonies. But there were often fierce debates about what these changes should be, and how they should be implemented. One debate which emerged very soon after the transfer of power was between economic rationalists and economic nationalists. Very often the arguments centred on Indonesia's economic and commercial ties with other countries. Many economic nationalists argued that during the colonial era, trade and investment links with the outside world had been based on the exploitation of Indonesia's natural resources and had brought little benefit to the great majority of the Indonesian population.

While these debates seemed to have been resolved in favour of the technocratic rationalists after 1966, they soon resurfaced and have continued to influence economic policy-making both before and after 1998. A mindset persisted in many political leaders and senior bureaucrats in both Java and the rest of the country that was often hostile to foreign trade and investment, especially when linked to resource exploitation. Another issue of great concern to economic nationalists was the role of the Chinese in the Indonesian economy, which has continued to be hotly debated through the Suharto era and beyond. Chapter 7 examines these various strands in the nationalist–rationalist debate since the 1950s.

Chapter 8 examines changes in living standards in Indonesia across the twentieth century. It is widely agreed that, while indicators relating to education, literacy and health have improved since 1949, poverty remains a serious problem. Indeed the perception that widespread poverty still persisted in Indonesia in the 1990s, after three decades of sustained growth, was one reason for the growing public disenchantment with the Suharto government. Since 1998 successive governments have implemented a range of 'social safety net' policies although their impact has been controversial. Data published by the World Bank and other agencies have shown that Indonesia, in the early twenty-first century, still has high levels of poverty in comparison with other countries in the Asian region including both China and Vietnam. Why have successive Indonesian governments been unable to spread the benefits of economic growth more widely among the entire population? Has the failure to implement agrarian reform policies since independence been responsible for continuing high levels of rural poverty, especially in Java? Chapter 8 addresses these questions.

Chapter 9 examines the changing role of government in Indonesia. Over the last four decades of Dutch rule, a broadly based tax system was put in place, together with a regulatory regime where the government took increasing responsibility not just for the provision of infrastructure but also for the regulation of production, and the provision of what became known as 'welfare' services. The first generation of post-independence leaders, many of them broadly socialist in their political views, thought that the state should take a leading role in the economy. While a strong central government was viewed as essential for rapid economic modernisation, there was also much discussion in the 1950s about the economic and financial links between the central government and the regions.

There were frequent accusations from those provinces producing most of the country's exports of a resource drain to Java, and they demanded a greater share of the tax revenues accruing from their exports. The problems were partially addressed in legislation passed in 1956, but the legislation was never implemented. The problems returned in the 1970s as revenues from the exploitation of natural resources, especially oil, became more important in the budget. It was only after Suharto left office that new legislation on centre-regional relations was passed. But it will be argued in Chapter 9 that the issues of the appropriate size and functions of the government in Indonesia, and the division of responsibilities between the centre and the regions, remained hotly contested.

When we look at Indonesian economic performance over the twentieth century and beyond, are we discussing success or failure? Certainly there has been considerable progress since the 1960s, not just in terms of GDP growth but also in terms of non-monetary indicators of living standards. But many Indonesians feel some disappointment that there has apparently been little catch-up with leading economies including the United States and Japan. In addition the gap in per capita GDP and other development indicators between Indonesia and other Asian economies including China, Thailand and Malaysia has widened since the 1960s. The final chapter presents an overview of Indonesia's economic performance, and discusses the constraints on future economic performance.

2   The colonial legacy

Colonial exploitation: some definitions

As was the case in many other former colonies, in Indonesia many people in the immediate post-independence era blamed most, if not all, of their problems on the legacy bequeathed to them by the colonial power. Many politicians, civil servants, academics and journalists took it as axiomatic that the Dutch had 'exploited the wealth of the Indies' and that this exploitation was the reason for the country's poverty. But what was meant by colonial exploitation? Landes (1961) suggested that a useful definition would link colonial exploitation to coercion, which leads to the employment of workers at wages lower than would prevail in a free labour market, or the purchase of products at prices lower than would obtain in free markets. More generally, according to Landes, colonial exploitation must imply constraints on the free operation of markets within the colonial territory.

This is a definition which has in fact been widely used in the literature in the decades since Landes suggested it; its relevance to Indonesia will be further discussed later. It can be extended to include the use of colonial markets as protected outlets for the surplus production of industries in the metropolitan countries. By the end of the nineteenth century, radical critics of Western colonialism attributed it at least partly to the need of industrial capitalism for ever larger markets. Metropolitan politicians wanting to justify colonial adventures to sceptical domestic electorates often used the argument that colonies could serve as captive markets for home produce (Landes 1998: 429–30). To what extent industrialisation in the metropolitan economies depended on colonial outlets remains a contested issue, with some economic historians denying the importance of colonial markets as an important factor in the industrial growth of the metropole (Bairoch 1993: Chapter 6; Lewis 1978: 30).

What seems more certain is that in most colonies, the metropolitan powers had little interest in fostering industrial growth, and indeed often pursued policies which led to de-industrialisation. The most famous

12

example is the demise of the textile industry in India in the nineteenth century, which lost not only most of its domestic market to foreign competition, but also its export markets. Williamson (2011: 64–5) has argued that similar de-industrialisation occurred in the Ottoman Empire, Indonesia and Mexico. Williamson, along with other economic historians, has analysed the impact of de-industrialisation on the terms of trade of tropical colonies. In most cases they became exporters of a narrow range of tropical commodities and importers of industrial goods. Thus they became very vulnerable to downturns in world prices of their major export commodities. In the Indonesian context, fluctuations in the prices of key commodities such as sugar, rubber and petroleum have had major consequences for economic performance, both before and after independence.

A further definition of colonial exploitation concerns the burden of taxation. Many pre-colonial governments in Asia and elsewhere taxed their populations heavily in labour and kind, as well as in money. Some defenders of European colonialism in Asia have argued that it brought about a rationalisation and lowering of tax burdens on the local populations, and thus curtailed the predatory nature of the state. But others have argued that colonialism simply replaced one form of fiscal predation with another. It has been argued that the imposition of cash taxes was frequently used as a means of forcing indigenous cultivators into the wage labour market, or into producing crops for sale. Following Landes, it has been asserted that, when workers were forced into wage labour to pay taxes, the wage rates were manipulated to benefit the main employers of labour, often large corporations domiciled in the colonial metropole. If they grew crops for sale, prices were often depressed below world market levels by export taxes or by state marketing boards.

Heavy taxation of indigenous populations could perhaps be justified if colonial governments used the revenues from taxes and non-tax revenues to provide infrastructure, education, health care and other modern services, which pre-colonial governments had neglected or been unaware of. Many studies in both Asia and Africa have stressed that colonial governments spent few resources in any of these areas. Infrastructure spending, when it took place, was usually skewed towards roads, railways and ports required by foreign enterprises in order to export agricultural and mineral products. For a range of reasons, little was done to provide either education or modern health services to indigenous populations; schools, hospitals and clinics, where they existed, were frequently provided by missions. To what extent did fiscal policy in colonial Indonesia conform to this pattern?

Another issue which has triggered a very large literature in the context of India, as well as in other colonial territories, concerns the 'drain' of capital out of the colony through the balance of payments. The argument is quite straightforward: metropolitan powers held back colonial development by implementing policies which led to substantial surpluses on the current account of the balance of payments, which in turn financed large and sustained outward flows of capital. The surpluses were the result of large surpluses of commodity exports over imports, which were not compensated by imports of services. Even where it could be demonstrated that the surpluses on the current account of the balance of payments were smaller than the trade balance, or even negative because of large deficits on services, the counter argument was that the service sector in most colonies was dominated by firms from the metropole, who often had monopolies over the provision of shipping, banking, insurance and other services and charged high prices. These debates have continued in studies of the economic history of many parts of Asia and Africa, but a consensus does appear to be emerging that at least some colonial economies did experience significant outflows of capital which were, in part at least, the result of large profits earned by companies based in the metropolitan power. We now examine this argument in the Indonesian context.

Economic development in Indonesia in the nineteenth century: the cultivation system

Virtually all discussions of Dutch policy in Indonesia in the nineteenth century focus on the system of forced cultivation of export crops, which was known in Dutch as the *cultuurstelsel*, and is usually translated into English as the cultivation system (CS). It was introduced by the Dutch government after the rather disappointing results from their attempts in the years from 1815 to 1830 to persuade private cultivators to produce crops for export (van Niel 1992: 137ff; see also Emmer 1998: 167, and van Zanden 2010: 159–62). Faced with a reluctance on the part of Dutch and other European capitalists to invest in agricultural plantations, the Dutch Governor-General, van den Bosch, persuaded the Dutch monarch to try a different approach to the cultivation of export crops which involved the imposition of government demands on individual villages to grow specific crops. It was argued that, given the fertility of the soils in Java, a family could produce enough rice and other foods for their own needs with only 120 labour-days. The Dutch plan was to coerce the population to use their 'surplus' labour time to produce export crops, such as sugar and coffee.

To begin with, the CS appeared to be successful. The growth in exports from Java accelerated rapidly and over the decade of the 1830s export growth was around 13 per cent per annum, and growth in per capita GDP was also positive (van Ark 1988: 114; van Zanden and Marks 2012: 50). The main reason for this success was that the principal political and commercial elites in Java (Dutch officials, the indigenous Javanese ruling class and the Chinese merchant community) all benefited from the system, and had an interest in making it work (van Zanden 2010: 163). But after 1840, growth of export production slowed considerably and never regained the dynamism of the 1830s. As a consequence, growth in GDP also slowed.

In addition, it became evident that the CS was having a detrimental impact on native welfare in at least some parts of Java. The Dutch authorities expected that the system would lead to a lightening of the tax burden on cultivators compared with the land tax imposed by Raffles, who headed the British administration in Java from 1811 to 1816 (Booth 1998: 19). It was therefore expected that the system would lead to an improvement in native welfare. But the reality was rather different. The 1840s were marked by growing food shortages and indeed famines in some parts of Java (Elson 1994: Chapter 4). A considerable proportion of the money paid out in crop payments was taken back by the government in the form of taxes, especially the land rent. Some money did stay in the villages; certainly the entire period seems to have been characterised by quite rapid growth of the money supply in Java (van Laanen 1989). But increasingly it was clear that the main beneficiaries of the CS were the indigenous ruling class, Dutch officials and the home government in the Netherlands.

The development of the CS had important implications for the Dutch economy, which several economic historians of the Netherlands have discussed. Van Zanden and van Riel (2004: 143) have described the growth of a 'colonial complex' in which industries such as shipbuilding, sugar refining and textiles in the Netherlands benefited from the growth in trade between the Netherlands and Indonesia. In the case of textiles, the Dutch limited exports from Britain into Java in order to protect the market for Dutch products (Booth 1998: 138). The budget of the Netherlands also benefited from the *batig slot*, which was the term used for the remittances on government account to the home budget. Van Zanden and van Riel (2004: table 5.1) estimate that in the 1830s, the remittances already accounted for around 32 per cent of tax income in the Netherlands, rising to 53 per cent by the 1850s, which was almost 4 per cent of Dutch GDP.

Given the benefits which the metropolitan government derived from the CS, not least in terms of a substantial contribution to the home budget, it might seem surprising that by the 1860s pressure was mounting in the Netherlands for a reform of the system. While moral outrage at the exploitation of native labour might have been one reason for this pressure, another was the realisation that a system based on coercion was expensive to maintain, especially as, with growing population, free wage labour was becoming more abundant (Boomgaard 1990). Van Zanden and van Riel (2004: 181–2) argue that one consequence of the growth of exports from Java after 1830 was that a rising merchant class became more influential, and by the 1860s they were confident that they could manage export agriculture more efficiently and at less cost to the budget than the increasingly discredited system of forced labour.

By 1850, the population of Java has been estimated to be 14 million, compared with 7.5 million in 1800 (Boomgaard and Gooszen 1991: 82). Part of this growth was probably due to higher birth rates, and part to public health measures, especially vaccination against smallpox, which reduced death rates. Some historians have argued that the higher birth rates were the direct result of intensified labour demands made on rural households although the evidence for this is contentious (White 1973; Alexander and Alexander 1971). The CS was formally terminated, at least in Java, with the liberal reforms of the 1870s but the legacy lasted well into the twentieth century. In particular, as Furnivall (1944: 174–5) argued, the idea that the colony was a business concern (*bedrif*) became entrenched in the minds of Dutch politicians, and the post-1870 reforms were significant mainly in that they admitted more shareholders. While the remittances from the colony to the Dutch budget had dwindled to nothing by the end of the nineteenth century, private enterprise and private individuals continued to remit profits until the end of Dutch colonial rule. It was the expectation of the liberal reformers that free markets for land and labour, as well as goods, would replace coercion, but in fact the indigenous populations of both Java and other parts of the country remained subject to coercion until well into the twentieth century.

Some Dutch historians have been harsh in their evaluation of the impact of the CS, both on the colonial economy and in the Netherlands. Emmer (1998: 169) argued that 'the cultivation system retarded the introduction of a modern market economy in Java and it also retarded the adaptation of the Dutch economy to the competitive capitalism of the 19th century'. Van Zanden and Marks (2012: 72) claim that it was 'arguably the most extreme example' of an extractive institution to have been introduced in any non-settler economy. These views, which have also been echoed by other writers, conflict with the much more optimistic assessment of Elson (1994: 305) that the CS 'promoted a previously unknown level of general prosperity among the peasantry'. This argument is based on an assertion that living standards in many parts of Java were very low before the CS began, which is not easy to prove or disprove. The national income data

assembled by van Zanden and Marks (2012: 50) indicate that per capita
GDP in Java grew only quite slowly between 1815 and 1840, and fell
between 1840 and 1860. Household consumption expenditures probably
fell in per capita terms. These figures do not suggest that living standards
on average improved significantly as a result of the CS, even if they were
low before the system began. There were gainers and losers within indigenous society, but the net impact on incomes and living standards of the
majority was probably negative.

The liberal and ethical eras

The CS was followed by a number of liberal economic reforms. These
were intended to allow market forces a stronger role in the economy,
although the agrarian legislation in fact imposed controls on the sale of
land owned by indigenous cultivators to other parties, including Chinese.
The legislation was also intended to facilitate the long-term leasing of land
to estate companies. One of the most important consequences was the
growth of large estates in Java and Sumatra, especially in the area of
northern Sumatra around the town of Medan. But after more than two
decades of liberal policies, there was increasing concern about the direction of colonial policy. Growth rates of GDP per capita in Java were barely
positive in the decades from 1860 to 1880, although they accelerated to
around 1 per cent per annum between 1880 and 1900 (Van Zanden and
Marks 2012: 50). Van der Eng's estimates for Indonesia show a slower
growth in per capita GDP of around 0.5 per cent per annum over these
two decades, although export volume did accelerate in the last fifteen
years of the century (van Ark 1988: 115–16). There was considerable real
growth in expenditures on public works between 1880 and 1900, especially on irrigation and railways (de Jong and Ravesteijn 2008: 66).

The progress in construction of public works was not enough to stem
the criticism of the colonial system by influential commentators in both
Indonesia and the Netherlands. They were concerned that, far from
benefiting the indigenous population of Java, the liberal reforms had
actually led to declining living standards. Falling per capita availability
of rice in Java was a particular worry. The population of Java had continued to grow, and by 1900 was estimated to be around 30 million. There
was a growing fear that, with finite supplies of arable land, it would not be
possible to accommodate more people in agriculture in Java, or indeed in
some of the more densely settled regions outside Java. The Calvinist-
Catholic coalition, which came to power in the Netherlands in 1901,
announced a new approach to colonial management which became
known as the ethical policy (Penders 1977: 61).

The ethical policy was motivated mainly by a concern over living standards, especially in Java. Cribb (1993: 227–9) has argued that there were three main strands in Dutch policy. The first was a desire to provide administrative and legal protection to the indigenous population, especially against the powerful interests of Western capitalism. The second was to provide more educational opportunities for indigenous Indonesians, while the third was to intervene directly through government initiatives to improve the productivity and incomes of indigenous Indonesians. Dutch policy emphasised agricultural intensification through improved irrigation, which would lead to more double-cropping of rice land. There was also a recognition that more off-farm employment opportunities were needed for the indigenous population. In order to provide a range of government services, Departments of Public Works, Health and Education were created or expanded, and both expatriate and indigenous officials were recruited to staff them (Boomgaard 1986; de Jong and Ravesteijn 2008).

But some officials still worried that such policies would not by themselves be enough to stave off the threat of a Malthusian catastrophe in Java. Even if new land could be brought under cultivation, and existing land cultivated more intensively, it was still unlikely that a continually growing population could be accommodated in agriculture in Java. The obvious solution, especially at a period when large numbers of Europe's 'surplus populations' were moving across the Atlantic to settle in parts of North and South America, was to encourage more Javanese to settle in those parts of the archipelago where the Dutch thought that the agricultural potential was being held back by small populations and a lack of agricultural labour. Javanese had in fact been moving to Lampung at the southern tip of Sumatra for many decades. The Dutch plan was to accelerate movement to new agricultural settlements, in both Sumatra and Sulawesi through ambitious land development schemes. In addition, many Javanese were encouraged to move to northern Sumatra to meet the demand for wage labour on the agricultural estates. After 1900 the Dutch began to impose controls on in-migration from other parts of Asia, especially China. The Javanese were persuaded to move through a system of indentured labour contracts which some critics considered coercive.

The coercion of workers to move to Sumatra was supposed to have stopped after 1870, after which date the out-migration of Javanese was considered to be voluntary. But there was considerable controversy about the treatment of indentured workers on Sumatran estates. Particularly controversial was the Coolie Ordinance with its penal sanction clause, which permitted the criminal prosecution of workers who ran away from their employers.[1] The Ordinance was only repealed in 1931 (Lindblad 2002: 103–4). Those who moved from Java to Sumatra were often from families who owned little or no land, but the landed families in Java were not spared government coercion. As sugar production grew, the sugar companies used coercive tactics to secure the rental of land from native landowners. They almost always demanded that the better irrigated *sawah* land was rented to them, although in fact sugar cultivation could have taken place on rain-fed land, if the planting had coincided with the monsoon season.

By 1930, the impact of population movement in Indonesia was clear from the results of the population census of that year. More than 31 per cent of the population of the north-east coast of Sumatra was born in Java, as was over one quarter of the population of Lampung (Pelzer 1945: 260). Hugo (1980: 110) estimated that by 1930 there were almost 1.14 million people of Javanese descent living outside Java. This ethnic mixing caused some problems, both before and after independence, but it did help to create the idea of Indonesia as a single national entity. Although Javanese migrants still used their own languages among themselves, the *lingua franca*, Malay, became more widely used, especially after its adoption as the language of the independence movement in 1928. The independence movement itself consisted of people from various parts of the archipelago, with Sumatrans as well as Javanese playing a prominent role. Although Dutch policy was to encourage the use of local vernaculars in the expanding education system, the increasing use of a common language was an important factor in spreading the 'idea of Indonesia' among increasing numbers of people (Elson 2008: 64–5).

An important reason for the growth of nationalism in the early decades of the twentieth century was a widespread conviction among many indigenous Indonesians that neither the liberal reforms of the last part of the nineteenth century nor the ethical policies after 1901 had brought them much benefit. Influential merchant groups in urban Java, such as the *Sarekat Dagang Islam*, resented competition from the Chinese (Kahin 1952: 67–70). The better-off farmers in Java, who controlled irrigated rice land, resented the enforced renting of land to the sugar companies. Most of those involved in the growing nationalist movement, including growing numbers of indigenous business people, would probably have agreed with the judgement of a later economist that 'the developmental effort under the ethical system was too little and too late to be effective in raising levels of living of the Indonesian people' (Higgins 1968: 693).

---

[1] For a discussion of the debate over the treatment of workers and the role of the Labour Inspectorate, from the viewpoint of one of the main participants, see Breman (2002).

Table 2.1 *Annual average growth in GDP, 1900–1938: Indonesia, the Philippines, Thailand, Taiwan*

Country	1900–1913	1913–1929	1929–1938	GDP* (per capita, 1938)
Indonesia	2.5	2.6	1.1	1,175
Philippines	2.9	4.3	4.1	1,522
Thailand	2.4	1.7	2.9	826
Taiwan	4.7	4.3	2.6	1,302

* GDP in 1990 international dollars; the figure for Taiwan is probably too low.
Sources: van der Eng (2013); Hooley (2005); Sato et al. (2008: 382); Sompop (1989); per capita GDP: Maddison (2003: 182–3).

Is this a fair criticism? Defenders of the ethical policy argued that it did lead to sustained real growth in government expenditure after 1900, and a shift in the composition of expenditures away from administration and defence towards public works (Booth 1990: 224–9). There was also an acceleration in both export and GDP growth after 1900: export volume almost doubled between 1900 and 1913, and then almost trebled between 1913 and 1929 in spite of the fact that export prices began to fall after 1920 (van Ark 1988: 116–17). Between 1901 and 1913, GDP grew at around 2.5 per cent per annum, and accelerated to 2.6 per cent per annum between 1913 and 1929. Output growth was faster than in Thailand, although probably slower than in the Philippines and Taiwan (Table 2.1). But did the policies adopted after 1900 lead to improved living standards for the indigenous population, which was after all the key aim of the ethical policy? Although the years from 1901 to 1914 saw some improvement in food availability in Java, the post-1914 period brought worrying developments. Inflation accelerated, leading to sharp increases in the prices of food and non-food staples.

The growth in public sector expenditures after 1900 had been partly funded by borrowing, leading to a growth in the debt servicing obliga-tions, which caused official concern in both the colony and the Netherlands (Booth 1998: 144–6). If spending on infrastructure, health, education and land settlement projects outside Java was to be sustained, more revenues would have to be raised from taxation. But a report published in 1921 found that the indigenous population was already being 'taxed to the utmost limit' (Penders 1977: 96).

Dutch authorities feared that further taxation of agriculture would have been met with stiff resistance from the rural population. In fact, the land tax in Java fell in terms of nominal guilders per hectare of arable land between the 1870s and the 1910s, although it increased over the 1920s.

As a proportion of value added in farm agriculture, it fell continually until the end of the 1920s (van der Eng 2006: 42). From 1870 until 1920, the land tax in Java was a lower percentage of value added in agriculture than in Japan, although it was higher between 1920 and 1940. The land tax was not assessed outside Java, Bali, Lombok and a small area in South Sulawesi before 1942, but other taxes including export taxes fell on indigenous producers. The export tax levied on smallholder rubber producers in an attempt to curtail smallholder production led to considerable unrest in parts of Sumatra in 1935, and was subsequently removed (O'Malley 1979: 239–45).

After 1920, the Dutch authorities, facing criticism from powerful commercial interests at home about the trend towards welfare colonialism, tried to rein in budgetary expenditures. In 1920, budgetary expenditures per capita were higher than in most other parts of Asia, and were only surpassed by the three components of British Malaya and Taiwan (Booth 2007: table 4.4). But thereafter they fell in terms of nominal dollars, and relative to several other colonies including the Philippines. Expenditures on capital works were cut sharply, especially after the world depression began to affect revenues in the early 1930s. The comparative study of public finances in Southeast Asia carried out by Schwulst (1932) in 1930/1931 found that Indonesia was spending a lower percentage of the total budget on agriculture and public works, and a higher proportion on defence than any other colony, and about the same as independent Siam. But in spite of the fiscal austerity, the government debt continued to cause official concern; in 1935 it was still higher in per capita terms than in other parts of Asia, excepting British Malaya (Table 2.2).

Increased government expenditures, especially in the early years of the ethical policy, did produce improved infrastructure. By the 1930s, Java had a highly developed system of roads and railways, even more extensive

Table 2.2 *Public debt per capita (US$)*

Country	1935	1955
British Malaya	18.21	27.39
Indonesia	15.45	3.79
India	12.11	17.64
Philippines	4.99	23.87
Thailand	2.76	4.15
Egypt	31.62	NA
Portugal	60.21	41.93

Source: Booth (2013b: table 5).

than in Taiwan (Booth 2007: table 4.7). Irrigation development had also progressed further than in most other parts of monsoon Asia, and this in turn permitted greater double-cropping of rice land. The numbers of professional engineers working for the government more than quadrupled between 1878 and 1928. The majority were trained in Delft in the Netherlands, although by 1930 there were 45 who had been trained in Bandung (de Jong and Ravesteijn 2008: 60). The Dutch administration was very proud of its engineering achievements in Indonesia, but most of the infrastructure was concentrated in Java and a few export-producing regions in Sumatra. Most other regions outside Java had few roads, and rail development was restricted to northern and southern Sumatra. A plan to build a trans-Sumatra rail line was shelved after 1930. There was no rail, and only very limited road development in Kalimantan, Sulawesi or the eastern islands.

Another trend which attracted adverse attention after 1900 was the persistent current account surplus on the balance of payments. The current account surplus had fallen after the termination of the CS, partly because remittances to the Dutch budget ended, but also because of the growth of military expenditures associated with the war in Aceh. The surplus began to grow again after 1900 (Booth 1998: 212–13). For much of the period from 1900 to 1930, it amounted to between 2 and 5 per cent of GDP. During the CS, the surplus was used to finance subventions to the Dutch budget; after 1900 the outflows were mainly private. They were the result of higher levels of savings, both personal and corporate, part of which were remitted abroad. Defenders of Dutch policy over these years claim that, on average, private firms in Indonesia were not earning unusually large profits and that even if profits were remitted abroad, the colonial economy still benefited from the development of private enterprise whether in agricultural estates, mining, manufacturing, transport or banking and financial services. These enterprises paid taxes into the colonial budget and employed local workers. Debates over the cost and benefits of foreign investment were to continue after independence.

Defenders of Dutch colonial trade policies also argued that after 1900 the Dutch share of imports to, and exports from, Indonesia steadily declined (van der Eng 1998a: table 1). The Netherlands was not using its colonies as captive markets for high-cost home producers of manufactures to the same extent as France was doing after 1918.[2] Indeed it suited the interests of many Dutch and other investors in Indonesia that their workers could purchase low-cost wage goods. After 1920 that

---

[2] A good discussion of the economic aspects of French colonial policy can be found in Thomas (2005: 98–118).

increasingly meant imported manufactures from Japan, especially cotton textiles, garments and household goods. The increase in Japanese imports into colonial Indonesia was also assisted by the Dutch decision to stay on the gold standard after 1930, which caused a substantial real appreciation of the guilder relative to the yen. In 1934, the Dutch authorities, worried more by the political than the economic ramifications of Japan's growing penetration of the colonial market, began to impose quotas on Japanese imports, although Indonesia remained an important market for Japanese textiles until 1942 (Booth 1998: 219–20).

In 1936, the Netherlands government moved the Dutch guilder off the gold standard, and with it the Netherlands Indies guilder. The devaluation followed the adoption of policy measures intended to encourage the growth of the traded goods sectors, including large-scale manufacturing. Until the 1930s industrial growth was largely centred on agricultural processing. The new policy encouraged foreign investment in a number of sectors including automobiles, rubber tires and tubes, soaps and cosmetics, batteries, cigarettes, electrical appliances and brewing (Shepherd 1941: 73). A measure of protection was granted the domestic textile sector, mainly by placing quotas on Japanese imports.

Encouragement was given to small-scale weaving through the distribution of improved handlooms (Palmer 1972: Chapter 2). Attempts to regulate production in small-scale enterprises were often frustrated by the sheer number of establishments, although the government persisted in its attempts until 1942. Official concern about 'cut throat competition' led to the formation in 1937 of a Regulation Board. The increase in what one French observer called 'administrative tyranny' was an important legacy to post-independence governments (Bousquet 1940: 51). Writing almost thirty years later, Higgins (1968: 693) claimed that over the 1930s there was a shift from a relatively free to a highly regulated economy, although the relatively free economy of the years from 1870 to 1930 was itself a reaction against the *dirigisme* of the years from 1830 to 1870.

Whatever the merits of greater government regulation, the industrial sector (mining, manufacturing, utilities and construction) recovered from the depression and grew in real terms by 85 per cent between 1934 and 1941. In 1941, it accounted for 17.6 per cent of GDP (van der Eng 2013). Some observers saw the greater attention to industrial policy in Indonesia as part of a wider trend on the part of colonial regimes in Asia to take industrial policy more seriously in the 1930s (Shepherd 1941: 110). Dutch officials, like the French in Vietnam, could hardly have been unaware of the efforts by the Japanese to promote industrial growth not just in Japan but also in Taiwan, Korea and Manchuria. Increasingly they realised that if living standards were to improve, employment opportunities outside agriculture would have to increase. Labour-intensive manufacturing was an obvious candidate for official support.

Economic recovery after 1934 was not accompanied by greater political freedom. By the mid-1930s the Dutch had managed to stifle the nationalist movement by incarcerating most of the leadership in remote parts of Eastern Indonesia.[3] But by then the idea of Indonesia as a unified nation, and by implication a unified economy, had gained widespread support among educated elites both in Java and elsewhere. The Malay language was also being used more widely across the archipelago and after independence became the official language for government and increasingly in legal and commercial transactions, and in the media. Last but by no means least, the great majority of Indonesians shared a common religion in Islam, even if there were considerable variations in the degree of commitment to Islamic values and practices. With the ignominious defeat of the Dutch at the hands of the Japanese in 1942, and the release of key leaders from Dutch prisons, the nationalist movement rapidly recovered its strength, and by 1945 was ready to assert itself as the legitimate government for the whole country.

Living standards in Indonesia during the last decade of Dutch rule

By 1941, in spite of the ravages of the depression, per capita GDP in Indonesia had surpassed the level achieved in 1929 (van der Eng 2013). But Indonesian per capita GDP was below that in British Malaya and the Philippines, as well as that in Taiwan and probably Korea.[4] Indonesia was also ranked well below most other parts of Southeast Asia in terms of infant mortality rates, crude death rates and educational enrolments. The last indicator placed Indonesia below all other Asian colonies except French Indochina (Furnivall 1943: 111). Even as late as the 1930s, infant mortality rates among indigenous Indonesians in Batavia were estimated to have been 300 per thousand, although they were lower in Bandung (Table 2.3). The very high mortality rates in Batavia, and other coastal

---

[3] The Governor General in the latter part of the 1920s, de Graeff, was committed to reconciliation between the colonial government and the 'moderate' (i.e. non-communist) nationalists. But his attempts failed, and he was forced into harsher measures (McVey 1965: 355). Ricklefs (2001: 231) argued that some nationalists had imbibed socialist and Marxist views of imperialism in the Netherlands, although on their return from the Netherlands they were often in conflict with more doctrinaire Marxists who had been trained in the Soviet Union.

[4] See Maddison (2003: 182). It should be noted that his estimate for Taiwan is almost certainly an understatement; see Fukao, Ma and Yuan (2007).

Table 2.3 *Infant mortality rates in Southeast Asia by ethnic group,*
1930s

	Indigenous	Chinese	European	Indian
SS (1934)	235	154	25	145
Kedah (1928)	112	137	NA	263
FMS (1936)	149	139	NA	136
Batavia (1935/1937)	300	150	50–60	NA
Bandung (1935/1938)	145	111	35	NA
Saigon (1936)	250	220	NA	NA

Notes: SS, Straits Settlements; FMS, Federated Malay States.
Sources: Booth (2012b), table 6.

towns and cities, were attributed to the unhealthy climate, and also to a
lack of parental knowledge regarding the causes of infant and child deaths
(Booth 2012a: 1167–8).

As has been noted, government expenditures per capita fell in terms of
nominal dollars after 1920. Government revenues also declined in per
capita terms, especially over the decade of the 1930s, although by the
late 1930s, Indonesia had a more diversified revenue structure than
most other Southeast Asian colonies. Tax revenues comprised over
60 per cent of all revenues, with income taxes, both personal and corporate,
accounting for over 20 per cent of total revenues. But in 1938 total
revenues per capita were lower than in the Philippines, Taiwan and the
three components of British Malaya, and indeed lower than in several
British colonies in Africa (Booth 2007: table 4.3). While at least some
Dutch officials might have wanted to increase expenditures in sectors
such as health and education in the latter part of the 1930s, they were
constrained by limited revenues, and a reluctance to increase government borrowing.

One reason for poor health indicators would have been poor nutrition.
The evidence indicates that rice availability per capita in Java was, by the
inter-war years, low in comparison with many other parts of Southeast
Asia. It was almost certainly low in many regions outside Java as well, with
the exception of the less densely settled rice-producing regions such as
Aceh, West Sumatra and South Sulawesi. Van der Eng (2000: table 6) has
estimated that, for Indonesia as a whole, by the 1930s only around 40 per
cent of total calorie consumption came from rice. Given the paucity of
data outside Java, these figures must be treated with caution but it is
probable that in many regions outside Java, as well as in Java, corn, sago
and root crops played an important role in the diets of many people.

Cassava was eaten in several forms: many poorer families in Central and East Java consumed it in dried form (*gaplek*) in the *paceklik*, or months before the main rice harvest. Studies using the household survey data from 1970 found that *gaplek* was an inferior food, consumed largely by the lower income groups (Dixon 1984). This would also have been the case before 1940. Fresh roots were also widely consumed, usually with some form of sauce to make the taste more palatable. Cassava, whether consumed fresh or dried, was a cheaper source of calories than rice and indeed cheaper than corn or sweet potatoes (van der Eng 1998b: table 7). But in spite of the availability of cheap supplements to rice, average calorie consumption per capita in Java by the 1930s was, for most population groups investigated by Dutch officialdom, well below 2,000 calories per day, which in modern times would be considered a minimum intake, especially for people engaged in physical labour.

Protein consumption was under 50 g per day (van der Eng 2000: table 4). The sample of farmers living near estates investigated in the final report of the Coolie Budget Commission in the late 1930s found that average daily calorie consumption was only 1,391, and protein consumption per capita around 35 g. Plantation factory labourers living off the plantation were consuming about the same, while field labourers were consuming less (van Niel 1956: 108–11). This report also found that calorie consumption rose with increased household incomes, especially among those living off the plantation. This finding appears to hold also for the sample of rural households investigated in the Kutawinangun study in Central Java in the early 1930s, which found a strong positive correlation between income per capita and calorie consumption. Nonetheless, the medical experts who participated in the Kutawinangun study found the state of health and nourishment of the entire village to be 'most satisfactory' (de Langen 1934: 405).

One possible explanation for the reasonable state of health in such a densely settled area was that those households which owned little land cultivated their house gardens very intensively. The Kutowinangun study, and other studies carried out in Java in the inter-war years, found that as average holding size decreased, the amount of land allocated to house gardens, and the intensity of planting, increased (Ochse and Terra 1934: 355). This tendency for those households where land availability per capita was low to exploit their gardens more intensively was to persist into the post-independence era. The Kutowinangun study found a significant negative correlation between land owned per capita, and the percentage of household income derived from 'sideline' occupations, which suggests that land-poor households were able to get at least some income from off-farm activities, and this income helped them to maintain an adequate diet. On the other hand, the Kutowinangun data showed that there was a significant positive correlation between household income and calorie and protein consumption, for both agricultural and non-agricultural households. The correlation coefficient between income per capita and calories intake was 0.86 (and even higher for protein intake).[5] What the household earned determined what the household ate.

Elsewhere in Java, there was evidence of more severe malnutrition in the latter part of the 1930s, especially in regions where cassava was a staple food, and where opportunities for earning extra cash income were limited. In 1939, the Director of Public Health instructed the National Nutrition Institute (*Instituut voor Volksvoeding*) to carry out a dietary survey in the Bojonegoro region in north-eastern Java where the food situation was causing grave concern (Penders 1984: 131). In five villages selected for detailed fieldwork, it was found that most families were receiving well below the stipulated minimum of 1,500 calories per day. Poor diet made the population more prone to malaria, which in turn made hunger oedema more widespread.

The governor of the province of East Java, Charles van der Plas, argued that effective programmes to combat hunger oedema across East Java would cost millions of guilders, and the money might be better spent on other policies including improved irrigation and agricultural extension in poor areas, and better education about child nutrition. Other senior officials such as H. J. van Mook argued that the situation in Bojonegoro was extreme, although it was widely acknowledged that the growing dependence on cassava as a source of calories was causing dietary problems in other parts of Java, and that, given the expected growth in population, out-migration and the provision of more non-agricultural employment would have to play a greater role in improving living standards on Java (Penders 1984: 142).

Social stratification at the end of the colonial era

Detailed village studies such as the one in Kutowinangun revealed that, by the 1930s, access to land in rural Java was skewed with only a small proportion of villagers owning more than one hectare of irrigated *sawah*. Indeed some scholars have argued on the basis of surveys carried out in 1904/1905 and in the 1920s that Javanese society was already quite polarised in the early part of the twentieth century, with at least one-third of the agricultural population owning little or no land (Alexander

[5] Data refer to twenty households surveyed; fifteen agricultural and five non-agricultural.

and Alexander 1982: 601–5). Their main source of income was as agricultural labourers, working either for farmers who owned land, or for agricultural estates (Husken and White 1989: 240–1). The breakdown of the 'native population' of Java given by Meyer Ranneft and Huender in 1923 and subsequently used by Wertheim (1956: 96–7) showed that wealthy farmers comprised only 2.5 per cent of the indigenous population, with middle-class farmers a further 19.8 per cent and poor farmers 27.1 per cent. Although there was less pressure on arable land outside Java, a study carried out in West Sumatra also found a skewed distribution of land, with 13 per cent of household heads owning 82 per cent of the land, and the remaining 87 per cent owning less than one hectare.

The 1930 population census for the first time in colonial Indonesia provided detailed information on the structure of the labour force. The results showed that in Java around 30 per cent of the labour force was in non-agricultural employment, although some of those classified as 'other' may have been at least partly engaged in agriculture. There was also a sharp difference between the male and female data, with little more than half the female labour force engaged in agriculture and around one-third in manufacturing and trade.[6] The 1930 census also produced surprisingly high female labour force participation rates, especially in some parts of Java. In Yogyakarta almost 60 per cent of women were found to be gainfully employed, compared with 46 per cent in the neighbouring province of Central Java. For Java as a whole female participation rates were 37 per cent. These figures were much higher than in much of Europe, including the Netherlands, at the same time (de Vries 2008: 212).

The census data also showed that indigenous workers comprised a very high proportion of the non-agricultural labour force, especially in comparison with other Asian colonies (Table 2.4). The increase in employment in government occupations, which resulted from the ethical policy, meant that by 1930 well over 90 per cent of all workers in government and the professions were indigenous Indonesians. This was a higher proportion than in other parts of colonial East and Southeast Asia with the exception of the Philippines and independent Thailand (Booth 2007: 121–8).

Wertheim (1956: 128–9) pointed out that over the 1930s, there was a tendency for the number of 'European' posts in the civil service to

---

[6] For a detailed discussion of the labour force data from the 1930 census, see Mertens (1978). He stresses the rather different results in Tables 18 and 19 in Volume 8, especially as they refer to female non-agricultural employment. See in particular Appendix Table 1.6 in his paper.

Table 2.4 *Indigenous workers as a percentage of the labour force in manufacturing, commerce, professions and government service*

	Indigenous workers as percentage of the labour force		
	Manufacturing	Commerce/trade	Government and professions
Indonesia (1930)	95.3	84.3	93.6
SS (1931)	7.2	3.9	20.5
FMS (1931)	3.0	2.4	32.9
Burma (1931)	80.8	73.3	86.7
Philippines (1939)	97.6	82.7	96.5
Thailand (1937)	55.2	60.6	95.2
Korea (1930)	89.7	85.1	59.8
Taiwan (1930)	78.5	86.9	49.2

Notes: SS, Straits Settlements; FMS, Federated Malay States. Data for Taiwan refer to male workers only.
Sources: Booth (2007), table 6.4.

decline. Between 1928 and 1938 the percentage of technical, administrative and financial posts occupied by indigenous Indonesians rose. This was partly done for budgetary reasons; Indonesian staff were paid less. But whatever the reason, many thousands of Indonesians had by the late 1930s been brought into the world of public administration. Some went on to occupy senior posts in the bureaucracy after 1949. The 1930 data also showed that indigenous workers were a majority in commerce and trade, although these were the occupations where most of the Chinese were engaged, and there was often direct competition between the two ethnic groups. Wertheim used the evidence from the 1930 census, and earlier surveys, to take issue with Kahin (1952: 124–5) who argued that a class of indigenous business people never really emerged in the late colonial era, mainly because of increased Chinese competition. Wertheim (1956: 125) considered that the evidence pointed to the emergence of an 'incipient native middle class', which broke through the 'old traditional order of society' and was beginning to exert a more individualistic influence on the behaviour of at least a minority of indigenous Indonesians.

But as more Indonesians moved into the world of trade and commerce, as well as into the public sector, resentment against both European and Chinese dominance of the non-agricultural economy grew. Movements such as *Sarekat Islam*, which was dominated by Moslem traders, assumed a strong anti-Chinese orientation. *Sarekat Islam* was important in the early phase of the independence movement, which became, from its inception, hostile to 'foreign Asians' and especially the Chinese. Reid (2010: 61) has argued that the anti-Chinese orientation of the nationalist movement in Indonesia could be contrasted with the situation in the Philippines, where the nationalist movement began earlier, and embraced many Filipinos of mixed Spanish and Chinese descent. The fact that so few Chinese were Moslems caused further divisions in the non-agricultural economy which persisted after 1949.

A colonial balance sheet

Drawing up a balance sheet for the colonial era in Indonesia is no easier than for many other former colonies, and debates continue over the costs and benefits of Dutch policies. On the benefit side, Dutch engineers undeniably provided modern infrastructure both in Java and in some regions outside Java, although most regions of Kalimantan and the eastern islands were neglected. In Java, infrastructure development, including roads, railways and irrigation, proceeded further than in most other parts of colonial Asia (Table 2.5). Length of roads relative to area was higher than in any other Asian colony, including Taiwan and Korea. Irrigation development in Java was also more advanced than in most other parts of colonial Asia. By the early twentieth century, administrative structures reached deep into indigenous society in Java, and these structures survived largely intact after independence. Their purpose was partly to control the indigenous population, but increasingly after 1900, the various layers of regional and local government assumed responsibility for service delivery as well. Java also benefited from the development of government credit systems, including the district and village banks and the pawnshops; their influence on post-colonial credit policies will be examined in more detail in Chapter 7.[7]

Outside Java, the Dutch made greater use of local traditional rulers to maintain law and order and to ensure that Dutch and other foreign companies obtained access to land for the development of mines and estates. After independence some of these local rulers were viewed as little more than tools of the Dutch and were removed from power. In Aceh and North Sumatra, the post-1945 attacks on the old aristocratic elites led to considerable violence. But elsewhere, especially in Eastern Indonesia, the old elites remained powerful players in post-independence regional and

---

[7] The credit system developed rapidly after 1910, and attracted studies by several foreign experts including Henry (1926) and Furnivall (1934a, 1934b). More recent evaluations have been less positive; see Alexander and Alexander (1991), Boomgaard (1993) and Cribb (1993).

Table 2.5 *Infrastructure endowments, late 1930s*

Country/year	Roads (km per thousand km^2)	Railways (km per thousand km^2)	Electricity* (installed capacity)
Taiwan (1937)	94.4	43.3**	38.32
Korea (1940)	107.2	25.7	29.05
Manchuria (1938)	35.6	7.0	NA
Philippines (1939)	70.5	4.5	4.76
Indonesia (1940)	27.7	3.9	2.97
Java	171.9	40.5	3.01
Outer Islands	17.0	1.1	2.86
Indochina (1936)	38.8	3.9	3.82
British Malaya (1938)	100.1	12.5	36.06
Burma (1938)	45.2	3.4	3.69

* Data refer to installed capacity in kilowatts per 1,000 population for the following years: 1938 (Philippines), 1937 (British Malaya) and 1940 (Indonesia, Korea and Taiwan). For Burma the data refer to the capacity of the large plants with an estimate for smaller plants.
** Data exclude 2,098 km of special track for the transport of sugar.
Sources: Philippines: Bureau of Census and Statistics (1947: 279, 304–7); Indonesia: CBS (1947: 56, 97); Indochina: Robequain (1944: 94–7, 285); British Malaya: Department of Statistics (1939); Burma: Andrus (1948: 226, 237); Korea: Kim et al. (2008: 488, 608); Taiwan: Grajdanzev (1942: 118–19); Barclay (1954: 42); Manchuria: MYB (1941: 575, 595).

local governments. For the most part they lacked either the knowledge or the financial resources, or the inclination, to develop modern infrastructure, or services including education and health care. Some education and health care was provided by Christian missions in some regions outside Java, but elsewhere such services were neglected.

The land tax system, and with it the development of land cadastres and individual property rights in land, was extended from Java to Bali and Lombok and a small part of South Sulawesi in the early twentieth century, but not to Sumatra, Kalimantan or Eastern Indonesia. Recent scholarship has viewed the development of secure individual property rights as a pre-condition for accelerated economic growth, although the rapid growth of smallholder agricultural production often took place in those regions where traditional tenure systems were in place. These seemed to have functioned quite well, especially for tree crops, which take some years to mature. Smallholder producers of tree crops such as rubber, coffee and pepper would not have made considerable outlays in terms of both time and money if they had not thought that their rights to the income from the mature trees were guaranteed by local laws and customs.

By the 1920s, many millions of Indonesians, both in Java and else-where, were working in the monetised economy, either as producers of agricultural products and manufactures for sale, or as wage workers or as traders. Lack of infrastructure, formal credit or individual land rights did not prevent the rapid growth of smallholder production of export crops, especially rubber, in both Sumatra and Kalimantan. Marketing networks developed to get rubber to coastal ports, to the Singapore entrepot, and ultimately to destinations in the USA and Europe. Although these net-works were often dominated by Chinese traders, indigenous Indonesians were also involved in large numbers.[8] To some observers, both Dutch and foreign, this diversification of the indigenous economy seemed to vindi-cate the original aims of the ethical policy.

But others were disappointed with the results of the ethical policy, and argued for a change in the direction of policy. Probably the best-known critique was that of Boeke (1927: 296) who argued that 'the population of Java has reacted to all these welfare policies in only one clear way: by growing like a flash flood'. Boeke and other Dutch officials were aware that population growth in the Netherlands had been quite rapid through much of the nineteenth century; fertility rates had remained quite high although mortality had fallen. But by the early twentieth century, fertility in the Netherlands, as in other parts of northern Europe, was falling. But this did not seem to be the case in Indonesia. Modern demographers would argue that one reason for the persistence of high fertility was the high infant and child mortality in many parts of the country. Some Dutch officials might have agreed with this but Boeke (1927: 298) argued that what was needed was a new development strategy which moved away from 'welfare socialism' and encouraged differentiation in native society by 'concerning itself with the vigorous, energetic, advanced elements'.

As Wertheim (1964: 265) later suggested, this was a policy of betting on the strong, which in fact some colonial agencies had already adopted by the latter part of the 1920s. Wertheim considered that the rural devel-opment policies, including the credit system, which were implemented in the final decades of Dutch rule in Indonesia effectively reached only the top 10 per cent of the rural population. This was also the case with education policies. Here the achievements of the Dutch were modest, especially when compared with the Americans in the Philippines. As late as 1940, only a small number of indigenous Indonesian children were able to progress beyond a few years in a rural school which taught a limited number of subjects in a vernacular language.

---

[8] Thomas and Panglaykim (1976) analyse the development of rubber marketing networks in South Sumatra and discuss the reasons for Chinese dominance.

Very few Indonesian children managed to secure places in the Dutch-language schools. In 1939/1940, 47,282 students were enrolled in the European elementary schools, of whom 5,150 were indigenous Indonesians and a further 1,281 foreign orientals. The proportion of non-Europeans in the European schools had in fact been falling since the peak in 1920 when 20 per cent of enrolments were non-Europeans. Chinese children were able to gain a Dutch-language education in the Dutch-Chinese schools of which there were several hundred. In 1939/1940 these schools enrolled almost 25,500 pupils most of whom were ethnic Chinese although there were small numbers of students from other ethnic groups (Govaars 2005: 257). Govaars (2005: 91) estimated that very few Chinese or native children were able to progress to the academic-track secondary schools. Even if they had wanted to continue their studies, places in the academic-track secondary system were limited, and many parents were unable to afford the fees. A small change in a family's financial position often meant the end of a child's school career (Booth 1998: 272–3).

Given that many subsequent scholars have equated colonial exploitation with distortion of markets, to what extent did the final decades of the Dutch era lead to freer markets? Although the policy changes of the 1870s were intended to end forced cultivation of crops, and usher in an era of free markets, the reality was rather different. In Java, smallholders had little option but to rent their rice land to the sugar estates, regardless of whether or not they had more profitable alternative uses. While taxation in labour and kind did end in some parts of the country, it was still in use in parts of the outer islands until well into the twentieth century. In Java a range of cash taxes fell on the indigenous population, which pushed them further into either the wage labour market or other cash-earning activities. These imposts might have been tolerated if indigenous Indonesians were able to see benefits from increased expenditures on agricultural development, credit facilities and other services including health and education. But the trickle-down effect was for many very limited, especially for those owning little or no land.

There was also the vexed issue of large private sector remittances, which in the eyes of many nationalists resulted from the fact that foreign companies were exploiting Indonesia's resources and remitting most of the profits, with little benefit accruing to the indigenous populations. While it was probably true that many Dutch and other foreign businesses operating in Indonesia did not make large profits, some certainly did. Royal Dutch Shell, formed in 1907 as a result of a merger between a Dutch and a British oil firm, was very profitable, and was able to use profits from Indonesia to finance its expansion to other parts of the world (van Zanden and Marks 2012: 87).[9] In their defence, Dutch investors argued that they brought new technologies and management expertise to the country and took risks in developing new commodities for world markets. Their profits were thus a fair commercial return. Most nationalists in Indonesia in the colonial era did not agree with this argument, and the resentment against foreign exploitation carried over into the independence era.

[9] Henri Deterding, the CEO of Royal Dutch Shell used his considerable influence in the Netherlands to lower taxes which he considered detrimental to Shell's profitability in Indonesia (Van Zanden and Marks 2012: 127).

3 Occupation, liberation and the challenges facing the new republic, 1942–66

A decade of struggle

In 1942, the armed forces of imperial Japan swept through British Malaya, Indonesia and the Philippines, inflicting humiliating defeats on the colonial governments and armies. The myth that European colonialism was invincible was destroyed in a few weeks of conflict. In many parts of Indonesia the Japanese were greeted as liberators and especially in Java there was little overt opposition until 1944 (Abdullah 2010). Nationalists were released from prison; Sukarno and Hatta cooperated with the Japanese, mainly 'in the interest of the greater goal of independence' (Ricklefs 2001: 251). Other prominent nationalists, including Sjahrir, avoided overt cooperation with the Japanese, and built up an underground network based on former colleagues.[1] For their part the Japanese promoted many Indonesian government officials into more senior posts to replace Dutch nationals who had either fled or been imprisoned.

The Japanese placed considerable emphasis on mobilising and indoctrinating youth. Following Japanese policy in both Taiwan and Korea, the school system was used to instil Japanese values into children along with a sense of nationalism. The evils of Dutch colonial policy were also stressed (Kurasawa 2010: 323). On the economic front, the Japanese gave top priority to the petroleum sector, where they urgently needed supplies to replace imports from the USA and elsewhere. Technicians quickly repaired the damage inflicted on the oilfields in Sumatra and Kalimantan by the departing Dutch. Crude oil production doubled between 1942 and 1943. Rubber production was also encouraged, but other export crops including sugar, spices, coffee and tea were not accorded high priority. Sugar was procured from Taiwan, and scarce shipping capacity could not be used to transport luxury goods such as coffee and spices to the Japanese mainland.

---

[1] Sutan Sjahrir was, like Hatta, from West Sumatra and they had both been educated in the Netherlands. While he and Hatta kept in close touch through the Japanese occupation, his relations with Sukarno were less close and became increasingly strained after 1945.

The Japanese paid little attention to the colonial borders and governed Southeast Asia according to their own strategic needs. Sumatra along with peninsular Malaya was governed from Singapore, while Borneo and most of the eastern islands were controlled by the navy. Problems of food supply rapidly emerged across the archipelago (Sato 2010: 267–79). Indonesia as a whole had been a net rice importer prior to 1942, relying on Thai, Burmese and Vietnamese imports to supply deficit areas in Sumatra, Java and elsewhere. These supplies were greatly reduced, partly because the Japanese needed the rice to supply to their own troops and partly because it was decreed that regions should be 'self-sufficient'. To a considerable extent this was the result of mounting pressures on transport capacity, including shipping and road transport. These pressures became more acute as American air and submarine attacks intensified.

By 1943–1944 the food situation was increasingly serious, especially in those parts of Java where food supply had already been precarious in the 1930s. In Bojonegoro, it has been estimated that population declined from 1.84 million in 1942 to 1.76 million in 1945. This decline may have been in part due to out-migration, or to lower fertility. But it was also in part the result of increased mortality. One estimate suggests that in Java as a whole, the population declined in absolute terms between 1942 and 1945 (van der Eng 2002: table 5). In 1950, it appears that the population of Indonesia was around 2.4 million less than what it would have been had the growth rate in the 1930s continued over the 1940s.[2] It would be an exaggeration to claim that these 'missing people' had all perished as a result of food shortages. Fertility dropped as marriages were postponed, in part at least because many young men were conscripted as labourers by the Japanese, and sent to other parts of the country or abroad. Some never returned. But increased mortality due to malnutrition was certainly part of the explanation for the population decline.

The brief declaration of independence, signed by Sukarno and Hatta, was read by Sukarno outside his house in Jakarta on the morning of 17 August 1945. A few weeks later, the British Army arrived to carry out what was expected to be a 'Red Cross' function. Japanese soldiers were to be disarmed and repatriated as soon as transport was available while the prisoners of war, mainly Dutch, were to be released, and also repatriated, or resettled in Indonesia. Compared to other parts of the region, especially

---

[2] The population census planned for 1940 never took place; the estimates of population in 1940 are based on the 1930 figures, and an assumption that population grew through the 1930s at 1.5 per cent per annum. According to the Central Bureau of Statistics (CBS 1947: table 8), the indigenous population of Indonesia was 68.63 million in 1940. Assuming a growth of 1.5 per cent per annum, it would have been 79.65 million in 1950; in fact it was officially estimated to have been 77.2 million.

Burma and the Philippines, Java had escaped massive devastation of infrastructure, and it was expected that ports, roads and railways could be quickly rehabilitated. But the British soon realised that a national revolution was underway, and the returning Dutch would have to deal with the situation. The Dutch for their part were determined to re-impose the colonial system as it was when they had been forced out by the Japanese in early 1942. They were convinced that the nationalists were led by Japanese collaborators, and had little support among the great majority of the population. Underpinning this view was a realisation that the Netherlands economy was itself in a very bad shape after years of German occupation, and that the 'loss of the Indies' would impose an even greater economic burden on the Dutch people.[3]

The USA had emerged as by far the strongest economic and military power in both Western Europe and Asia, but the Americans were themselves uncertain about how to treat the Indonesian nationalists. Only after the Madiun rebellion was put down in 1948 did the Americans decide that the Indonesian leaders were not pro-communist, and their legitimate aspirations for independence should be supported. The negotiations with the Dutch which led up to the transfer of power in December 1949 were difficult, and often acrimonious, especially regarding the role of Dutch commercial and financial interests after independence. The Dutch demanded that the newly independent country must take over the entire debt of the Netherlands Indies, and 'insisted on obtaining necessary guarantees for unrestricted operations by Dutch business enterprises in independent Indonesia' (Thee 2012: 6).

The Dutch reluctantly agreed to some reduction in the debt, to allow for the cost of the war against the nationalists waged from 1945 to 1949. According to Kahin (1997: 26), the work of Sumitro Djojohadikusomo was particularly important in getting the Dutch to agree to this reduction: the final amount was set at $1.13 billion. The American representative at the conference 'encouraged the Republic's leaders to expect that American aid would be generous' but in the end they only received a loan of $100 million from the Export–Import Bank, which had to be repaid with interest, and which was considerably less than the credits given to the home government in the Netherlands (Kahin 1997: 26).

---

[3] A memorandum circulated by J. Derksen and J. Tinbergen during the German occupation used a simple multiplier model to estimate the effect of the loss of colonial remittances on the Dutch economy. Their prediction that the loss would have a serious negative impact on the home economy influenced official opinion after 1945, although it turned out to be incorrect. American aid together with rapid recovery in Germany led to a fast recovery in the Netherlands, and by 1960 the gap between Dutch and Indonesian GDP per capita was greater than it had been in the late 1930s.

Table 3.1 *Index of per capita GDP in pre-war peak, 1950, 1955 and 1960 (pre-war = 100)*

Country	c. 1941	1950	1955	1960
Indonesia (1941)	100	71	82	88
Malaysia (1942)	100	93	87	91
Singapore (1939)	100	93	82	83
Thailand (1938)	100	99	114	131
Burma (1938)	100	54	63	76
India (1943)	100	89	97	108
Philippines (1939)	100	74	93	101
Taiwan (1938)	100	70	91	103
South Korea (1937)	100	52	71	75

Sources: Malaysia, Thailand, Burma and South Korea: Maddison (2003: 182–5); Indonesia: van der Eng (2013); Singapore: Sugimoto (2011: 49, 185); India: Sivasubramonian (2002: 136–9); Philippines: Hooley (2005: table A-1); Taiwan: Sato (2008: 233–4, 395–6).

The struggle against the Dutch lasted over four years and the economic consequences were severe. Guerrilla warfare against the Dutch army caused considerable devastation and prevented economic rehabilitation. By the end of the decade most of the important export industries were producing only a small fraction of their pre-1942 output. Smallholder agricultural output in Java was also well below pre-1942 levels. De Vries (1949: 132) observed that many seed farms had been destroyed, irrigation systems had not been maintained and 'vast areas of hill country' had been damaged by soil erosion. In the final years of the Japanese occupation, the widespread issue of Japanese banknotes caused mounting inflation, which continued after 1945. Food continued to be scarce, especially in urban areas. By 1949, per capita GDP was only 64 per cent of the 1941 level (van der Eng 2013).

Indonesia was hardly alone in Asia in experiencing per capita output declines over the 1940s. Only Thailand had recovered to pre-war levels of GDP by 1950 (Table 3.1). In Taiwan, and the Philippines, the output decline was much the same as in Indonesia, while it was much worse in South Korea and Burma. But compared to most other former colonies, the conditions imposed by the Dutch in the negotiations leading up to the transfer of power were harsh. The Financial-Economic Agreement (*Finec*) signed in November 1949 guaranteed that Dutch businesses in Indonesia could continue business as usual including the remittance of profits. Apart from having to take over much of the colonial debt, there was also an obligation on the part of the Indonesian government to 'consult' with the Netherlands on all monetary and financial measures which might affect Dutch business interests (Dick 2002: 171; Lindblad 2008: 73). The Java Bank, which had many of the functions of a central bank, was still controlled by the Dutch, making an independent monetary possible difficult (Thee 2012: 6–7). It was hardly surprising that many nationalists were bitter about these terms and blamed Hatta in particular for conceding too much.

In addition, Indonesia in the early 1950s faced some fundamental political and economic dilemmas which during the independence struggle had not been confronted, let alone resolved. What sort of constitution should the country embrace? The federal system, adopted under duress in 1949, was abandoned in favour of a unitary state in 1950, but many Indonesians realised that some way would have to be found to accommodate the legitimate demands of the smaller, export-oriented regions outside Java. The fear that Javanese colonialism would replace that of the Dutch was widespread outside Java in the early 1950s, and ultimately led to the rebellions in the latter part of the decade. Kahar Muzakar, who led the rebels in South Sulawesi, accused Sukarno of a 'new Madjapahitism', and argued that he was seeking to impose Javanese hegemony on other parts of the country (Muzakar 1960).

There was also the legacy of the 'plural society', so graphically depicted by Furnivall, who claimed that while most visitors to both Burma and Java were impressed by the 'medley of peoples', the different ethnic groups 'mix but do not combine'. They met in the marketplace to buy and sell, but did not integrate socially or culturally. Even in the economic sphere, there was a division of labour along racial lines, with different ethnic groups having different functions (Furnivall 1948: 304–5). In the private sector, Dutch and Chinese businesses played a dominant role in the late colonial era, and in the view of many nationalists not much changed after 1949. With production in most sectors of the economy substantially below pre-1942 levels, how could the new government meet the increased expectations regarding employment and living standards which political independence had brought?

Tackling the challenges

There were certainly several among the first generation of post-independence politicians who grasped fully the difficulties facing the new state. In his statement to the national parliament after taking office as prime minister in September 1950, Mohammad Natsir (1951: 54) argued that changes from a colonial to a national economic structure 'cannot be achieved in one or two years' and warned that political independence would not automatically be followed by greater prosperity. It would take time and much hard work to create a 'balanced economic structure' in place of the colonial system, and in the meantime Indonesians would have to continue to depend on foreign capital and expertise. Even more important than capital accumulation, there was an urgent need to develop the 'knowledge, comprehension and organizing ability' of the Indonesian people, and improved access to education was the key to such development.

The Natsir statement reflected the views of the two leading technocrats in the cabinet, Sjafruddin Prawiranegara (Minister of Finance) and Sumitro Djojohadikusumo (Minister of Trade and Industry). But the position of the Natsir government was weak. It excluded the main nationalist party, the *Partai Nasional Indonesia* (PNI), and only survived until March 1951, when it was succeeded by the Sukiman cabinet. The Natsir cabinet did achieve some progress in improving administration, and in establishing a framework for planned economic growth. It was able to implement some important reforms in tax policy including the introduction of a sales tax. But it failed 'to build itself a basis of political support' (Feith 1962: 176). This indeed was to be the fate of most of the cabinets of the 1950–1957 period; they were in office for too short a period to be able to implement effective economic policies, even where there was a clear vision about what policies were needed. Increasingly as the 1950s progressed, vision was replaced by haggling over the division of government resources, which in turn were limited by the weak capacity of the government apparatus to mobilise revenues.

But in spite of the political instability which characterised the decade as a whole, there was in fact some progress towards the goals laid out in the Natsir statement, and especially towards improving the 'knowledge, comprehension and organizing ability' of the Indonesian people. These achievements have often been overlooked by subsequent scholars who have tended to stress the improvements which occurred during Suharto's long period in office. They are all the more impressive when assessed in the light of the legacies bequeathed by the Dutch, the Japanese and the independence struggle, as well as in the light of the macroeconomic problems which beset successive governments post-1950. The next section examines these macroeconomic problems in more detail.

The macroeconomic environment: 1949–1967

Several series are available which show growth of national income and its components after the transfer of power in 1949. The series published by the United Nations Economic Commission for Asia and the Far East

Table 3.2 *Real per capita government revenues and expenditures, 1938–1964 (guilders, rupiah per capita: 1953 prices)*

	Revenues	Expenditures
1938	135.4	151.2
1951	166.7	149.9
1953	165.8	191.0
1955	97.9	122.3
1957	135.7	169.0
1959	77.0	111.2
1962	44.8	74.0

Sources: Population data: CBS (2014: table 2.1). Revenue and expenditure data; 1938: Creutzberg (1976: table 4); 1951–1962: CBS (1971: 317). Price deflator: Jakarta retail price index for 15 home and 15 imported goods; CBS (1963: 260–1).

shows that GNP at 1955 prices grew by 33 per cent between 1951 and 1959 (ECAFE 1964: 240). This is much the same growth rate as that shown in the more recent series prepared by van der Eng (2013). Given that population grew over the years from 1951 to 1959 by around 16 per cent, it seems clear that there was some growth in per capita GDP over the 1950s, although not enough to permit a return to the 1941 level. Both government revenues and government expenditures rose in real terms over the 1950s. According to the ECAFE study government total expenditures almost doubled in real terms between 1951 and 1959, although the increase in real revenues was slower (ECAFE 1964: 242).

Several points should be made about the growth in government expenditures. First, in spite of the real growth which occurred after 1950, it is probable that real per capita government expenditures were lower in the 1950s than in the latter part of the 1930s. Using the Jakarta Retail Price Index as a deflator, real expenditures per capita were higher in 1953 than they had been in 1938, but fell back sharply after that year (Table 3.2). Second, most expenditures were devoted to current rather than capital expenditures, especially capital expenditures on public works and transport. Indeed expenditures on public works, power and transport together with health and education never appear to have amounted to more than about 15 per cent of the total over the decade, while defence expenditures had risen to more than one-third of the total by 1960 (Booth 2010: table 4). Defence outlays peaked at around half of total expenditures in 1962. Total investment expenditures declined relative to national expenditure over the 1950s and by 1960 were only about 7 per cent of GNE, most of which was contributed by the private sector (ECAFE 1964: 243). In 1957, government investment expenditure at 2.6 per cent of GDP was lower than in any other Asian country except the Philippines. The share of government in total investment expenditure was also low in comparison with other Asian countries (Booth 1998: 167).

A third point relates to the much faster growth in budgetary expenditures than in revenues after 1951. In fact, after 1951, total revenues fell steadily in real terms and only returned to the 1951 level in 1959 (ECAFE 1964: 242). The inevitable result was widening government deficits, and the debt/GDP ratio increased. This increase in itself could have been manageable if the debt was funded in non-inflationary ways such as through domestic or foreign borrowing. But by 1960 the floating debt was over 63 per cent of the total; this represented borrowing from the central bank. The government sector was adding to the money supply without any compensating decline in other sectors of the economy, and this led to increasing inflation.[4] In contrast to Indonesia, most other countries in Southeast Asia had quite modest rates of inflation through the 1950s.

The poor performance of revenue policy after 1950 can be ascribed to several factors. Per capita GDP was still lower than at the end of the Dutch period, which meant that the revenue base was lower, and there was a reluctance on the part of many Indonesians to pay taxes, such as land and excise taxes, which were associated with 'colonial exploitation'. Many policy-makers were convinced that Indonesia possessed vast natural resource wealth, exploitation of which would yield large revenues to the government without the need for additional taxes whose incidence would fall on the indigenous population. This attitude was to persist in Indonesia for several decades. In fact, revenues from the extraction of natural resources remained quite small, and for most of the 1950s, government revenues were very reliant on foreign trade taxes, whose incidence fell in part on the incomes of indigenous producers of export crops such as rubber. Revenues from export and import taxes were high during the Korean War boom of the early 1950s, but even after world prices of rubber and other commodities fell, trade taxes continued to account for between one-third and one-half of total government revenues (CBS 1963: 219).

A general sales tax was introduced in the early 1950s, and the proportion of revenues from the sales tax and excises did increase between 1951 and 1954, although fell thereafter. But direct taxes on personal and corporate incomes proved difficult to collect especially as inflation

---

[4] Ahrensdorf (1959) compared the causes of inflation in Indonesia with three Latin American countries which also had high inflation over the 1950s. He found that in Indonesia, the expansionary effect of government cash deficits exceeded that of credit expansion to the private sector, except in 1951.

accelerated, and they fell as a percentage of total revenues after 1955 (Booth 2010: table 5). Much of the growth in revenues after 1956 was due to increases in 'other revenues', which included contributions from state trading companies and 'excess profits' from sales of oil and other goods.

Measuring the extent of inflation was itself a difficult statistical exercise; different indices gave different results. Most of the cost of living indices published by the Central Bureau of Statistics in the years from 1950 to 1967 were based on colonial-era series, often using the same weights. In addition, with the publication of both nominal and real national income data, an economy-wide deflator could be estimated. Especially after 1957, the national income deflator showed a markedly lower rate of inflation than the cost of living indices, especially that which was based on prices of thirty home-produced and imported goods in the Jakarta market (Booth 2010: table 6). The rural food index was close to national income deflator until 1957, but diverged thereafter. It seems clear that after 1957, the impact of inflation varied considerably by region and social class. This point should be borne in mind in assessing real growth in income and wages in different parts of Indonesia over the entire period from 1950 until the late 1960s.

At the aggregate level, the private consumption component of gross national expenditure rose by slightly over 30 per cent between 1951 and 1957; this was considerably faster than population growth of around 12 per cent over these years (Table 3.3). This suggests that on average, real per capita consumption was rising. But how evenly distributed was this rise? Did differential rates of inflation mean that some groups

Table 3.3 *Growth of population, GNP, GDP and private consumption expenditures in Indonesia, 1951–1970 (1955 = 100)*

	POP	GNP	GDP	PCE
1951	92	81	85	82
1955	100	100	100	100
1957	104	110	107	108
1960	111	110	117	98
1963	118	126*	117	NA
1967	129	139*	124	NA
1970	137	149*	174	NA

* Estimated from the ECAFE model.
Notes: GNP refers to GNP at 1955 market prices. GDP is in 2000 market prices. PCE is private consumption expenditures at 1955 prices.
Sources: Population: CBS (2014: table 2.1); GNP and PCE: ECAFE (1964: 240, 243); GDP (van der Eng 2013).

benefited less than others? The price data might indicate that rural populations were more protected from the ravages of inflation than urban dwellers, although rural populations were by no means completely insulated from increases in market prices as many depended on purchased food and other basic needs. The impact of accelerating inflation on living standards is further examined later.

In October 1956, President Sukarno delivered a speech in which he claimed it was time for Indonesia to 'bury the parties' and embark on a new political and economic course. In March 1957, the second cabinet formed by Ali Sastroamidjojo fell, and Sukarno formed an extra-parliamentary emergency business cabinet (Legge 2003: 326). The prime minister was an engineer, Dr Juanda, who had served in earlier cabinets. Later in 1957, the defeat of the West Irian motion at the United Nations was the trigger for the takeover of Dutch companies across the country.[5] Thousands of Dutch nationals left. In January 1958, several key leaders from the parliamentary period including Natsir, Harahap and Sjafruddin Prawiranegara gathered in West Sumatra to form an alternative government. Their rebellion was not secessionist; their aim was to formulate a new constitution which gave the regions greater autonomy, making Indonesia in effect a federal state. During the second part of 1959, the leaders based in West Sumatra held meetings to draw up a new constitution for the proposed federal state where the component elements would be able to choose a form of government 'to accord with the culture and wishes of its people' (Kahin 2012: 136).

Faced with mounting challenges to the authority of the central government, Sukarno made it clear that he was no longer satisfied with his role as a figurehead president. He wanted a more powerful role, such as that accorded the office of president in the 1945 constitution. The idea of a return to the 1945 constitution was not new; it had been suggested by both political and military leaders as disillusionment with parliamentary democracy mounted (Legge 2003: 342). Finally in a short ceremony at the presidential palace on 5 July 1959, Sukarno dissolved the Constituent Assembly and adopted the 1945 constitution by decree. Such a decree in itself was probably unconstitutional, but was welcomed by at least some sections of Indonesian society as bringing to an end the instability of the

[5] The province of West New Guinea, or West Irian, was left under Dutch control in 1949, and became an increasingly contentious issue between Indonesia and the Netherlands in the 1950s. In August 1957, a group of Asian and African nations placed the dispute on the agenda of the General Assembly of the United Nations, but the subsequent resolution failed to secure a two-thirds majority. For a detailed discussion of the subsequent events see Lindblad (2008), Chapter VIII.

previous two years. By the end of 1961, the rebellion in Sumatra had been defeated, although in Sulawesi fighting continued for longer.

Over the five years from 1960 to 1965, the performance of the economy deteriorated, and inflation accelerated. By 1965, the consumer price index, which stood at 100 in 1954, reached 61,400 (Arndt 1971: 373). Sukarno himself had little interest in, or understanding of, economic issues (Legge 2003: 373). While he might have grasped that inflation had a detrimental effect on the living standards of many millions of Indonesians, in his speeches he claimed that Indonesia was a 'Great Nation' and was not going to beg for aid, especially if conditions were attached. It was better to eat poverty rations of cassava and be independent than eat beefsteak and be enslaved (Sukarno 1963: 395). By the early 1960s many Indonesians, although almost certainly not Sukarno himself, were eating poverty rations of cassava, and very few had access to beefsteak.

It is doubtful if Sukarno understood that the principal cause of the inflation was the increasing budget deficit which in turn was the result of stagnating revenues and growing military expenditures. He was not prepared to curtail the role of the military and after West Irian was incorporated into Indonesia, he launched another campaign against Malaysia. There was also a rapid growth in bank credit to fund the president's special projects including the national mosque, various monuments around Jakarta, luxury hotels and conferences of the 'new emerging forces' (Arndt 1971: 380–1). The final serious attempt at stabilisation occurred in May 1963, when a package of reforms were announced to stimulate exports and reduce the budget deficit through reduction of subsidies and increased revenues (Booth 1998: 172). But political support for the package was tenuous; many Indonesians were suspicious of its foreign, especially American, backing, and so its effect was short-lived.

Sukarno was increasingly under the influence of socialist views in his final years in office and in the power struggle between the military and the Indonesian Communist Party seemed more inclined to support the latter. Yet his attempts to increase government control over the economy were only partly successful. Most of the Dutch enterprises taken over in 1957–1958 became state enterprises, and the state-owned sector probably produced about 20 per cent of GDP by 1960 (Booth 1998: 175). Smallholder agriculture accounted for around 50 per cent of GDP; this sector remained the preserve of uncollectivised peasants (Castles 1965: 23). The residual share of GDP, around 30 per cent, was produced by privately owned non-agricultural enterprises. Many of the larger enterprises not owned by foreign interests were controlled by Chinese, often in conjunction with influential indigenous politicians or civil servants who were in a position to get access to import licenses and bank credit. The implications of these 'Ali-Baba' arrangements for private sector development will be discussed further in Chapter 7.

In spite of the growth of the state-owned sector after the nationalisations of the late 1950s, and in spite of the growing rhetoric about Indonesian socialism, it can be argued that the role of the government in the economy from the late 1950s onwards became weaker rather than stronger. Government budgetary expenditures never exceeded 11 per cent of GDP in the years from 1962 to 1967, and the amount devoted to non-military expenditures was usually much lower. Government provision of services including health, education, and agricultural extension was limited, although in some regions provincial and local governments took an active role in building schools and clinics, and paying for staff. But much infrastructure, including roads and irrigation, was not maintained. Outside Java, the control of the central government became increasingly tenuous, and especially in the export-producing regions, 'de facto federalism' prevailed (Mackie 1980: 675). Castles (1965: 30) argued that by the early 1960s, the prevailing ideology in government circles was hostile to all forms of capitalism, but 'de facto capitalism' was still alive and indeed flourishing in many parts of the country.

The performance of the export sector and the grievances of the export-producing regions

By the early 1960s, it was increasingly clear that some countries in Southeast Asia had recovered more quickly from the ravages of war, and were achieving faster economic growth than others (Table 3.1). One reason for the difference in economic performance was the different international trade and investment policies adopted in different parts of the region. Myint (1967) argued that policy in Indonesia and Burma became 'inward-looking' after 1950; exchange rates were overvalued and governments did little to assist smallholder producers of export crops. Official attitudes to foreign investment became more hostile; after the expropriation of Dutch assets in the late 1950s, Indonesia received little new investment outside the oil sector. This contrasts with Thailand where the Board of Investment was established in the early 1960s, and the government set out to attract foreign investment, especially in manufacturing.

Myint's assessment of export performance, especially in Indonesia, Burma and the Philippines, was distorted by statistical factors. The official exchange rate in these countries was overvalued and traded goods were thus undervalued in national income statistics compared with non-traded goods. The series on export volume produced by Rosendale (1975: 73) for Indonesia shows a 40 per cent increase between 1938 and 1957. This was higher than the increase in GDP over these years estimated by van der Eng (2013). Paauw (1963: 570–1) argued that the growth in export volume was mainly the result of growth in oil exports which in turn was the result of the so-called let-alone contracts which had been negotiated by the Dutch with the oil companies in the late 1940s. These contracts allowed the companies to repair infrastructure damaged by the Japanese in return for some free-dom in the disposition of foreign exchange earnings (Hunter 1966a: 260; Lindblad 2008: 41). They were unpopular with most nationalists but were honoured after 1949 until they expired.

While it is true that oil output did grow after 1950, rubber and tin exports also increased, although in the case of tin, there was a sharp decline in export volume after 1957 (Rosendale 1975: 74). The rubber story illustrates both the resilience of the export sector and also the problems it faced after 1949. By the late 1930s, smallholder production had accounted for almost half of total production. In the years from 1954 to 1960, the proportion rose to 65 per cent. Total rubber exports in 1954–1956 reached almost 700 million metric tons, compared to just over 400 million tons in 1938–1940. It seems likely that much of this increment was due to smallholders. While both estates and smallholders received a boost from the high prices in the early 1950s, it was the smallholders who were better able to weather the price falls after the temporary boom was over. They were also far less vulnerable to the political problems of the late 1950s which resulted in the nationalisation of the Dutch estates, and labour difficulties in other foreign-owned companies.

After 1957 export volume became more volatile. Accelerating infla-tion led to further real appreciation of the exchange rate. In several of the major producing regions outside Java, illegal trade grew, much of it the result of deliberate mis-invoicing of legal trade (Pitt 1991: 76). Indeed Pitt argued that by the mid-1960s, so much trade was conducted illeg-ally that for many exporters outside Java, the trade regime was not too different from that which would have prevailed under a more open system, with market-determined exchange rates. But even if that was the case, the export-producing provinces still had legitimate grievances against the central government, which piled up over time. The most serious grievance concerned the imbalance between export revenues and imports in several provinces outside Java.

In 1956/1960 the percentage of exports from Java had fallen to only 14 per cent compared with 35 per cent in the late 1930s (Table 3.4). The main reason for this decline was the demise of sugar exports; sugar production was only around 40 per cent of the average for 1938–1940

Table 3.4 *Exports from and imports to Java as a percentage of total exports and imports from/to Indonesia, 1911/1915–2006/2010*

	Exports	Imports
1911/1915	57	70
1916/1920	60	71
1921/1925	53	71
1926/1930	49	64
1931/1935	45	67
1936/1940	35	65
1956/1960	14	68
1961/1965	13	78
1966/1970	12	75
1971/1975	13	70
1976/1980	11	76
1981/1985[*]	18	70
1986/1990	28	78
1991/1995	43	82
1996/2000	48	80
2001/2005	48	81
2006/2010	41	78

Note: [*] After 1981, the CBS revised the export data; total exports increased by around 13 per cent but exports from Java increased by more than threefold. It is probable that the percentage of exports from Java between 1950 and 1980 was understated. *Source:* Booth (2015), table 2.1.

in the mid-1950s and almost all went into the domestic market. At the same time, the proportion of imports going into ports in Java grew. While some of these imports would have been shipped out again to smaller ports outside Java, many stayed in Java. This was because both government and private demand for imports of capital and consumption goods, especially food, was higher in Java. In addition, it is probable that government expenditures became more skewed towards Java, although this is more difficult to quantify.

The main complaint of the exporting regions was that, although they were the main generators of the nation's wealth, they were neglected when decisions were made on its expenditure (Feith 1962: 487–8). The whole issue of regional finance was subjected to detailed investigation in the mid-1950s by a committee headed by M. Nasroen, a senior civil servant in the Department of the Interior, and composed of fiscal experts from various government agencies. The committee's report proposed a complex system which would fund local governments through two streams; one would be exclusively local and the other composed of a share of central government revenues from income, company and wages taxes, stamp taxes, property taxes and customs and excise duties (Paauw 1960: Appendix D; Legge 1961: 189–200).

The Nasroen proposals were criticised by Paauw (1960: 411) on the grounds that they neither simplified the tax structure nor attacked the problem of an extremely complex administrative system. Other observers also pointed out that most of the taxes assigned to local governments were never going to yield much revenue. This was a criticism which was to recur again in most assessments of regional finance in Indonesia until the present day. It was also argued that the formulae suggested for distributing central revenues did not appear to be based on either the needs or the capacity of the local governments. In spite of these criticisms, many of the findings of this committee were incorporated in Law No. 32 of 1956, concerning financial relations between the centre and the autonomous regions. This law did make some important concessions to the regions in that it allowed the proceeds of both income taxes and foreign trade taxes to be shared between the provinces where the tax revenues originated and the central government. But as Legge (1961: 193) pointed out, implementation of this law was slow, even before the constitutional changes of 1959.

The return to the 1945 constitution, and the military campaigns against the PRRI/Permesta rebels in Sumatra and Sulawesi, created an environment where the centre had little appetite for further reform of trade and investment policies, or of centre–region financial arrangements. Mackie (1980: 674) argued that by the early 1960s 'a politics of manipulation and compromise replaced the earlier confrontational pattern of politics'. But while the army had managed to subdue the regional rebellions, it had neither the capacity nor the will to stop the smuggling; indeed some regional commanders were heavily involved in illegal activities. As the public finances deteriorated, grants to the regions diminished in real terms, and provincial and local governments tended to go their own way, disregarding central government regulations when it suited them. It was only after the violent events of 1965–1966 and the demise of Sukarno that a long process of recentralisation of power began.

Access to land and employment

Over the 1950s, economic planners in Indonesia had no clear idea of how employment patterns had changed, if at all, since the 1930 census. While it was expected that a substantial part of the increment in population had been accommodated in the agricultural sector, there was no way of knowing to what extent the growing labour force had access to land, and if not what alternative wage employment opportunities were available. What was clear was that disputes over access to land were becoming increasingly violent, both in Java and elsewhere. The Wilopo cabinet fell over disputes in North Sumatra, when the government was seen to be siding with the estate companies, many of them Dutch-owned, against the squatters who had moved onto land controlled by estates in the Japanese period and subsequently (Feith 1962: 292–7). The problems in North Sumatra were aggravated by the large influx of Toba Batak migrants who had left their traditional lands in the interior to seek land and work closer to Medan.

Cunningham (1958: 143) estimated that after 1948 around 100,000 hectares of former plantation land had been lost to the estates. To the extent that it had been occupied by squatters from the interior, this caused tensions with the local Malay population who considered themselves *orang asli*, with strong rights to land in the coastal regions. Contemporary observers pointed out that the problems in North Sumatra were the tip of a very large iceberg, and the problem of squatting, not only on foreign-leased estate land but also on public lands in towns and forests in many parts of the country, continued to be a major problem for subsequent administrations.

After 1900, Dutch colonial authorities had realised that the land frontier in Java could not be extended much further, and that more Javanese would have to move either to non-agricultural occupations or to agricultural settlements outside Java. Transmigration became part of the ethical package, and funds were allocated for the creation of new settlement sites in Sumatra and Sulawesi. It is estimated that 47,613 Javanese moved to other parts of the archipelago during 1938–1941, and through the 1950s another 40,000 moved (Jones 1966: 57). But these numbers were probably more than matched by in-migrants to urban Java from other parts of the country seeking education and employment, mainly in the service sector. The 1961 census data showed that the percentage of the total population living in Java had changed little from 1930, at around 65 per cent (Hunter 1966b: 37).

The 1961 census did show that there had been a slight decline in the proportion of the labour force in Java employed in agriculture (from 71 to 69 per cent) and a slight increase outside Java (Jones 1966: 54). But the absolute growth was considerable, in both Java and other regions. The most striking change shown by the 1961 census was the decline in the proportion of the labour force employed in manufacturing and the growth in the proportion employed in services. There was an absolute decline in the numbers of women working in manufacturing. This might have been the result of changing definitions but could also have reflected the demise of some handicraft industries (Booth 1998: 67–8). Although there was a considerable expansion in government employment after 1950, most of the new jobs in the service sector were in small-scale private enterprises, often family-based, and in domestic service.

The total number of government employees, including those working in central and local government and in state enterprises, came to around 1.033 million in 1961, which can be compared with the 1961 Population Census estimate of total employment in services (not including trade, financial services and transport) of 3.095 million (CBS 1963: 269–73). The balance of service workers not employed by government were in community and personal services. Many probably worked as household servants. There can be little doubt that government employment grew rapidly over the 1950s; it is probable that many former fighters in the independence struggle were given government jobs. But in spite of the growth in numbers after 1950, the total size of the government payroll was only about 1 per cent of the population in 1961. This was lower than in Thailand or Malaysia (Evers 1987: table 1). The evidence also indicated that many government employees were poorly educated with at most primary school education. This only changed after 1970.

The growth in numbers employed at least partly in agriculture explains the increase in squatting, and in the 1950s and early 1960s, the rights of those seeking access to land were vociferously supported by the Indonesian Communist Party (Mortimer 1974: Chapter 4). Indeed Mortimer (1980) argued that the remarkable recovery of the Indonesian Communist Party after the debacle in Madiun in 1948 was in large part due to their exploitation of rural grievances, especially in Java and Bali. But it was clear to many observers that even if all the land controlled by estates in Java, estimated to be around 627,000 hectares in 1961, were to be redistributed to the landless, there would not be sufficient land to provide them with an adequate living. This was probably the case in other parts of the archipelago as well. More off-farm employment would have to be provided to the growing labour force. In many densely settled parts of Java, employment in manufacturing and petty trade was an important sideline for families cultivating small parcels of land. The study carried out by the Institute of Economic and Social Research at the University of Indonesia in Djabres, Central Java, found that 88 per cent of households controlled less than 0.5 hectares of land. Nearly half the working population was engaged in secondary activities, especially in the roof-tile industry in which the village specialised (Widjojo 1956: 780).

But for many in Indonesia, employment outside small-scale agriculture in the 1950s and 1960s was limited in availability and poorly remunerated. The wage series assembled by Papanek (1980: tables 4.3–4.8) indicated a decline in real wages for estate workers in Java and Sumatra and household servants, especially after 1957. If these trends reflected developments in wages for other categories of unskilled workers including casual agricultural labourers, it is probable that many millions of Indonesians who owned either small parcels of land or no land at all experienced falling incomes and living standards.

Trends in fertility, mortality and per capita consumption

The problem of inadequate employment opportunities, which was very obvious in the early post-independence years, was a particular source of concern because demographic trends suggested that it would get much worse over the 1960s. The number of people entering the labour market over the 1950s was smaller than might have been expected given pre-1940 demographic trends because of the fall in birth rates and the rise in mortality associated with the Japanese occupation and the liberation struggle. But the 1950s saw both a fall in mortality and a rise in fertility. Estimates prepared by Widjojo (1970: 158) indicated that crude death rates fell over the 1950s to around twenty-six per thousand, compared with twenty-eight per thousand in the late 1930s and thirty-five per thousand in the early 1940s. Life expectancy also increased to an estimated forty-six years by 1967 (Table 3.5). Falling mortality and rising fertility pushed population growth rates to around 2 per cent per annum by the latter part of the 1950s. As a result of the post-1950 surge in births, in 1961 more than one-third of the population was under ten, and 42 per cent was under fifteen (Hunter 1966b: 39).

The decline in mortality, and the consequent increase in life expectancy, could be interpreted as showing an improvement in overall living standards compared with the late colonial era. But the acceleration in population growth rates implied that there would be huge problems in supplying even basic needs of food, clothing and shelter to the growing population, let alone improving access to health, education, transport and other services. In fact the official data showed that rice consumption per capita in Java was slightly higher in 1955/1959 than in 1936/1940, although total consumption of all cereals and root crops was lower (Table 3.5). The increased consumption of rice in part reflected growing reliance on imports, which in turn meant that scarce foreign exchange was being diverted from urgently needed imports of raw materials and capital equipment. Outside Java, per capita availability of the major food crops in

Table 3.5 *Per capita GDP, food consumption, life expectancy, literacy and educational enrolments, 1936–1940, 1955–1959 and 1960–1964*

Indicator	1936/1940	1955/1959	1960/1964
Per capita GDP*	2,157	1,996	2,093
Per capita rice intake ** (kg per year)			
Java	86.2	87.6	84.4
Indonesia	NA	94.6	91.7
Per capita cereals and roots intake ** (kg per year)			
Java	198	176	175
Indonesia	NA	177	176
Per capita pulses intake ** (kg per year)			
Java	7.8	8.5	9.0
Indonesia	NA	6.4	6.0
Life expectancy			
(years)	35	37.5	45.7 (1967)
Literacy	NA	NA	46.7 (1961)
Enrolments***	3.6%	7.4%	15.5%

* Rupiah per capita: 2000 prices for 1938, 1957, 1962.
** Food availability, accounting for imports and exports.
*** Enrolments in primary and secondary schools as a percentage of total population.
Sources: Per capita GDP: Van der Eng (2013); per capita rice and food availability: CBS (1959: 215), CBS (1963: 245), CBS (1968: 359). Life expectancy and crude death rates: Widjojo (1970: 158, 191), CBS (2006b: 87); Educational enrolments: CBS (1968: 47).

calorie terms was often lower than on Java; in Sumatra it was only about 84 per cent of the Javanese figure (Mears 1961: table 1). This cast a doubt on the casual assumption, made by many Javanese, that food availability was always higher outside Java.

Trends in average indicators such as food availability do not tell us anything about distribution. To estimate distributional indicators, comprehensive households surveys are needed, and these were not carried out in Indonesia until the 1960s. A cost of living survey carried out in Jakarta by the Institute of Economic and Social Research (LPEM) at the University of Indonesia in 1953/1954 made comparisons with the survey conducted in 1937 of the living conditions of coolies employed by the municipal government in Batavia. The sample for the 1953/1954 survey was small (only 250 families) and it is possible that it was more skewed towards very poor households than the 1937 survey. But the analysis showed that a much higher percentage of household budgets was spent on food in 1953/1954 compared with 1937 (74 per cent compared with 56.5 per cent), and that in real terms monthly per capita food expenditures in 1953/1954 were substantially lower.[6] If this were the case in Jakarta, it is likely to have been true in other urban areas as well, and probably also in many rural districts.

The first national socioeconomic survey was carried out by the Central Bureau of Statistics in 1963/1964 but only in Java. A further survey in 1964/1965 covered most, but not all provinces outside Java, while the one carried out in 1967 again only covered Java. These three surveys gave an alarming picture of poverty trends in Java. In 1963/1964 and 1964/1965 around 61 per cent of households were spending less than a very modest poverty line, the equivalent of 20 kg of rice per capita per month.[7] In 1967 this percentage increased to 67 per cent (Booth 1988: 193). Outside Java 52 per cent of the population was below the 20 kg threshold in 1964/1965. In 1964/1965 only 8 per cent of households in Java were considered self-sufficient, and about 10 per cent outside Java. The 1963/1964 survey also showed that there were very sharp disparities in per capita rice consumption in Java between the top 20 per cent of the expenditure distribution and the bottom 20 per cent; the richest group were eating more than three times the amount of the poorest (Timmer 2015: 103). Disparities in rice consumption probably reflected even larger disparities in non-food consumption expenditures.

The grim picture given by the socioeconomic surveys was confirmed by data on food availability in different parts of the country. In colonial times, nutritionists were already aware that rice consumption per capita in many parts of Java was insufficient to furnish an adequate caloric intake, let alone sufficient protein and vitamins. A range of food supplements would be needed for a balanced diet. Many poorer households relied on corn and root crops to supplement whatever rice they could obtain. The evidence assembled by the Evaluation Study of the Applied Nutrition Project found that average per capita consumption of basic foods in Java when measured in rice equivalents had fallen in 1956/1959 compared with 1936/1939 from 204 kg per capita to

---

[6] Weinreb and Ibrahim (1957: Tables 14 and 15). These authors show that nominal expenditures on food rose almost nine-fold between 1937 and 1953/1954, which was a much lower rate of increase than that shown by the main cost of living indicators reported in *Statistical Pocketbook 1959*, 223–34.

[7] These poverty lines based on rice prices were proposed by Sajogyo (1975) and were used in poverty assessments until the BPS put forward a national poverty line based on a broader basket of basic needs. The choice of poverty lines in Indonesia is discussed further in Chapter 8.

175 kg per capita (Sajogyo 1975: 67). By 1965/1969 it had fallen even further to 154 kg per capita. Per capita consumption of peanuts and soybeans had also fallen, from around 9.2 kg per capita in 1936/1939 to 6 kg per capita in the late 1960s.

By the early 1960s it was estimated that in thirty-five of the eighty districts (*kabupaten*) in Java, cassava consumption exceeded 50 kg per capita per year, indicating that many people used it as their staple food, and would probably be suffering from malnutrition as a result. In 85 per cent of districts, rice and corn consumption per capita in 1961 was below the caloric minimum (Napitupulu 1968: 65). Neither was the problem of poor diet confined to Java. In parts of Eastern Indonesia, including Maluku and East Nusatenggara, where sago and tubers were staple foods, malnutrition was likely to be a problem unless people could get access to supplementary fruits, vegetables, fish and meat. For many poorer households these were luxuries they could seldom enjoy.

Educational development and the rise of 'new classes'

Before 1900, very few Indonesians were able to access Dutch-language schools, and there were a limited number of secular schools teaching in the vernacular languages. One of the goals of the ethical policy was more educational provision, although the Dutch were concerned that education might raise the employment expectations of young Indonesians far beyond the capacity of the economy to provide appropriate jobs. Thus schooling was provided in the main languages of the archipelago, and was intended to impart basic literacy and numeracy and useful skills to young people, which would improve their productivity in traditional occupations such as farming and trading. In spite of the economic problems of the early 1930s, it was estimated that by 1940 around 45 per cent of children aged six to nine were enrolled in vernacular schools compared with 35 per cent in 1930 (van der Wal 1961: 7). This might appear a reasonable achievement for a colonial regime which was often accused of neglecting education, although many children failed to complete even the three-year cycle, and the vast majority did not continue to secondary school, or beyond.

The comparative data assembled by Furnivall (1943: 111) indicated that by the late 1930s, the ratio of total school enrolments to population was only about 4 per cent in Indonesia, which was lower than in any other colonial territory in Southeast Asia except French Indochina, and lower than in the Japanese colonies of Taiwan and Korea. An important reason for the slow growth in enrolments and the high dropout rate was the fee structure. Even the vocational schools designed exclusively for indigenous Indonesians charged fees which were high in relation to average incomes and students usually had to live away from home and pay board. As van der Veur (1969: 16) argued, even the slightest change in family circumstances could spell the end of a child's educational career.

But the lucky few who gained some kind of vocational diploma joined what Wertheim (1956: 126) called the 'new class of intellectuals' who, as was pointed out in the previous chapter, occupied a special position in late colonial society. Their grasp of Dutch and familiarity with events in the wider world gave them considerable prestige and many made socially advantageous marriages. Young men who had achieved some education in the Dutch language (the great majority were male) began to envision careers for themselves, especially in government and public administration, which would have been beyond the dreams of their parents. The abrupt end of Dutch colonialism and the arrival of the Japanese in 1942 opened up new opportunities which they were not slow to grasp.

It seems probable that there was some expansion of educational opportunities for boys in particular during the Japanese occupation. Many young men joined the various militias which the Japanese established, and which could have served an educational function as well as instilling military virtues and loyalty to the regime. In the latter part of the 1940s, more schools were opened, especially in those areas where the forces of the republic were in control. That literacy was still low was obvious; a leading authority estimated that more than 60 per cent of the population was illiterate in 1947.[8] But the 1961 Population Census revealed a sharp increase in literacy in the younger age groups, especially for males under the age of twenty-five who would have been five or younger in 1940 (Booth 2010: table 8). This suggests some expansion in educational opportunities over the 1940s, or at least an increase in opportunities for young people to gain basic literacy.

After independence, there were ambitious plans to increase educational enrolments at all levels. Many nationalists argued that education in the national language was a crucial means of welding the many ethnic groups of the archipelago into a coherent entity. The old division between Dutch and vernacular language schools was abolished, as were the schools for Indonesians of Chinese descent. All children were to experience the same schooling in the same language. But inevitably, given the

---

[8] Van der Wal (1961: 7) quotes estimates of Professor H. Djajadiningrat, head of the Department of Education in Batavia in 1948, that using the American definition of illiteracy, the percentage was 69 per cent in 1930, dropping to 63 per cent in 1947. The 1961 Population Census reported total illiteracy rates as 53 per cent, but probably used a different definition (Nugroho 1967: 141).

post-1950 surge in the birth rate, and the fact that in most regions enrolments were starting from a low base, most of the growth was at the primary level. The growth was impressive; primary enrolments in 1955/ 1956 were almost three times the numbers recorded in 1939/1940. Perhaps more surprisingly, teachers were found to put in front of the classes; the student–teacher ratio was lower in 1960/1961 than in the late 1930s (Booth 2010: table 9). The momentum continued even into the troubled years of the early 1960s. For much of the period from 1950 to 1965 the growth in primary and secondary enrolments in Indonesia was well above the Asian average.

But, inevitably, rapid growth brought with it many problems. Many of the teachers were poorly trained and their real salaries were in most cases well below pre-1942 levels. Hutasoit (1954: 53) pointed out that many school buildings had been neglected or destroyed during the 1940s. After 1950 some were taken over by other government departments, especially in the larger cities. In Jakarta alone it was estimated that thirty-four school buildings had been converted to other uses. Given the growth in enrolments, most urban schools had to operate on a two-shift basis. Basic teaching aids including books and writing paper usually had to be provided by the students. In many parts of the country community groups were responsible for the building and maintenance of school buildings; often they also supplemented inadequate teacher salaries (Daroesman 1972: 65; Beeby 1979: 43–4). In Maluku, Hutasoit (1954: 53–4) claimed that all schools had been 'provided by the people' via levies in cash or kind; this may well have been true of other provinces also.[9] Pupils were also required to make up-front payments, and also to pay monthly fees, which acted as a barrier to entry, and in many cases led to high dropouts.

In spite of the problems, several million Indonesian children, both boys and girls, were enrolled in primary schools by the early 1960s. The 1961 census indicated that 77.4 per cent of boys and 72.4 per cent of girls aged seven to thirteen in urban areas were attending school (Booth 2010: table 10). Figures in rural areas were lower but on average more than half of all children were enrolled. But what about progression to post-primary education? Here the figures were less encouraging. Of the 9.9 million students enrolled in schools in 1960/1961, 9.2 million were

---

[9] Paauw's analysis of the Interior Ministry's data on provincial and district budgets for 1953 revealed considerable capital expenditure by both levels, at least some of which went on school buildings. In addition provinces spent over 18 million rupiah on subsidies to primary schools. Paauw argued that the total value of investment projects completed by local governments without the support of the Interior Ministry would have been much greater, especially outside Java. See Paauw (1960: 291–6).

at the primary level, 541,500 were attending lower and upper secondary schools and the balance were enrolled in vocational and university-level courses which would presumably lead to some kind of technical or professional qualification (CBS 1963: 31). Of most interest are the 29,000 enrolled in universities, as these would comprise most of the recruits into the senior civil service positions and into professional and technical jobs in the private sector over the 1960s and beyond.

What kind of background did they come from? The survey conducted by Palmier at Gadjah Mada University in the early 1950s found that around 60 per cent of the students were the children of government officials; the percentage was higher in the Faculty of Medicine than in the less prestigious faculties such as agriculture and literature (Palmier 1957: 370–1). It was higher still in the government academic high schools, which were the path to a university career. At the lower levels of the school system, Palmier (1957: 331) argued that the schools attended by the children of officials had a much better record of passes in the final examination than those where government officials were only a small proportion of all parents. In his sample of twenty-four schools, there was significant positive correlation between the percentage of children who passed the final examination and the percentage of parents who were government officials. Palmier concluded that:

The road to the University lies from the elementary through the State and subsidized secondary and high academic schools. Though it may not be true to say that the higher one goes the smaller the share of available places that the non-officials obtain, it appears to be the case that, generally speaking, the higher schools have most of their places given to the officials. This is much more so for the institutions which prepare for the more remunerative and esteemed professions. While the same general pattern applied in the vocational schools ... they were much more the preserve of children of non-officials. (Palmier 1957: 371–2)

Palmier also pointed out that both the Moslem schools and the unsubsidised secular schools, although dissimilar in many ways, had several features in common. They catered largely for the children of non-officials and the education they provided was unlikely to permit their graduates to enter the upper levels of the government service, as it did not provide them with the necessary qualifications. But the educational experience gained by students in these schools did inculcate similar expectations regarding careers and remuneration. As economic growth slowed in the late 1950s and early 1960s, these students would have found it very difficult to get jobs either in government or in the stagnating private sector. Their frustrations added to the social unrest of the period.

Palmier's research suggests that during the 1950s, a powerful new 'official class' of administrators, teachers and professionals was developing whose members were using the education system to advance their own careers, and those of their children. Wertheim (1956: 140) argued that, by the early 1950s, the 'social supremacy of the upper layer of the new class of Western-educated Indonesians' appeared assured, not least because many Europeans and mixed-race residents were leaving. Many of this upper layer were among the fortunate minority who had managed to get some post-primary education in the colonial era, and who then had moved into more responsible positions during the Japanese occupation, and after 1950. Although some had retired by the time that Suharto came to power and some with the wrong political affiliations saw their careers abruptly terminated in 1965/1966, it was in many cases their children who gained the necessary tertiary qualifications in the years from 1955 to 1965, and who in turn benefited from the boom years of the 1970s.

Many of the new official class of the post-independence era were influenced to a greater or lesser extent by socialist ideas and espoused views which were hostile to private enterprise and to capitalism. The majority of officials may have had little sympathy with the egalitarian and populist rhetoric of the Indonesian Communist Party and its affiliates. But neither did they necessarily support even the mildly pro-private enterprise views of the Natsir statement. The implications of this for private sector development will be examined further in Chapter 7. As a result of the growing hostility, the position of the Indonesian Chinese became more difficult in the latter part of the 1950s. Some of the anti-Chinese regulations were adopted because of pressure from the military and indigenous business groups, rather than because of government hostility. Sukarno himself was never an advocate of overt discrimination (Legge 2003: 372–3). Even so, many Chinese took the exit option and left for China, Hong Kong, Singapore and the Netherlands.

The 1961 Population Census did not break down the labour force by ethnicity, so it is impossible to tell whether the Chinese share of the non-agricultural labour force had changed markedly compared with 1930. But given that indigenous Indonesians already accounted for a high share of the non-agricultural labour force in 1930, even in occupations such as trade which were often thought to be the preserve of the Chinese, it is highly unlikely that their share would have fallen by 1961. What upset nationalists was that the Chinese were perceived to control the larger and more profitable private enterprises which were not in foreign hands, and also dominate the more lucrative professions. Indigenous Indonesians were small shopkeepers and school teachers but the Chinese owned the large stores and were the doctors and the lawyers.

Williams (1952: 59) argued that during the last part of the colonial era, the Chinese in Indonesia 'failed to achieve entrepreneurship' and were indeed unable to do so in the colonial environment. This might seem a strange assertion, given the prominent role which Chinese businessmen were to play in business and commerce in the Suharto era. But it was true that many Chinese who had lived in Java for several generations wanted their children to gain some Dutch-language education, and move into the professions if possible, or at the very least work for the government or for private firms owned by Dutch and other foreign interests. This type of employment was considered more secure and conferred higher status than self-employment in business. In the post-1949 era, many Chinese businessmen were 'totok' (that is 'new comers'; migrants from China, or the children of migrants), rather than Dutch-speaking Chinese whose families had been in the Indies for several generations. The assimilated Chinese gravitated to the professions, although in the 1950s quotas were introduced in the universities, especially in faculties of law, medicine and engineering.

Gainers and losers from economic change: 1950–1967

In spite of the evidence that per capita GDP had not returned to pre-1940 levels by the late 1950s, it could still be argued that human development more broadly defined had improved somewhat in the latter part of the 1950s compared with twenty years earlier. Life expectancy had increased, which was mainly due to the dissemination of new medicines such as antibiotics and national campaigns including the use of DDT to destroy mosquitos.[10] There had been an improvement in educational enrolments relative to population. Literacy rates had also increased especially among the younger age cohorts. But at the same time there was mounting evidence that the economic growth which had undoubtedly occurred between 1950 and 1957 had benefited some groups more than others. The 'new class' of senior officials and politicians almost certainly benefited in real terms, and urban-based employers and employees in the private sector probably also experienced some real income growth. But taken together these groups were still a very small proportion of the total population.

A much larger proportion of the labour force were unskilled or semi-skilled labourers. By the end of the 1950s, it was clear that inflation had

---

[10] It is more difficult to quantify post-independence improvements in health than in education. But there can be little doubt that access to services did improve especially in urban areas, and this was reflected in increasing life expectancies over the 1950s.

taken its toll on wage labourers, and that for several important categories of worker such as estate labourers, daily wage rates in real terms were falling. This continued through the early 1960s. For those largely or wholly dependent on wage labour, this could only mean falling incomes and expenditures. But many millions of Indonesians who derived some income from wage labour also controlled some land, and at least part of their income came from agricultural production. Trends in their real income depended on the market prices of the crops they produced. These fluctuated considerably, but families who could produce enough rice and other food crops for most of their household needs were at least insulated from sharply rising prices. The minority of farmers who produced a substantial surplus of food crops over and above their own needs could well have experienced rising real incomes over the 1960s. On the other hand, it is clear that food consumption per capita for the great majority of the population in Java in the 1960s either stagnated or fell compared with the late 1930s.

Those farmers producing export crops experienced fluctuating fortunes after the end of the boom of 1950–1951. Rubber prices had actually recovered to levels close to 1950–1951 in the latter part of the decade, and those smallholders who were able to expand output over the decade may well have experienced some improvement in their income terms of trade, depending on the prices which they had to pay for food, clothing and other basic necessities. Export unit values for other important smallholder crops such as pepper, copra, tobacco and coffee fell more sharply from peaks in the early 1950s (Rosendale 1975: 74–5). Unfortunately, estimating the terms of trade for smallholder producers outside Java is very difficult as rural price data for consumption goods are not available. But it seems reasonable to assume that for most producers life was becoming more of a struggle by the early 1960s, and real incomes could only be maintained, if at all, by expanding output. The problem of falling international prices for some crops was of course aggravated by the increasingly over-valued exchange rate. By the early 1960s smuggling of exports to neighbouring countries was accelerating.

Given the data problems, it is unrealistic to expect that we are ever going to be in a position where we can state with certainty who gained and who lost from the economic changes which occurred in the years from 1949 to 1965. In terms of broad indicators of welfare, the most impressive gain was in education, but even here the main beneficiaries were those Indonesians whose families had been able to obtain non-agricultural employment, especially in government administration, in the 1930s and 1940s, and who moved into more responsible jobs after

1949. Perhaps that was inevitable, but the consequences for the future evolution of Indonesian society were considerable. Those who gained access to education and thence to secure and well-remunerated jobs in either the public or the private sector after 1950 were able to put their children through the academic high schools and universities. These graduates were in turn the main beneficiaries of economic growth in the Suharto era, and their descendants will continue to benefit from this legacy well into the twenty-first century.

4   Suharto's economic record
Successes and failures

Challenges facing Suharto's New Order

By the mid-1960s, most economists were painting a dismal picture of the Indonesian economy. In one of the most widely read textbooks of the decade, Higgins characterised Indonesia as the 'chronic dropout' and claimed that the country 'must surely be accounted the number one economic failure among the major underdeveloped countries'. He pointed out that all the available evidence pointed to prolonged stagnation throughout the colonial era, the Japanese occupation and the first two decades of independence and argued that such stagnation

in the form of virtually constant levels of per capita income or an unchanging structure of employment and production or both- is certainly not unknown among underdeveloped countries; but the Indonesian experience, in which a whole series of concepts of economic organisation, first in a colony and then in an independent nation, failed to bring significant or lasting improvements in levels of living at any time, seems to be unique. (Higgins 1968: 678)

At the time these words were written, few expected that there would be any dramatic improvement in Indonesia's economic fortunes. In September 1965 an attempted coup resulted in the murder in Jakarta of six senior generals. This provided an excuse for the military to begin to purge members of the Communist Party and ultimately Sukarno himself. In March 1966, the hitherto obscure Lieutenant-General Suharto together with the former diplomat Adam Malik and the Sultan of Yogyakarta assumed effective power. The new regime was backed by most of the army and also had the support of many groups within the intelligentsia, the student body and the Islamic community. Its anti-communist complexion guaranteed the new government considerable support from major Western bilateral and multilateral donors, support which had been spurned by Sukarno. But Indonesia's 'New Order' faced daunting tasks in rehabilitating the economy.

Per capita GDP in 1967 was lower, in real terms, than in 1941, and lower than in many other Asian and African countries (Table 4.1). Gross

Table 4.1 *Per capita GDP in 1967: Indonesia and other African and Asian countries (2005 international dollars)*

Asia		Africa	
ASEAN-5			
Indonesia	647	DR Congo	709
Thailand	1,324	Egypt	1,067
Philippines	1,696	Ghana	1,146
Malaysia	1,846	Nigeria	1,155
Singapore	5,320	Ivory Coast	1,212
		Senegal	1,287
Bangladesh	675		
China	716		
India	809		
Korea (Republic)	2,199		

Note: Data refer to per capita GDP, at 2005 prices, derived from growth rates of c, g, and i.
Source: Heston, Summers and Aten (2012).

domestic capital formation had sunk to 6 per cent of GDP in 1962, and remained at below 10 per cent until 1968 (CBS 1970: 47). The failure to invest was evident not just in the absence of new infrastructure and productive enterprises, but also in the poor condition of existing factories, roads, railways, electricity generation facilities, ports, airports, irrigation systems and so on. Visitors to the major Indonesian cities in Java and Sumatra were greeted with scenes of poverty, squalor and dilapidation. The situation was as bad or worse in Eastern Indonesia where, in the years from 1949 to 1967, only the most intrepid foreigners ventured. Transport and irrigation infrastructure in Java and Sumatra had deteriorated since 1945, but in other parts of the archipelago it had never been constructed. Shipping services were erratic and food supplies inadequate.

As a result, in 1960 road and rail densities (length divided by area) in Kalimantan, Sulawesi, Maluku and West New Guinea were lower than in most other former colonies in East and Southeast Asia, and in many colonies in sub-Saharan Africa including the Belgian Congo (Booth 2013: table 3.4). Irrigated agriculture was also restricted to a few regions in Bali and Sulawesi; in 1963, over 80 per cent of all paddy grown on irrigated land was produced in Java and Sumatra (CBS 1963: 71). In most regions in Eastern Indonesia, ports had developed in the colonial era to ship agricultural and mineral products to Java, or directly to Singapore, and roads were constructed to link ports to a few inland towns. Beyond these urban settlements transport was by river or by rough tracks. There were no railways and few airports. Inter-island shipping services had declined since independence, especially after the nationalisation measures in the late 1950s. In the early 1950s, freight carried by the Dutch line (KPM) was higher than in 1938 (Ali 1966: table 4). But after the nationalisation measures, efficiency was subordinated to the political aim of building up an Indonesian-owned system.

The problem of regional disparities in infrastructure was only one of many facing the new regime in 1966, and not the most urgent. Two statements issued in April 1966 by the Sultan of Yogyakarta, who had become Deputy Premier in charge of Economic Affairs, painted 'a picture of economic breakdown' with 'few parallels in a great nation in modern times' (Pang and Arndt 1966: 1). Most of the evaluations of Indonesia's economic prospects carried out in the latter part of the 1960s were pessimistic in tone, and argued that, given the magnitude of the problems facing the country, economic recovery would be slow. Top priority was given to stabilising prices, rescheduling repayments on the foreign debt, reducing the balance of payments deficit, and bringing order to the public finances. Some top officials known to be close to Sukarno, including the Governor of the Central Bank, were removed from office and detained, but most stayed in post and cooperated with the new leadership.

Suharto and his advisers realised that restoring credibility with Western aid donors was an essential prerequisite for a programme of sustained economic recovery. In order to enhance the legitimacy of his administration in the eyes of sceptical Western nations, several Western-trained academic economists from the University of Indonesia were recruited to advisory positions and then to the key economic portfolios in the cabinet announced in June 1968. Some of them had been educated at the University of California, and they became known as the 'Berkeley Mafia'. Although some radical groups in the USA and Europe claimed that this group, led by Professor Widjojo Nitisastro, was committed to an ultra-liberal, free-market policy agenda, the reality was a programme of cautious, pragmatic reform. 'Liberalism' in both its economic and political forms had been treated with great suspicion by many Indonesian intellectuals and policy-makers ever since independence, and the economist-technocrats who found themselves in the cabinet were only too aware that Suharto and his military advisers were hardly more enthusiastic about the merits of an open market economy than Sukarno had been.

The most immediate policy goal was to end the ruinous inflation. A crucial step to achieving this goal was to balance the budget by reducing expenditures, especially on defence, and by boosting revenues. In 1967, foreign credits were used to finance a considerable part of routine expenditure, but gradually domestic revenues were sufficient for this purpose.

Aid was targeted to the implementation of specific development projects. In addition, the new foreign investment law passed in 1967 facilitated investment by foreign companies in private sector development in sectors such as mining and manufacturing. The inflow of both public and private funds from abroad allowed both the budget and the balance of payments deficits to be brought under control without inducing a sharp domestic recession, although per capita GDP did not begin to rise until 1968. Between 1966 and 1969, the rate of inflation was reduced to single figures. Most controls on movements of capital into and out of the country had been removed, and by 1971 the exchange rate had been unified and pegged to the dollar.[1] In 1967 a poor rice harvest led to a sharp rise in domestic rice prices, which threatened to destabilise the recovery programme. This convinced the government of the importance of the food crop sector in the country's overall growth strategy. Agricultural development and the rehabilitation of rural infrastructure were thus accorded priority treatment in the first Five Year Plan of the New Order government, which began in April 1969.

Economic growth and structural change: 1968–1996

Between 1967 and 1981 the economy in fact grew at 8 per cent per annum, a faster rate than had been achieved at any time in the country's modern history. During most of these years and especially after 1974 when world oil prices began to increase rapidly, Indonesia enjoyed a substantial improvement in its terms of trade so that real income growth corrected for the terms of trade was over 10 per cent per annum between 1967 and 1981 (Sundrum 1986: 48). Real investment expenditures, which had stagnated through the years from 1962 to 1967, increased around nine-fold between 1967 and 1981. In 1981, they comprised more than 20 per cent of GDP. Consumption expenditure, which had stag-nated between 1962 and 1967, and fallen in per capita terms, increased by more than three-fold between 1968 and 1981 (Sundrum 1986: 49).

Although the fall in world oil prices in the early and mid-1980s was accompanied by a fall in growth rates, the government used the decline in the price of the country's main export as a pretext for initiating a wide-ranging programme of structural reforms, including two substantial devaluations of the rupiah, major taxation and banking reforms and a series of measures aimed at improving incentives for exporters.[2] By the

---

[1] A number of very useful studies on this period of stabilisation can be found in Glassburner (1971).

[2] These reforms have been discussed in detail in the 'Survey of Recent Developments' series in the *Bulletin of Indonesian Economic Studies*.

late 1980s, non-oil, and especially manufactured, exports were growing strongly, and the overall GDP growth rates had returned to around 7 per cent per annum. From being the 'chronic dropout' of twenty years earlier, the country was now being hailed by many in the international development establishment as a successful example of relatively painless structural adjustment in the wake of a commodity boom. In 1993 Indonesia, along with Thailand and Malaysia, the four 'Asian tigers' (Hong Kong, South Korea, Singapore and Taiwan) and Japan, was classified by the World Bank as one of Asia's 'miracle' economies, whose economic achievements 'set them apart from most other developing economies' (World Bank 1993: 2).

In reviewing economic achievements since 1969, the Sixth Five Year Plan (*Repelita VI*) emphasised both the record of sustained economic growth and the structural changes which occurred in the Indonesian economy over the twenty-five years from 1969 to 1994 (Booth 1994). GDP rose at an average rate of 6.8 per cent per annum; population growth over these twenty-five years averaged 2.1 per cent per annum, so per capita GDP growth was slightly under 5 per cent per annum. This rate of growth meant that per capita GDP was doubling every fifteen years. As a result of this sustained growth in per capita output, the economy became far more diversified, both in terms of the structure of production and in terms of exports.

If the sectoral composition of output and the labour force in 1971 is compared with 1995, the most striking difference is the decline in the role of the agricultural sector and the increase in the role of manufacturing industry. The share of industrial output in GDP (defined as manufacturing, construction and utilities) rose from 13.3 per cent in 1971 to 33.8 per cent in 1995 (Table 4.2). This was roughly equivalent to the share of industrial output in GDP in the Republic of Korea in 1970. Growth in manufacturing industry over the 1970s was exceptionally fast in world terms; Roepstorff (1985: 33) found that it was even faster than in Korea over the years from 1973 to 1981. The proportion of the labour force employed in manufacturing, construction and utilities also rose, although the structural change in the labour force over the two decades from 1971 to 1995 was not as dramatic as the change in national output. The proportion of the employed labour force in the agricultural sector fell from 66.3 per cent to 44 per cent, which was also similar to the Korean figure for the latter part of the 1960s.

It is well known that a process of sustained growth of GDP will over time lead to a fall in the share of agriculture in total output, and a similar, although usually slower, decline in the agricultural labour force as a proportion of the total labour force. But this does not mean that

Table 4.2 *Sectoral allocation of GDP and the labour force, 1971 and 1995*★

	GDP		Labour force		Relative★★ productivity	
	1971	1995	1971	1995	1971	1995
Agriculture	43.6	17.2	66.3	44.0	0.7	0.4
Mining	6.6	8.4	0.2	0.8	31.1	10.5
Manufacturing	9.4	24.2	6.8	12.6	1.4	1.9
Utilities	0.5	1.2	0.1	0.3	5.1	4.6
Construction	3.4	7.6	1.7	4.7	2.0	1.6
Trade	18.8	16.8	10.8	17.3	1.7	1.0
Transport	4.3	6.8	2.4	4.3	1.8	1.6
Banking	1.2	4.7	0.2	0.8	5.1	10.7
Dwellings	2.0	2.6	NA	NA	NA	NA
Public Services	5.6	5.9	10.3	15.1	0.8	0.6
Other Services★★★	4.8	4.6				
Total	100.0	100.0	100.0	100.0	1.00	1.00

★ GDP data are nominal; labour force data refer to employed workers only. In 1971, there were some employed workers whose occupations were not specified, so the data do not quite add to 100.
★★ GDP per employed worker in each sector as a ratio of GDP per employed worker for the labour force as a whole.
★★★ Labour force and productivity estimates refer to both public and other services.
Sources: CBS (1975a, 1975b, 1997).

agriculture is unimportant in the growth process. Indeed, successive New Order development plans gave high priority to agricultural and rural development. In the first phase of accelerated growth, from 1967 to 1973, when total GDP grew at around 8 per cent per annum, the agricultural sector accounted for almost 30 per cent of this growth (Sundrum 1986, table 13). Over these years, the government supported the introduction of the new seed–fertiliser–water technologies developed at the International Rice Research Institute in the Philippines, through the improved provision of irrigation and extension services, and provision of fertiliser at subsidised prices.[3] Rice yields began to increase, especially in Java.

After 1973, the world price of oil rose sharply. Indonesia was not a large oil exporter compared to producers in the Middle East but the higher

---

[3] Both in the colonial era and after independence, farmers in Indonesia did not pay for irrigation water. In the colonial era, the land tax was assessed on irrigated land at a higher rate than on other land in lieu of direct irrigation charges. After independence land tax revenues fell in real terms, but successive governments were reluctant to charge for irrigation water.

revenues earned from the exportable surplus of oil had important implications for both the balance of payments and the budget. Budgetary revenues from the oil company tax were used to further extend subsidies to the food crop sector, to encourage farmers to adopt the high-yielding varieties of rice. Irrigation systems were rehabilitated and extended, and chemical fertilisers such as urea and superphosphate were sold at subsidised prices on the open market. Central government grants to the regions for a range of infrastructure projects also increased. These efforts culminated in a burst of rice production growth between 1979 and 1984, when total output grew by 45 per cent. By 1985, the government was able to proclaim that rice self-sufficiency had been achieved.[4]

The fact that the oil boom years witnessed a rapid growth in both agriculture and manufacturing has led some commentators to argue that Indonesia managed to escape the 'Dutch Disease' or booming sector problem which affected other oil exporters in the 1970s. When a strong traded goods sector emerges, the absorption of revenues from the booming sector into the domestic economy will lead to an appreciation of the real exchange rate which puts pressure on exporters of other traded goods, and encourages a shift in output and employment towards non-traded sectors of the economy such as construction and services. Warr (1984) argued that there was some loss of competitiveness between 1971 and 1977. But the impact, during this period, of the exchange rate appreciation on food crop agriculture and manufacturing output was less severe than in other petroleum economies because of the assistance given to them through input subsidies in the case of food agriculture, and restrictions on imports through tariffs and quotas. In many sectors of manufacturing industry, effective rates of protection were very high through the 1970s and into the 1980s (Pangestu and Boediono 1986).

In the food crop sector, the growth in domestic output had a beneficial impact on domestic consumption. Food balance sheet data show that rice availability per capita increased from less than 100 kg per annum in the mid-1960s to 143 kg per capita in 1985. Production and consumption of other superior foodstuffs such as meat, milk and vegetables also increased over these years. However, after 1985 there was a marked slowdown in the rate of growth of rice production; total production rose by only 23 per cent in the decade from 1987 to 1997 (World Bank 1998: table 30). The slowdown was attributed to the fact that most rice farmers in the irrigated areas of Indonesia were achieving yields close to the technological maximum. Irrigated area outside Java also expanded, but the yields achieved

---

[4] A good overview of Indonesian rice policy in the years from 1968 to 1984 from the viewpoint of a key government adviser is given by Mears (1984).

tended on average to be lower. In addition, many farmers were finding that other crops such as vegetables were more lucrative than rice, and irrigated rice land was often used to cultivate these crops.

The overall contribution of the agricultural sector to total GDP growth in the years from 1983 to 1996 was only 15 per cent, while that of the mining sector was just over 6 per cent. The manufacturing, utilities, construction and financial services sectors were the main engines of growth. Together these sectors accounted for almost half of total GDP growth in these years, and the manufacturing sector alone for 27 per cent.[5] The rapid growth of the manufacturing sector was partly due to the growth of petroleum and natural gas processing, but in 1996 these two industries accounted for only about 10 per cent of total manufacturing output (World Bank 1998: table 6). The rest was accounted for by a range of manufacturing activities, some such as motor vehicles oriented largely to the domestic market, and some such as wood processing, garments and footwear, and electronics oriented mainly to the export market.

The growth of manufactured exports was an important reason for the striking change in the composition of exports which took place between 1983 and 1996. In the 1960s, Indonesia's export composition was typical of most undeveloped economies. There was heavy reliance on a narrow range of primary commodities, in particular rubber and crude petroleum. In 1965, around 70 per cent of official export earnings were derived from these two products. At the peak of the oil boom, oil revenues accounted for over 80 per cent of total export earnings. Export earnings from the petroleum and gas sector as a percentage of the total declined sharply between 1981 (the peak of the oil boom) and 1989, recovered somewhat in 1990, and then fell again. Non-oil export receipts grew rapidly, to 35 per cent of total export earnings in 1986 and to almost 78 per cent in 1995/96 (World Bank 1997: 11). Over 40 per cent of the increase in non-oil export earnings between 1986 and 1996 was derived not from traditional staples like rubber, palm oil, coffee or non-ferrous metals, but from new manufactured exports, dominated by processed wood products (especially plywood), textiles and garments, footwear, electrical appliances and a range of other goods including furniture, leather goods, pulp and paper products and chemicals. The rapidity of the growth of these 'new exports' surprised many observers. Several explanations for this success have been put forward.

First, the exchange rate had fallen sharply in real terms after the two large devaluations of the rupiah in 1983 and 1986, and the subsequent

---

[5] These percentages are estimated from the current price data given in World Bank (1998: Table 5).

decision to allow the rate to float downwards relative to the dollar. Warr (1992: 153) showed that the relative price of tradables to non-tradables rose sharply after the two devaluations of 1983 and 1986. On price and quality Indonesia began to compete successfully with producers of labour-intensive manufactures from other parts of the region, including China, Thailand and Malaysia. In addition, the very sharp appreciation of the Japanese, Korean and Taiwanese currencies after 1985 encouraged export producers in these countries to relocate their labour-intensive manufacturing processes to other parts of Asia where wage costs were lower. Indonesia along with Thailand and Malaysia benefited from an increase in foreign investment from Northeast Asia, much of it in export-oriented manufacturing (Thee 1991).

A further explanation for the non-oil export success lay in the policies adopted by the Indonesian government to improve the general incentive climate for export producers. A duty drawback scheme for exporters was introduced, and administered quite efficiently by the Ministry of Finance. The customs surveillance functions of the notoriously corrupt Directorate General of Customs and Excises were taken over by the Swiss firm SGS. This led to considerable improvements in the efficiency of the ports, and in the speed with which imports and exports could reach their final destinations (Hill 1996: 114–15; James and Stephenson 2002; Resosudarno and Kuncoro 2006).

Budget policy after 1968

It was argued in the previous chapter that the failure of budget policy was the main cause of the spiralling inflation in the years 1954–1969. After 1969, the budget deficit was brought under control; in that year rather more than a quarter of total budgetary revenues were derived from foreign aid and borrowing, and about 15 per cent from the tax on income from sale of crude oil and petroleum products. The balance was derived from a range of domestic taxes, most of which were inefficiently administered and yielded low revenues. With the rapid expansion of revenues from the oil company tax after 1973, revenues from this single source dominated budgetary revenues in the latter part of the 1970s and the early 1980s. Indeed for much of the period from 1971 to 1990, revenues from the oil company tax, together with foreign aid and borrowing, accounted for well over half of all budgetary revenues. The ready availability of such 'painless' sources of government revenue meant that there was little incentive to implement reforms of the domestic tax system. Even compared with other populated petroleum economies such as Nigeria and Venezuela, the proportion of non-oil to total government revenues in Indonesia in the mid-1970s was very low (Booth and McCawley 1981: 161).

As world oil prices fell, and Indonesian export revenues from oil and gas contracted in the 1980s, aid and foreign borrowing, especially the latter, assumed a more prominent role in total government revenues. But the government also began to tackle the problem of domestic tax reform with the introduction of a value-added tax and a comprehensive reform of the income tax system. As these tax reform measures took effect in the latter part of the 1980s, revenues from the value-added tax increased rapidly as a proportion of both non-oil tax revenues and GDP. The reformed income tax also grew relative to GDP. By the late 1980s, the proportion of total income tax derived from private corporations had increased to 35 per cent, compared with 27 per cent from state enterprises and 38 per cent from individuals (Asher and Booth 1992: 51–3).

A fundamental tenet of New Order budgetary policy was to maintain a 'balanced budget', with total budgetary expenditures not exceeding revenues from all sources (including aid and government borrowing). This definition of the budget deficit was not helpful in estimating the impact of the budget on the domestic economy; the concept of the domestic deficit (the difference between domestic revenues and domestic expenditures) was more useful, but was not shown in the Indonesian budget documents. As oil revenues increased as a proportion of total revenues in the 1970s, the domestic deficit increased both in absolute terms and as a proportion of GDP (Booth and McCawley 1981: 147–8).[6] However unhelpful from the point of view of analysing the economic impact of the budget, the official emphasis on the overall budget balance did reflect the government commitment to keeping budgetary expenditures below or equal to revenues from all sources, including aid and borrowing.

The official 'balanced budget' policy did allow the government to cut expenditures quite drastically in response to falling oil revenues in the early and mid-1980s (Asher and Booth 1992: pp. 60ff). But even given the government's willingness to prune back both routine and development expenditure, there was a rapid growth in government external borrowing, especially in the early part of the 1980s. As much of this borrowing was denominated in non-dollar currencies, particularly yen, the debt-servicing obligations grew rapidly as a proportion to total budget expenditures after the appreciation of the yen in 1985–1986. The problem was further

---

[6] In their survey of various concepts of the budget deficit, Booth and McCawley (1981: 149–50) examined the monetary deficit estimated from the money supply data. Using this concept, it appeared that foreign borrowing might have been understated in the official budget documents; tax revenues could also have been understated and government expenditures overstated.

aggravated by the subsequent rupiah devaluation of September 1986. By 1988, external debt service obligations, both public and private, reached 40 per cent of total exports of goods and services (Hill 1996: table 5.2). The fifth Five Year Plan (*Repelita V*) contained an explicit commitment to reduce the level of government indebtedness, and indeed by 1993/1994, government debt service obligations had dropped to 21 per cent of total exports, although the growth in the foreign debt incurred by the private sector meant that the total foreign debt service ratio still stood at 32.5 per cent (Booth 1994: table 8).

A further point about government expenditure policies over the Suharto era, which attracted considerable critical attention, was the tendency for state enterprises to borrow from the banking system. Sometimes this borrowing was to finance capital expenditures, but often it covered operational losses. In the case of the state-owned banks, which dominated the banking system until the reforms of the late 1980s, non-performing loans were a considerable problem. Some of these loans were to other state enterprises, and some to private firms owned by well-connected individuals. Outside observers often blamed the problems of the state enterprises, including the state banks, on poor management. In many cases this was true but it was often politically impossible for utilities to raise prices to a level which would allow a reasonable return on capital. Hill (1996: 61) uses the money supply data to argue that the public sector defined to include state enterprises ran large deficits in most years between 1969 and 1989.

The growth of the private sector

The steady growth of the manufacturing sector together with a rapid expansion of private sector activity in sectors such as utilities, transport, retail trade, banking and finance, and real estate meant that by the end of the fifth Five Year Plan (1993/1994), it was claimed that 73 per cent of all investment funds originated from the private sector (Booth 1994: table 4). While this figure might have been inflated, there seems to be little doubt that private sector investment grew more rapidly than government investment from the latter part of the 1970s onwards. Furthermore, domestic businesses accounted for much of the growth in private investment. The role of foreign direct investment (FDI) in gross domestic capital formation (GDCF) was quite modest until the early 1990s. A set of estimates prepared by Japanese economists indicated that in 1986–1991, FDI accounted for only 2.4 per cent of GDCF, compared with 29.4 per cent in Singapore, 9.7 per cent in Malaysia and 6.3 per cent in Thailand (Yoshida, Akimune, Nohara and Sato 1994: table 4.4).

After 1991, FDI inflows accelerated and Indonesian companies began to borrow extensively abroad to take advantage of the considerable differential in interest rates between the rupiah and the dollar, the Deutschmark and the yen. Both these trends were greeted with enthusiasm at the time by most commentators. It was argued that Indonesia, as a rapidly industrialising Asian economy, was an increasingly attractive investment location, both for firms looking for low-cost export platforms and foreign companies wanting to establish a production base to supply the rapidly growing domestic market. Foreign banks were keen to lend to Indonesian companies which had already grown rapidly and appeared to have the potential for further expansion. By March 1998, it was estimated that the total stock of foreign debt was $138 billion, of which $72.5 billion was private (World Bank 1998, table 2.1). Before the crisis of late 1997, this 'privatization' of foreign debt was widely regarded as a sign of the growing maturity of the Indonesian economy and few commentators appeared concerned by the trend.

Regional development policy

The economists and engineers who were appointed as ministers and senior civil servants in the early Suharto era were well aware that in a large, archipelagic country, the provision of national transport, telecommunications and other infrastructural networks was a crucial means of encouraging greater national unity as well as a prerequisite for the growth of modern industry and commerce. They were also well aware that little new infrastructure had been built since the 1950s, and roads, railways and irrigation networks built in the colonial era had not been maintained. Through the oil boom of the 1970s, and even after declining oil revenues led to a regime of fiscal austerity in the 1980s, the Suharto government consistently gave infrastructure development high priority in public expenditure.

In practice, this often meant the rehabilitation and expansion of existing road and irrigation networks, the rapid expansion of electric power production, the improvement of ports and airports, and the provision of clean water to both urban and rural households for drinking and bathing. In the 1980s and 1990s, the private sector took a greater role in infrastructure development, especially in the construction of toll roads and electricity generation facilities, with results which will be discussed further in Chapter 6. But for much of the New Order period, the provision of infrastructure was primarily a government responsibility. In one case, a wholly owned subsidiary of an American company developed Indonesia's first communications satellite. In 1980 the government decided to nationalise the company. After tough bargaining compensation was agreed, and the company became an Indonesian state enterprise (Wells and Ahmed 2007: Chapter 3).

The three principal channels for these expenditures were the 'sectoral' budgetary allocations to government departments, the system of grants to provincial and sub-provincial levels of government, known collectively as INPRES (*Instruksi Presiden*) grants, and loans channelled via the state-owned banking system to state-owned enterprises. Both sectoral and INPRES allocations expanded rapidly in the 1970s, and the government was thus able to utilise capacity at all levels of government from the centre to the village to carry out infrastructural projects. Projects that were more capital-intensive and technically complex were usually implemented by central departments and state enterprises such as the State Electricity Enterprise (PLN) through the sectoral budgets, often with substantial off-budget loans from the state banks, while the technically less demanding projects were carried out at lower levels using government grants, and whatever revenues as the local governments could raise from their own funds.

After fifteen years of steady growth, government development expenditures were cut back quite drastically during the fourth Five Year Plan (1984–1989), as oil revenues fell, foreign debt service obligations rose, and the government struggled to maintain a balanced budget. Although not all development expenditures were devoted to capital works, the cutbacks did severely affect the growth of government expenditures on infrastructure. However, the more buoyant economic climate of the early 1990s meant that government development expenditures grew rapidly relative to routine expenditures. If we compare provision of infrastructure in 1995 with 1968, we can appreciate how much was achieved during the Suharto era (Table 4.3). The length of asphalt roads increased over eight-fold, while production of electricity increased thirty-three-fold. As a result of rising incomes and better provision of infrastructure, the number of motor vehicles (cars, trucks, buses and motor cycles) increased rapidly. Visitors to Indonesian cities in the 1990s were impressed by the number of cars, but far more important for most Indonesians was the growth in bus services, particularly in Sumatra, Java and Bali. This growth, combined with much improved inter-island ferry services, meant that Bali, Lombok and the eastern islands were connected to Java and Sumatra through a network of ferry and inter-city bus routes, and people could move easily and cheaply to join friends and relations in different parts of the country.

During the fifth Plan of the Suharto era (1989–1994), there was a more deliberate attempt to skew the allocation of government investment, and INPRES funds in particular, more sharply towards the relatively

Table 4.3 *Growth in infrastructure, 1968–1995*

Type of infrastructure	1968	1995	Percentage in Java and Sumatra 1995
Asphalt roads (×1,000 km)	20.85	175.36	68.3
Other roads (×1,000 km)	NA	197.06	51.4
Total roads (×1,000 km)	83.27	372.41	59.4
Electricity production (×1,000 MWh)	1,780.46	59,280.9	92.9
Cars (×1,000)	201.74	2,107.3	88.2
Trucks (×1,000)	93.42	1,336.2	83.6
Buses (×1,000)	19.61	688.5	90.6
Motorcycles (×1,000)	308.40	9,076.8	81.2

Sources: 1968: CBS (1974: 293); 1995: CBS (1997: 385); Department of Information, *Lampiran Pidato Kenegaraan 1996.*

neglected eastern part of the country. In the mid-1990s the Central Bureau of Statistics began to publish poverty data broken down by province. The 1996 figures showed that the highest incidence of poverty was found in the six provinces of West Kalimantan, West and East Nusatenggara, Timor Timur, Maluku and Irian Jaya (CBS 1997: 572). These provinces all received a high share of INPRES allocations relative to their populations. A study of INPRES allocations in the mid-1990s confirmed the rural bias of many of the central grants to the regions which in effect meant that the rapidly urbanising regions in Java and elsewhere lost out relative to more remote, rural regions (Silver, Azis and Schroeder 2001: 351).

The larger allocations of at least some government expenditure programmes towards Eastern Indonesia reflected a growing official concern at the evidence of a widening development gap between Java/Bali and Sumatra on the one hand, and the rest of the country on the other. The regional income data showed that the four provinces on the island of Sulawesi, together with Maluku, West and East Nusatenggara and Timor Timur shared only marginally in the three main types of industrialisation which occurred in Indonesia from the 1960s to the 1990s. Import-substituting industrialisation was mainly based in Java, especially in Jakarta and West Java, in order to benefit from the large market concentrated in that island. The growth of labour-intensive, export-oriented industry was also largely based in Java, to take advantage of both superior infrastructure and abundant reserves of cheap labour. By the early 1990s, over 40 per cent of total exports were coming from Java, a higher proportion than at any time since the early 1930s (Table 3.3).

Resource-based industrialisation was for obvious reasons concentrated in those provinces which were well endowed with oil, gas and minerals. But the provinces of Aceh, Riau and East Kalimantan, which produced a large share of oil and gas revenues, saw much of their income going to the centre. The difference between exports and imports as a percentage of GDP was over 60 per cent in these provinces in the 1980s (Booth 2015: 31). There was some decline in the export surpluses in the 1990s, but these provinces continued to resent the fact that they received little benefit from the exploitation of their resources. The situation was even worse in Irian Jaya, where per capita GDP was much higher than the national average, but poverty was also well above the level in Java and Sumatra. The problem of high rates of poverty in some of the richest provinces in the country will be examined further in Chapter 8. Chapter 9 analyses the policies adopted to remedy the grievances of these provinces after Suharto left office.

By 1996, the eight provinces of Eastern Indonesia including Sulawesi but excluding Irian Jaya accounted for around 12 per cent of Indonesia's population, but only 6.6 per cent of total GDP, and an even smaller percentage of GDP accruing from the manufacturing sector. Given their lack of natural resources, poor infrastructure and dispersed population, the prospects for rapid industrial growth in these provinces, and indeed in other relatively isolated provinces such as West, Central and South Kalimantan, did not seem very bright in the 1990s. Even the prospects for the kind of rapid agricultural growth which had taken place in Java, Bali and Sumatra in the 1970s and 1980s did not seem good. Rural infrastructure such as roads and irrigation was still undeveloped, as it had been in the colonial era. Unfavourable biophysical conditions such as low rainfall and poor soils prevailed over most of the region, and there was a dearth of new agricultural technologies appropriate to the local situation.

Although agro-industry, based for example on fishing, livestock or fruit and vegetable growing, was commercially viable in some eastern regions, it hardly appeared likely to provide a basis for the kind of rapid export-oriented manufacturing growth already underway in Java, Bali and parts of Sumatra by the early 1990s. Indeed some argued that the best hope for the more isolated provinces outside Java was to become exporters of labour, with inward remittances accounting for a growing proportion of regional income. Certainly there was little evidence that the increased allocations of development funds from the central government budget from the early 1990s was sufficient to make up for decades of neglect of infrastructural development in Eastern Indonesia. These problems remained to be tackled in the very different political and economic climate after 1998.

The revolution in fertility and education

Indonesia emerged into independence as the sixth largest country in the world; with the subsequent breakup of Pakistan and the USSR it had by the early 1990s become the fourth largest. The first post-independence census was held in 1961 and estimated that the population was 97.1 million of which half was under 20. The census also found that the vast majority of the country's population had either had no schooling or had not completed primary school. More than 50 per cent of the population over ten was illiterate. Moreover, population growth was rapid; in the period between the 1961 and 1971 censuses, population grew at slightly over 2 per cent per annum. Most demographers concurred that population growth had been proceeding at roughly this rate since the early 1950s. Population growth in Java, one of the most densely settled regions in Asia, was only slightly lower than the national average.

During the Sukarno era, population policies had been pro-natalist (Hull and Mantra 1981). To the extent that the government had been concerned about problems of over-population and poverty in Java, the official policy 'solution' was transmigration rather than family planning. The term transmigration was used for government-sponsored movement of people from Java and Bali to less densely settled regions in Sumatra and Sulawesi. In most cases the settlers were given land, and it was envisaged that they would make their living as farmers. The policy had been initiated in the colonial era, and continued after independence, although budgetary constraints and lack of administrative capacity meant that only small numbers of people were actually moved under official government settlement programmes in the 1950s and 1960s (Hardjono 1977: 25–6). Nevertheless, Sukarno and his ministers considered that movement of population was the best way of easing population pressure in Java. They did not support limiting family size and family planning was a 'taboo subject' in most government circles, although there were community leaders and women's groups which did understand the need for modern birth control practices in Java, and indeed elsewhere.

In 1968, the new government moved cautiously to change official policy. A National Family Planning Institute was established, and the following year it was given full responsibility for the implementation of a family planning programme in Java and Bali. Support from foreign aid donors was solicited, and by the mid-1970s there was clear evidence of fertility decline, not just in Java and Bali but in Sumatra as well. The two main reasons for the decline were an increase in the age of marriage, and adoption of birth control practices within marriage. Both in turn reflected the impact of social modernisation on consumption norms and on aspirations for social mobility (Hull and Mantra 1981: 274ff). While there was some debate about the impact of the government family planning programme, several observers drew attention to the effective contraceptive distribution system and the importance of public information campaigns about contraception and family size issues. In addition, local government and community groups felt empowered to persuade couples to practise contraception (McNicoll and Singarimbun 1983: 98).

As a result, families began to realise that children must be educated if they were to move up the social scale, but education, like health care, was often a considerable drain on household resources. Small families meant better-educated and healthier families. Accompanying the drop in fertility was a decline in infant and child mortality, reflecting more widespread access to health facilities, and a greater willingness on the part of parents to seek medical help when children fell ill. For Indonesia as a whole, infant mortality rates fell from 145 per thousand live births in 1967 to 47 per thousand in 1996, and there was a corresponding increase in life expectancy at birth, from 46 years in 1967 to 65 years in 1996 (CBS 2006b: 72–87). As with falling fertility and falling mortality, the growth in educational enrolments after 1969 reflected both greater provision of government services and changing parental aspirations for, and expectations of, their children.

In 1968, only 41.4 per cent of the children aged between seven and twelve were in primary school. By 1993, the primary school participation rate had risen to over 90 per cent. Already by 1988/1989 it was argued that the great majority of children in the seven to twelve age groups were attending primary schools, and the focus of government attention shifted to the secondary level, where it was projected that the numbers enrolled, and participation rates would grow rapidly (Booth 1989: tables 11 and 12). But these ambitious targets were not met; in fact at both the junior high school (*sekolah menengah pertama*) and senior high school (*sekolah menengah atas*) levels the number of new students were lower in 1993/1994 than in 1988/1989. Total number of students also fell, except in the vocational senior high schools, as did number of graduates (Table 4.4). The *Repelita V* document forecast crude participation rates at the junior high school level of 67 per cent by 1993/1994. In fact the actual rate was around 43.4 per cent, and 52.7 per cent if enrolments in the Islamic schools (*madrasah*) were also included.[7] At the senior high school level, crude participation rates of 45 per cent were forecast; the actual rate was

---

[7] In Indonesia, the *madrasah* are supposed to follow the same curriculum as the secular schools, although they are under the control of the Ministry of Religion.

Table 4.4 *Numbers[a] in secondary and tertiary education, 1988–1989, 1993–1994 and 1997–1998 (millions)*

	1988/1989	1993/1994	1997
New pupils			
Lower secondary (general)	2.55	2.15	2.85
Lower secondary (vocational)	0.04	–	–
Upper secondary (general)	1.09	0.84	1.13
Upper secondary (vocational)	0.42	0.51	0.72
Teacher training	0.08	–	–
Higher education	0.34	0.42	0.61
Total pupils			
Lower secondary (general)	6.57	5.75	8.05
Lower secondary (vocational)	0.11	–	–
Upper secondary (general)	2.76	2.39	2.89
Upper secondary (vocational)	1.18	1.37	1.96
Teacher training[b]	0.28	–	–
Higher education	1.66	2.06	2.69
Graduates			
Lower secondary (general)	1.93	1.63	2.18
Lower secondary (vocational)	0.03	–	–
Upper secondary	1.15	1.10	1.28
Higher education	0.16	0.20	0.48
Teachers			
Lower secondary	0.41	0.36	0.46
Upper secondary	0.29	0.30	0.39
Higher education	0.06	0.09	0.11
Participation rates[c]			
Lower secondary	53.4	43.4	60.0
Upper secondary	37.1	30.3	36.3
Higher education	8.5	9.5	11.2

[a] Excludes data from the *madrasah*.
[b] Refers to teacher training high schools (SPG), which have been phased out.
[c] Crude participation rates: numbers of students as a proportion of the 13–15, 16–18 and 19–24 age cohorts, respectively.
Source: Department of Information *Lampiran Pidato Kenegaraan 1994*, Chapter XVI; *Lampiran Pidato Kenegaraan 1998*, Chapter XVIII.

only 30 per cent, and slightly higher if enrolments in the Islamic schools are included.

The reasons for these disappointing results were complex and several different explanations were advanced. In discussing the *Repelita* v results, the official *Lampiran Pidato Kenegaraan* (Appendix to the State Speech) of 1994, argued that many young people in the senior high school (SMA) age groups (16–18) found the cost of continuing on to senior high school too great, both in the sense that the fees, uniform, transport and other costs were a considerable burden on the family budget, and in the sense that the income foregone from earnings became steadily greater as children grew older (Department of Information 1994: XVI-23). Certainly the direct financial burden of SMA attendance by the early 1990s had become considerable. A study prepared by the Central Bureau of Statistics, based on the 1992 *Susenas* module, estimated the average annual cost of senior high school attendance in urban areas to be around $140 per annum in 1992 (CBS 1994). This represented over one-third of average per capita consumption expenditures in Indonesia in that year, and for many households the cost was too great.

In addition, as the 1995 Inter-censal Survey showed, the probability of a long period of post-graduation unemployment increased considerably at the SMA level compared with lower levels. In 1995, 14.2 per cent of economically active male senior high school graduates in urban areas were unemployed and looking for work, and 10 per cent of male university graduates. The corresponding figures for female graduates were 29 and 20 per cent (CBS 1996: tables 39.1 and 39.2). The implications of these figures were certainly not lost on parents who saw little point in spending large sums on SMA education if the young graduate was then either unemployed or forced to take a job which he or she could just as easily have taken with a junior high school diploma. By 1997/1998, numbers enrolled in upper secondary school as a proportion of the sixteen to eighteen age cohort were still lower than in 1988/ 1989 (Table 4.4).

To some extent these reasons also applied at the junior high school (SMP) level, although at that level the main deterrent for many parents, especially in rural areas, was the direct financial cost of continuing beyond primary school. The CBS study found that the average annual cost of SMP attendance in urban areas was $94.50 and $54.70 in rural areas (CBS 1994: 106–8). This study also found that 91 per cent of boys currently enrolled in primary schools and 89 per cent of girls wanted to continue their education to higher levels. Almost half of the people in the five to twenty-nine age groups who were no longer in school gave financial reasons for their dropping out (CBS 1994: 46–7). Only 8 per cent said that they had dropped out in order to work, and 11 per cent claimed that they, or their parents, considered that they had had enough education. The results of this study suggested that there was widespread unsatisfied demand for education in Indonesia in the early 1990s, and that financial constraints were the main factor influencing the decision to continue in the education system.

The opportunity cost of having a child in junior high school in the early 1990s, although high for many families, was still relatively low compared with senior high school and university. A junior high school certificate was often used as a 'screening device' by factories recruiting for low-skilled jobs. Thus many parents would probably have been prepared to invest in the extra three years of junior high school education in order to secure factory employment, if the direct cost to the family could have been reduced. Such a reduction could only have been achieved (as indeed it was at the primary level in the 1970s and 1980s) by building and equipping more junior high schools in rural areas, and by training more teachers. This indeed was a main thrust of education policy in the sixth Five Year Plan (*Repelita VI*), and the proportion of the thirteen to fifteen age cohort in school did increase between 1993/1994 and 1997/1998 (Table 4.4). The aim of the twenty-five-year plan, published in 1994, was to achieve universal compulsory education to SMP level. This was to be done in steps with the crude participation rate rising to 66.2 per cent in 1998/1999, and 87 per cent by 2003/2004.[8] In the next chapter, progress towards these targets will be assessed in greater detail.

Given the disappointing enrolment figures at the secondary level in the decade from 1988 to 1998, it was inevitable that much of the debate on educational policy in Indonesia in the 1990s centred on the goal of compulsory nine-year education. But much remained to be done at the primary level. Although it was widely believed that the goal of universal primary education had been attained in Indonesia, the reality was somewhat different. Over *Repelita V*, the refined participation rate at the primary level (the proportion of children aged seven to twelve who were attending primary school) actually fell from 99.6 per cent in 1988/1989 to 90.1 per cent in 1990/1991, although it increased again to 93.5 per cent in 1993/1994 (Department of Information 1994: table XVI-1). These figures could have reflected some inflation in the figures for the late 1980s. They were also national averages, and in some of the more isolated rural areas they would have been lower. Although virtually all Indonesian children probably had some exposure to primary education by the mid-1990s, it was clear that not all spent the years from seven to twelve in school.

The study based on the 1992 *Susenas* results indicated that around 90 per cent of children in the seven to twelve age group were in school, 7 per cent had not yet enrolled and 3 per cent were no longer in school (CBS 1994: 5). These figures were broadly confirmed by the 1991

---

[8] *Rencana Pembangunan Lima Tahun Keenam, 1994/1995–1998/1998*, Vol 4 (Jakarta: Department of Information 1994), table 32.2.

Demographic and Health Survey which found that 87 per cent of children in the seven to twelve age group were in school. Various measures were taken to bring education to children in remote rural areas; for example, a pilot programme of 'guru kunjung' (visiting teachers) was developed in the Riau islands. Other initiatives involved using village halls and other facilities as schools where no buildings yet existed, and offering special training and incentives to teachers working in isolated areas. While all these measures were obviously desirable, there were still, in the mid-1990s, major problems with many existing primary schools, even in the densely settled parts of Java. Buildings were often in poor repair, teaching materials inadequate, and the teachers lacked the motivation to attend regularly and devote their full attention to the curriculum.

The sixth Five Year Plan (*Repelita VI*) document acknowledged the need to improve the quality of primary education, but offered little in the way of new policy initiatives. Some observers argued that the government would be better advised to improve the quality of primary education before embarking on the programme of compulsory nine-year education. Poor teacher remuneration was often given as a reason for low motivation and high rates of teacher absenteeism, although given the fact that school teachers accounted for 46 per cent of all tenured civil servants in 1994, the problem could only have been tackled within the wider context of reform of the civil service pay structure. A further problem was that many teachers were not permanent civil servants and received an honorarium rather than a regular civil service salary. Their job insecurity influenced their motivation to attend regularly and teach the full curriculum.

The ongoing debate about education, employment and remuneration in Indonesia in the 1990s was both encouraging and disturbing. It was encouraging because it indicated that the Indonesian policy-making establishment had taken to heart the argument that educational attainment is an extremely important factor in explaining why some economies have been more successful than others in sustaining rapid rates of economic growth since the 1960s. The argument was particularly relevant to the experience of the Northeast Asian 'hyper-growth' economies including Japan, South Korea and Taiwan. But the disturbing aspect of the debate in Indonesia centred on the apparent lack of policy solutions for the disappointing trends in educational enrolments at the high school level, or indeed for the emerging mismatch in tertiary enrolments. Put simply, by the mid-1990s, too many children were dropping out of school too early, and of those who stayed in education until the upper secondary and tertiary levels, too many were opting for courses in law, business studies and arts, and too few in foreign languages and basic sciences, or in engineering and technology.

Thus even before the economic situation deteriorated sharply in late 1997, it was clear to many observers that Indonesia would have to devote more resources to improving the quality of both primary and secondary education, to increasing enrolments as a proportion of the age cohort in secondary education, and to increasing the number of tertiary places in scientific disciplines. This would involve not just increased resources for the educational sector, but also major changes in the way that educational services were delivered to a growing population. In the early 1990s Indonesia was devoting less than 10 per cent of budgetary expenditures to education, compared with 19.6 per cent in Malaysia, 21 per cent in Thailand and 22 per cent in Singapore. Government expenditure on education was only 2 per cent of GDP, one of the lowest figures in East Asia.[9] Thus Indonesia faced the new millennium with pressing needs to expand access to, and quality of, education but with fewer government resources to fund the necessary programmes.

Suharto and his critics

In the early years of the Suharto era, the press was reasonably free to criticise government policies. While the newspapers and journals associated with the Indonesian Communist Party had been shut down, others, including student newspapers, flourished and enjoyed a wide readership in urban areas. Not infrequently these papers picked up critical analyses of the performance of the Suharto government from abroad and recycled them, together with domestic commentary, to Indonesian readers. By the early 1970s, many observers were expressing disappointment that the benefits of accelerated growth were not trickling down to more people especially in rural areas. Attempts by government to disseminate the new seed–fertiliser rice technologies developed at IRRI in the Philippines appeared to be having only a modest impact on rice yields, at least until the mid-1970s. Critics also claimed that the benefits accrued largely to those farmers who owned irrigated land. They were a minority in most parts of Java and also in many areas of settled agriculture outside Java. There was also criticism of the 'rice bias' of the government's agricultural policies and the failure to address the problems of smallholder producers of crops such as rubber, coffee and coconuts. These farmers had suffered from the real exchange rate appreciation of the 1970s, and had not benefited from the subsidies granted to food crop farmers (Paauw 1978).

[9] These figures are taken from *Government Finance Statistics Yearbook 1994* (Washington, DC: International Monetary Fund 1994), pp. 64–5, 92–3.

In addition, many social scientists working in Java in the 1970s pointed to the impact which new agricultural technologies, such as the replacement of hand-pounding by small rice mills, were having on poorer people in rural areas who had depended on these labour-intensive processing tasks for part of their income. Some critics tied their discussion of what they perceived as development failures in Indonesia to the wider international discourse on economic and social development of the 1970s. This was a period when many social scientists were sceptical that the poor, densely populated countries in Asia could ever emulate Japan and catch up with the industrial West. Some thought they were wrong even to try, and should instead focus on self-reliance, repudiating the traps of foreign dependence, mechanical adoption of foreign models, and fixation on growth as the overriding consideration (Mortimer 1973: 65). For such writers the appropriate models to follow were those of China, North Vietnam and Tanzania, where the egalitarian ethic was supposedly strongest and where it was argued that 'peasant-centric' policies were most effective.

Over the 1970s, the critical commentary grew, even after the crackdown on the media and student organisations which followed the Malari riots of 1974. Some foreign observers questioned whether Indonesians had the 'moral discipline' to succeed under either communism or capitalism (May 1978: 411). Such writers seemed to have accepted the views of at least some Dutch officials, that Indonesians had little interest in improving output and incomes, and would not respond to either market incentives or government coercion. Others, including many Indonesians, pointed to the growing corruption and signs of high living among a small elite in Jakarta and other cities, and argued that all the rewards of accelerated growth were accruing to these people and that the great 'floating mass' in both urban and rural areas benefited little, if at all. The evidence from the household surveys carried out in 1970 and 1976 was mixed and some analysts argued that when appropriate allowance had been made for the impact of inflation on the purchasing power of the lower income groups, there was little evidence of a substantial poverty decline over these years. In addition, the Pertamina collapse of the mid-1970s demonstrated quite dramatically just how little control technocrats in the Ministry of Finance and elsewhere had over the finances of state enterprises, especially those operating in the lucrative mining and forestry sectors (Arndt 1975; McCawley 1978).

One Suharto biographer has argued that the period from the mid-1970s to the early 1980s was the most difficult phase in his presidential career, when his administration was plagued by a series of crises, both economic and political (Elson 2001: 233). But with a combination of tactical astuteness, and ruthlessness where necessary, he and his close associates weathered the storms. Even the departure from the cabinet in 1983 of key technocrats such as Widjojo Nitisastro and M. Sadli, and the death of his chief security adviser, Ali Moertopo, did not greatly affect his grip on government. He found replacements and soldiered on. On the economic front, he gave considerable latitude to Ali Wardhana and a team of technocrats in the Ministry of Finance to implement a package of reforms in trade and taxation policy, and a substantial liberalisation of the domestic banking system. The 'unambiguous change in direction' signalled by these reforms 'unleashed a surprisingly swift supply response', particularly in the non-oil manufacturing sector (Hill 1996: 155).

In spite of these positive developments, the critics of Suharto's economic policies were far from silenced. By the early 1990s, the 'alternative' development models of the 1970s no longer looked so persuasive. By then China, Vietnam and Tanzania had themselves turned away from inward-looking policies of self-reliance, and were embarking on sweeping economic reforms. Suharto's critics instead looked to other models for their inspiration. By the early 1990s, there were several on offer. Economists, while acknowledging the positive outcomes of the post-1985 reforms, stressed that some industrial sectors were still receiving considerable government assistance. Particular targets for criticism were the industries established by the influential Minister for Research and Technology, Dr B. J. Habibie, under the Strategic Industries Board, and the so-called national car project, under the control of Suharto's youngest son. Funding for these projects was opaque, but widely assumed to come from the state-owned banking sector.

Many younger Indonesians joined the growing number of non-government organisations which focused on environmental issues, human rights, the rule of law, and egalitarian economic and social policies, including greater government support for small enterprises owned and managed by indigenous Indonesians. Concerns over these issues were often tinged with Islamic notions of justice and fair play in the face of government policies which appeared to favour relatively wealthy Christian and Chinese minorities. Characteristically, Suharto reacted quickly to defuse Moslem discontent by creating an officially sanctioned association of Islamic intellectuals under the leadership of Dr B. J. Habibie. In the 1988–1993 cabinet, three key economic posts had been occupied by Christians; in 1993 these ministers were all removed and in two cases replaced by Moslems. But the critics were not silenced. In the final phase of the Suharto era, their objections to economic policy centred around four key issues.

The first, and probably the most contentious, concerned the role of large, diversified business conglomerates in the economy. In the 1980s, the work of Muhaimin (1982) and Robison (1986) had drawn attention to the rise of large-scale business groups in Indonesia usually controlled by Indonesians of Chinese descent. Other studies, including a number by Indonesians, quickly followed; these studies drew attention not just to the Chinese conglomerates but also to those owned by members of the Suharto family. One such study ranked the top forty business groups in Indonesia in terms of estimated sales in 1988; the top ten were controlled by Chinese and the eleventh largest by Suharto's second son, Bambang Trihatmojo (Widyahartono 1993: 70–1). Another ranking of the top thirty conglomerates according to asset values in 1996 showed that all the Suharto family businesses together ranked eighth, after seven large Chinese-owned groups, most operated by families with close links to senior political figures (Rokhim 2005: 17).

To the growing numbers of Indonesians running small and medium-sized enterprises in the 1990s, and indeed even to those who owned or managed quite large concerns, such lists showed clearly that a small number of business people had become extremely rich through exploiting their links to Suharto himself and to other key political figures. While these tycoons might have possessed considerable business acumen, their success was in large part based on their preferential access to lucrative contracts and monopoly privileges across the entire economy from flour milling to the petroleum sector. The resentment which this caused in the wider business community was considerable, and in turn it fuelled other resentments about continuing poverty and inequality in Indonesian society. The official figures which showed rapid poverty decline since the mid-1970s were not met with universal acceptance, especially as the poverty line was considered very low.

The evidence on conglomerates and poverty will be examined in more detail in Chapters 7 and 8. In addition to these two concerns, there was mounting criticism of the impact that some of the government's most cherished development programmes were having on the environment and on relations between Indonesia's many ethnic groups. A particular focus of critical attention was the transmigration programme which had had massive funding from the World Bank, the Asian Development Bank, several bilateral donors, and from the domestic budget, especially over the third Five Year Plan (1979–1984). By the latter part of the 1980s it was clear that much of the land being opened up for settlement in Kalimantan, Sulawesi and Irian Jaya was of poor quality. Surveys carried out by the Central Bureau of Statistics in the 1980s showed that a large part of incomes of transmigrant families was derived from off-farm work. The World Bank, in a report which was intended to justify its expenditures on transmigration to an increasingly sceptical audience, conceded that in some of the sites the land was so poor that it was unlikely to furnish settler families with an adequate income in the medium term (World Bank 1988: xvii). To many in the environmental movement, the Indonesian programme was not only producing dubious results in terms of settler livelihoods, but was also contributing to an alarming increase in deforestation outside Java.

A combination of international pressure and domestic budget cuts reduced funding for the transmigration programme after the mid-1980s. But people continued to move on a voluntary basis in large numbers, encouraged by cheap transport, and the lure of more remunerative employment opportunities outside Java. Concern about economic development policies outside Java, and the environmental problems with which they were associated, did not abate. By the early 1990s, following statements by the president and other leading officials, attention was focused on the problems of the isolated provinces of Eastern Indonesia where headcount measures of poverty remained stubbornly high, and where tensions between different religious and ethnic groups were escalating. Increasingly the problem of rich provinces and poor people was seen as the inevitable result of a highly centralised, indeed predatory, fiscal system, which drained the provinces of their resource wealth and gave little back in return.

Conglomerates, poverty, wasteful development projects which produced little but environmental degradation, and regional imbalances in development, were all attracting criticism from academics and NGOs by the mid-1990s. To some observers all these problems reflected a more basic problem of lack of accountability on the part of both central and regional governments, which went well beyond the lack of effective government audit procedures, serious though that lack was. After thirty years in power, the Suharto government appeared to many to be remote, out of touch, and increasingly concerned with self-enrichment. The cabinet announced in 1993 was shorn of most of the more technocratic ministers whose economic management had won respect both at home and abroad. They were replaced by lesser-known figures, few of whom were either willing or able to tackle the abuses of power by Suharto's family, or by the military. But few observers, either Indonesian or foreign, predicted the magnitude of the problems which would confront the government in 1997 and 1998.

5   The 1997–98 crisis and its legacy
Dropping out again?

The onset of the economic crisis

By early 1997, episodes of ethnic and religious violence were erupting in several parts of the country, while the ongoing problems in Aceh, Irian Jaya and East Timor appeared incapable of resolution. Many were wondering for how much longer Suharto could continue to rely on the loyalty of the army in carrying out brutal and unpopular 'pacification' activities in far-flung parts of the country. But to most observers, both within Indonesia and abroad, the economy still appeared strong.[1] Both domestic and foreign economists, including respected economic journalists and multilateral lending organisations such as the World Bank and the Asian Development Bank, praised the Indonesian government for its adherence to sound macroeconomic management. Budget deficits had been kept low, inflation was well under control, and the balance of payments deficit at around 4 per cent of GDP seemed far less worrisome to most observers than the much higher deficits in Malaysia and Thailand.[2] Certainly there was some concern that there was a growing reliance on short-term capital inflow to fund the current account deficit but again this trend did not seem nearly so pronounced as in Thailand. It was known that some conglomerates were borrowing large sums offshore but this was not seen as something the government could or should concern itself with.

The problems in Thailand came to a head in early July 1997, when the Thai authorities were forced to float the baht, which then depreciated rapidly. The rupiah came under pressure soon after the Thai decision to float the baht, and after apparently futile attempts by Bank Indonesia to

---

[1] See, for example, Jay Solomons, 'What Political Risk?', *Far Eastern Economic Review*, 20 February 1997. The country report published by the World Bank in May 1997 was entitled *Indonesia: Sustaining High Growth with Equity* (Report 16433-IND), and had a generally optimistic tone, while calling for further deregulation measures.

[2] See 'Emerging Asia's Sombre Era', *Economist*, 24 August 1996 for a discussion of macroeconomic imbalances in Southeast Asia and South Korea and a comparison with Mexico.

stabilise the rupiah, it was decided that from 14 August, the rupiah could float freely. This was a decisive break with previous exchange rate management in Indonesia, and IMF officials were quoted as applauding the move. The president and other senior officials stressed that economic fundamentals in Indonesia were sound, and that there was no reason for panic (Lindblad 1997: 5–8). But by early October, serious problems were emerging. Capital outflow was accelerating, and the rupiah was trading at 3,600 to the dollar, compared with 2,500 in July. The government then turned to the International Monetary Fund (IMF) for a standby loan. It appears that both the IMF and the technocrats within the government hoped that, by adhering to the conditions of this loan, Indonesia would convince both the domestic and international business community of its serious commitment to ongoing economic reform. By taking the medicine, which included the closure of sixteen banks, the president and his advisers expected that the health of the economy would be rapidly restored (Boediono 2002: 386).

But if the purpose of signing the first IMF letter of intent was to affirm that Indonesia was serious about fundamental economic reform, the strategy backfired. As Sheng (2009: 227) pointed out, the attempt to curb Suharto's power to allocate largesse to the business groups controlled by his family 'led to a highly publicised impasse' between the president and the IMF. Events in the following months made it clear that the government had little stomach for implementing most of the reforms which the IMF, as well as domestic reformers in the Finance Ministry and elsewhere, demanded. The authority of the president was increasingly compromised by rumours of his poor health. He disappeared from view at the end of November after returning from a foreign trip, and did not appear in public for two weeks. It now seems clear that he had suffered a stroke. In January 1998 a budget was announced which appeared quite unrealistic in its growth predictions for 1998. Suharto signed a second letter of intent with the IMF which was supposed to withdraw support for projects such as the national car which were closely linked to his family. But as a senior Indonesian economist later admitted, although he appeared to go along with the IMF's demands, 'his heart lay elsewhere' (Boediono 2002: 386).

The rupiah fell further in January to below 10,000 to the dollar and capital flight accelerated. Suharto and some members of his family seemed to be supporting the establishment of a currency board, an idea opposed by both his economics team and the IMF. In March 1998 he was re-elected as president for a further five years and announced a cabinet consisting mainly of his close associates, including his eldest daughter, whom he appeared to be grooming as his successor. As it became clear to many observers within

Indonesia and abroad that Suharto was simply not prepared to accept economic reforms which might in any way prejudice the business or political interests of his family and their associates, confidence in his regime collapsed. Student protests became widespread and violent riots occurred in several cities in May 1998. In Jakarta, it was widely believed that elements in the army or the police were behind the shooting of several students on a university campus, and attacks on Chinese property, which caused hundreds of deaths. By mid-May, Suharto had lost the confidence of most of his cabinet, and finally on 21 May, he stepped down in favour of his vice-president, Dr B. J. Habibie.

By late 1998, it was clear that the magnitude of the collapse, both economic and political, which had occurred in Indonesia since mid-1997, was far greater than anyone would have predicted two years earlier. Total GDP contracted by over 13 per cent in 1998, and per capita GDP fell by over 14 per cent. The problems in the financial sector and in sectors such as manufacturing and construction were compounded by a severe drought in some parts of the country. A further alarming development in 1998 was the rapid rise in prices; the rising inflation was due to the rapid growth in the money supply which had occurred in late 1997 and early 1998 as a consequence of the liquidity credits to the banking system. Public confidence in economic management in the latter part of 1998 remained fragile, and even with Suharto gone, the international community seemed reluctant to extend aid to a regime with little popular support and which was still tainted with corruption and nepotism. From being, a few years earlier, one of the much-hyped Asian miracles, Indonesia approached the new millennium with a contracting economy, growing numbers in poverty and no clear strategy for reversing the decline. After thirty years, commentators again began to question whether Indonesia could long survive as a single political entity.

What caused the crisis of 1997/1998?

Debates about what caused such a dramatic reversal of fortune, not just in Indonesia but also in Thailand, Malaysia and the Republic of Korea, began in 1998 and have continued down to the present. In the immediate aftermath of the crisis several well-known economists, not all of whom had displayed much interest in Southeast Asia prior to the crisis, rushed in with diagnoses and explanations. The World Bank, which had, in public at least, been bullish about the economies of East and Southeast Asia until 1996, was, like many other agencies, caught completely off guard by the events of late 1997 and early 1998 in Indonesia. A report published in July 1998 stated that:

Indonesia's problems began with contagion but nobody could have guessed the speed and severity of the crisis that followed. The confidence of domestic and international investors, built painstakingly over years, was shattered in months . . . Years of progress in development and poverty reduction are at risk. (World Bank 1998: 1.15)

The World Bank argued that the crisis in Indonesia was not brought about by macroeconomic errors; the government had not made the same mistake as Thailand in trying to maintain the impossible trinity of a pegged exchange rate, an open capital account and a reliance on monetary policy to stabilise the domestic economy. Until August 1997, the exchange rate was allowed to float within clearly defined bands, a system which most foreign and domestic business groups seemed happy with. According to the World Bank (1998: 1.8–1.9) there were four 'microeconomic causes of the crisis': a rapid build-up of private external debt, a flawed banking system, deteriorating standards of governance and rising corruption, and the political uncertainty brought about by Suharto's age and health, and the lack of a clear successor. Each of these explanations deserves closer scrutiny.

That there was a rapid build-up of private debt in the 1990s was clear; about 85 per cent of the increase in external debt between 1992 and 1997 was due to private sector borrowing (World Bank 1998: 1.9). In their analysis of the crisis, Firman and Stiglitz (1998: 28) pointed out that roughly two-thirds of the external debt of Indonesian banks reporting to the Bank for International Settlements was incurred by the nonbank private sector, which was 'among the highest proportions of any country in the world'. Foreign banks were eager to lend to both Indonesia and Thailand, given their track records of high growth, low inflation and prudent fiscal policy. For its part, the Indonesian government was 'steeped in the importance of private sector freedoms and wedded to openness in the capital account', and the authorities, while expressing some concern about the growth of private external debt, 'genuinely held that this was a matter for the private sector to handle on its own without government interference' (World Bank 1998: 1.8). The report of the independent evaluation office of the IMF, published in 2003, claimed that the large volume of capital inflows was discussed at official meetings with the Indonesian government, but acknowledged that 'IMF surveillance grossly underestimated the magnitude of short-term debt' and hence the vulnerability of the economy to a shift in market sentiment (IMF 2003: 61). This was perhaps surprising, given that by the mid-1990s, Indonesia had become well known in international banking circles for the unusually high inward and outward flows of capital, much higher indeed than in Thailand or Malaysia (Kuroyanagi and Hayakawa 1997: table 6).

The second microeconomic problem identified by the World Bank concerned flaws in the banking system. Reforms which began in 1988 had, by the mid-1990s, led to a rapid rise in the number of domestic private banks, many of which were linked to large business groups. The state-owned banks lost market share. They had dominated the banking system until 1988, and had acted mainly as 'agents of development' channelling funds to priority projects selected by the government and implemented for the most part by state enterprises. The private banks expanded their branch networks and competed for deposits, but many of their loans were made to firms connected to the conglomerates which controlled the banks. As Sheng (2009: 231) pointed out, Indonesia after 1988 experienced a problem which has frequently occurred after banking de-regulation in many parts of the world: credit growth at the expense of credit quality. Unfortunately the government institution charged with bank supervision was the central bank, Bank Indonesia, which proved unable to monitor the lending policies of the growing number of private banks, let alone liquidate those banks where imprudent lending had in effect made them insolvent (Sheng 2009: 236–9).

Both the IMF and the World Bank had, over the 1980s, been very critical of the lending policies of the state banks, and applauded the move towards greater liberalisation, which led to the rapid growth of private domestic banks. So did many academic economists within Indonesia and abroad. Until the crisis erupted, very few gave much thought to the potential risks to which the liberalised banking system had exposed the broader economy. In the early 1990s, there were several highly publicised problems in banks associated with the Suharto family and the large conglomerates. Bank Duta had experienced difficulties after an employee made large losses on foreign exchange speculations, and had to be bailed out with money from Suharto family foundations, while Bank Summa had to be rescued by the Soeryadjaya family with funds from the sale of their stake in their conglomerate with further assistance from other conglomerates close to the president (Booth 2001: 32–3). In both cases Bank Indonesia was not directly involved in the rescues. While some observers were worried by the absence of effective prudential supervision in Indonesia, very few considered that a failure of the entire system was possible. The IMF, as the international agency most concerned with problems in the financial system, was subsequently criticised by its own independent evaluation office for its failure to flag up or evaluate the potential risks to the macro-economy of a collapse of confidence in the financial system in Indonesia (IMF 2003: 63–4). But until early 1998, the risk of a systemic collapse seemed remote.

The third microeconomic problem identified by the World Bank concerned problems of 'governance' which included government corruption (often seen as resulting from too much red tape and unnecessary regulation of the private sector), insider trading on the stock market, a weak and venal judiciary, and a general lack of transparency in government decision-making, which was at least partly the result of the influence of the large conglomerates controlled by people with family or other links to powerful political actors. The World Bank, together with many other commentators, argued that these problems were hardly new in Indonesia, and probably did not precipitate the crisis. But they did influence perceptions 'of how Indonesia would manage the crisis, and whether it had the institutional capacity to respond quickly, fairly and effectively' (World Bank 1998: 1.10). This was true enough, but at the same time it could also be argued that public tolerance for corruption and collusion in Indonesia had declined sharply over the 1990s. Many educated young people who had chosen careers in the private sector over the 1980s and 1990s deeply resented what were seen as unfair privileges conferred on a few 'businessmen' simply because of their family backgrounds. Thus when serious problems first surfaced in mid-1997, there was already little expectation among the business community that the government would be either able or willing to act in the national interest. Most business people had few scruples about sending funds abroad when they were convinced that the powerful and well connected were doing the same.

That corruption made tackling the crisis much more difficult can be seen in the use made of the Bank Indonesia liquidity credits (BLBI), which were supposed to be used to support banks experiencing short-term liquidity problems. By mid-1998, it was estimated that 144 trillion rupiah (14 per cent of GDP) had been injected into the banking system. According to a report of the Supreme Audit Agency (BPK), irregular practices were pervasive in the management of the funds; almost all the money in fact went to a few private banks and one state bank (Bank Exim), where the support covered fraudulent losses in its treasury operations, rather than deposit withdrawals (IMF 2003: 72). Three banks, all connected to powerful conglomerates, received most of the funds given to the private banks (BCA, BDNI and Danamon). The report of the independent evaluation office claimed that it took several months for IMF staff to find out that corrupt practices were involved in the allocation of BLBI funds (IMF 2003: 79). One suspects that many Indonesians in the banking and business community realised much earlier what was going on, contributing further to the collapse of confidence in government management of the crisis.

A further factor contributing to the crisis, according to the World Bank (1998: 1.11), was the 'unfortunate political juncture' at which it occurred. Suharto was coming to the end of his five-year term and while few doubted that he would seek re-election, his age and health did create uncertainties. The cabinet announced in early 1998 did nothing to assuage these uncertainties. Suharto himself seemed to be in denial that there were serious issues of economic management which needed to be confronted. In some public speeches he appeared to support the IMF-mandated reforms, but when the former American vice-president, Walter Mondale, sent by President Clinton to assess the situation in March 1998, interviewed him, he could only assert that in the past he had been able to manage crises, and that many of the reforms demanded by the USA and the IMF were 'suicidal' (Borsuk and Chng 2014: 368). Many Indonesians thought that the appointment of Dr Habibie as vice-president was a further insurance policy for the ageing president. Given Habibie's well-known support for pouring public funds into costly technology projects, and his contempt for the orthodox economists who criticised these projects, it is possible that Suharto felt that, were he to resign, Habibie would have little legitimacy as president. In fact Habibie, after taking up the presidency in May 1988, was quite receptive to the advice coming from the economists in the cabinet (Boediono 2002: 387–9). He realised that, if he were to be re-elected in the following year, he would have to give top priority to economic recovery, and the support of the IMF was necessary to restore confidence, both at home and abroad. In the event, Habibie was not re-elected and economic recovery was slow, for reasons that are discussed in the following section.

Some foreign analyses of the crisis were inclined to see the problems as caused by investor panic, and blamed international agencies, especially the IMF, for advocating policies, such as the closure of banks in Indonesia, which aggravated panic. Williamson (2004: 835) argued that a crucial error was to abandon the 'crawling band' system which had allowed the rupiah to slowly depreciate, and claimed that if the IMF had been prepared to give a large loan to Indonesia of around 30 billion dollars, conditional on the retention of the crawling band, events in the latter part of 1997 and early 1998 might have taken a very different course. While it is true that the decision to move to a free float added more uncertainty to a situation where business confidence was already fragile, this argument seems to ignore the wider problem of declining business confidence. Other analysts have argued that a different approach by the IMF in the latter part of 1997, involving fewer demands for reforms in the real economy, might have stabilised the situation (Grenville 2004).

But the problems in the banking system were already very serious, and would have had to be addressed at some future time. It is unlikely that Suharto and the cabinet he formed in 1998 would have had the motivation to introduce the necessary reforms.

The behaviour of the IMF attracted much criticism from many quarters, and there can be little doubt that the IMF, the World Bank and many Indonesian economists both inside and outside government underestimated the gravity of the situation in the latter part of 1997. It appears that until late 1997, the IMF agreed with official growth predictions of four to 5 per cent in 1998, only slightly less than the 1997 figure (Grenville 2004: 78). There was widespread confidence that the 'strong economic fundamentals' which had supported three decades of rapid growth in Indonesia would triumph over short-term jitters brought on by the problems in Thailand. Both the Indonesian government and international agencies ignored the weaknesses and vulnerabilities not just in the financial system but in other sectors of the economy as well. As Sheng (2009: 224) pointed out in his analysis of these vulnerabilities, there was a tendency on the part of most observers to be impressed by the apparently benign macroeconomic indicators and to downplay or ignore the problems created by Suharto and his family over many years. When Suharto finally resigned in May 1998, he left his successors to deal with not just a devastated banking system but also the monumental task of restoring both domestic and international confidence in the Indonesian economy.

A slow recovery: 1998–2004

The Habibie cabinet was criticised as containing too many faces from the Suharto era, and too few real reformers. But once sworn in, it moved quickly to tackle at least some of the economic problems facing the country, and achieved more success than most observers would have considered possible a few months earlier. The new president was persuaded by his economics ministers to pursue a tight monetary policy to curb inflation and stop capital flight. These goals he managed to achieve quite quickly; by early 1999, inflation had slowed and the rupiah had recovered some of its value. The very pessimistic predictions regarding the continuing impact of the crisis on real output proved incorrect; real GDP contracted by over 13 per cent in 1998, but grew slightly, by just under 1 per cent, in 1999. As Marks (2009: 49) argued, Habibie was under intense pressure from the *Golkar* Party, which had routinely won most elections during the Suharto era, to gain political support through populist economic policies, including introducing 'social safety nets' to protect the population from the consequences of economic contraction.

Subsidised rice was distributed to many households deemed 'poor' and schools were given assistance to prevent dropouts. Habibie also introduced two laws which were intended to give more grants to sub-provincial levels of government to carry out a range of functions relating to regional and rural development, health and education. The impact of these changes will be assessed in Chapter 9.

In spite of many gloomy predictions to the contrary, the parliamentary elections promised by President Habibie did take place in June 1999 and were considered by most observers to have been reasonably fair with little voter coercion. The People's Consultative Assembly (the newly elected parliament plus a number of appointed members and representatives of the provinces) met in October to elect the new president, and although the atmosphere was tense, the proceedings took place quite smoothly. President Habibie's speech accounting for his brief period in office was delivered but the subsequent vote failed to ratify it, and he then announced he would not be a candidate in the upcoming election. Habibie's defeat was attributed to several factors, including ongoing economic hardship, the Bank Bali scandal which concerned illicit payments to senior *Golkar* figures, and the violence in East Timor following the vote to secede from Indonesia. In what then became a two-horse race, the leader of the PKB party, Abdurrahman Wahid, beat Megawati Sukarnoputeri by a comfortable majority. Megawati's supporters vented their disappointment in street riots in Jakarta and elsewhere but the potentially explosive situation calmed down when she was voted in as vice-president by a large majority. The new cabinet contained some well-known reformers, although it was clear that some of the members were there to pay off political debts rather than because of their ability or mass following.

Thus at the end of 1999, Indonesia had a new parliament and a new president, both enjoying greater democratic legitimacy than any since the early days of independence. But both the economic and the political challenges facing the new administration remained formidable. Regional tensions were mounting; conflicts in Maluku and Central Sulawesi were being exploited by both military and religious groups from Java and elsewhere. Deaths and incidents of non-secessionist collective violence had climbed from virtually nothing in the early 1990s to disturbing levels in 1999 (van Klinken 2007: 5). Rumours of a possible military coup against the new government began to circulate almost as soon as it was sworn in. Although on the production front the economy was no longer in free fall, per capita GDP and per capita national income in 1999 were considerably lower than in 1997; in fact per capita GDP did not return to the 1997 level until 2004 (Table 5.1). The cabinet led by

Table 5.1 *Per capita GDP, unemployment and labour force participation rates, 1996–2008*

	Per capita GDP (Rp ×1,000)	Unemployment (%)	Labour force participation rates (%)
1996	7,479	4.3	66.9
1997	7,724	4.2	66.3
1998	6,595	5.1	66.9
1999	6,523	6.0	67.2
2000	6,738	5.8	67.8
2001	6,895	8.0	68.6
2002	7,113	9.1	67.8
2003	7,358	9.9	67.9
2004	7,630	10.3	67.5
2005	7,962	11.9	66.8
2006	8,271	10.9	66.2
2007	8,660	10.0	67.0
2008	9,040	9.4	67.2

Note: Per capita GDP in 2000 prices. Unemployed is the percentage of the labour force currently not working and actively seeking work. The labour force participation rate is the labour force, including both those working and seeking work, as a percentage of the total population over fifteen. Data refer to the month of August, with the exception of 2005 (November).
Sources: GDP data: van der Eng (2013); unemployment and labour force data: www.bps.go.uk.

Abdurrahman Wahid proved unable to function effectively as a team, and confidence eroded rapidly. In July 2001, a special session of the MPR (People's Representative Council) voted to replace him with Megawati, who became the third president to take office after the resignation of Suharto.

The economic problems remained serious, with only a modest increase in output and continuing problems in the financial sector. Critics blamed the slow recovery on tight fiscal and monetary policies mandated by the IMF as conditions for further assistance. But in fact fiscal policy was tightened only to a modest extent in 1997, and through 1998 the deficits permitted by the IMF increased to 10.1 per cent of GDP, the highest in any IMF-supported programme (IMF 2003: 67). The actual deficit in 1998/1999 was much lower than 10 per cent of GDP, reflecting both rigidities in spending, especially on the newly introduced social safety nets, and the fiscal conservatism of the Ministry of Finance. The IMF admitted that its team was slow to realise that the severe GDP contraction in 1998 was mainly the result of a collapse in private sector investment expenditures. This collapse was ascribed to both the very sharp depreciation of the rupiah, which raised the cost of servicing foreign loans for many firms, and to the general political and economic uncertainty. The report by the independent evaluation office of the IMF rejected the argument that high interest rates were to blame for the output contraction. They argued that real interest rates were negative from late 1997 to early 1999 because of the high inflation and the reluctance of government to raise rates, at least until Suharto left office. But real interest rates did rise after mid-1998, and probably adversely affected some private companies seeking working capital from their banks.

In 1998 and 1999, there were steep declines in the volume of real bank credit, of 25 per cent and 57 per cent. There was some positive growth in 2000, but in 2001 there was again a real decline. The extent of the decline was more severe than in Thailand. The reluctance of banks to lend was partly the result of the high proportion of non-performing loans to total loans, which was still over 40 per cent in 2002, although it fell thereafter (Dowling and Yap 2008: 83). The lack of credit, together with falling demand for many luxury products, caused serious problems for many businesses, which lingered even after growth rates had begun to improve. By 2005 the number of large and medium-scale manufacturing enterprises had fallen to 20,729 compared with 22,615 in 1996. Employment in this sector also fell from 4.7 million in 1996 to 4.2 million in 2005. Perhaps surprisingly, small industries and household enterprises seem to have experienced fewer difficulties, although there was some decline in numbers of household industries between 1996 and 2000.[3] The report of the IMF Evaluation Office did admit that a strategy designed to protect small and medium-scale enterprises would have been helpful, although it would have been difficult to design (IMF 2003: 70).

The large devaluation of the rupiah might have been expected to boost the income of exporters and producers of import substitutes, but here the evidence was mixed. By mid-1999 there was growing evidence that many smallholder producers of export crops (rubber, coffee, cocoa, pepper, etc.) were benefiting from higher real incomes, although inflation was eroding the real value of the large increase in the nominal prices they received. These producers relied on credit from the formal financial sector only to a very limited extent, and in the short term could increase output to benefit from rising prices. But exporters of manufactures were badly hit, in part because of the tightening of domestic credit, but also because of the reluctance of many foreign banks to accept Indonesian letters of credit. Growth of manufactured exports, which had been rapid until 1996,

[3] These figures are taken from the *Statistical Yearbooks* for 2003 and 2006.

slowed to less than 1 per cent per annum from 1997 to 1999. There was some recovery after 2000, especially in resource-based sectors including hydrocarbons and inorganic chemicals, and electronics (Aswicahyono, Hill and Narjoko 2010: 1093).

Rates of open unemployment increased after the crisis, and in 2003 had reached 10 per cent of the labour force, compared with 4.3 per cent in 1996 (Table 5.1). Even after per capita GDP had recovered to its 1996 level, open unemployment remained at around 10–11 per cent for several years. Labour force participation rates were fairly stable after 1996, which indicates that rather than withdraw from the labour force, most workers who lost their jobs continued to search for new ones. How many of these workers were able to find productive employment is unclear. Employment in agriculture, which was falling as a percentage of the labour force in the early 1990s, increased between 1997 and 2000 from 41 to 45 per cent of the employed labour force. In other sectors, employment was either stable as a share of the total or fell, especially in public services (World Bank 2001: table 6).

The rise in unemployment between 1996 and 2003 could plausibly be attributed to the impact of the crisis on output, and the slow recovery between 1999 and 2003. Not only did employment in construction contract, but there was also considerable labour-shedding in labour-intensive manufacturing sectors such as textiles, garments and footwear. During the Megawati presidency, measures were adopted which were designed to give workers greater protection, including quite generous provisions on minimum wages and severance pay, as well as limitations on hiring workers on short-term contracts and on outsourcing. Most of these measures were enshrined in the 2003 Manpower Act. There can be little doubt that the provisions of the act deterred some employers from hiring new workers, and also led to the departure of some foreign investors, especially Korean, from the garment and footwear sectors (Alisjahbana and Manning 2002: 298). Thus, however well intentioned, the stricter regulatory climate probably contributed to the slow growth in non-agricultural employment after 2003. In addition, international markets for labour-intensive manufactures became much more competitive, as China and Vietnam rapidly expanded their exports. Several commentators pointed out that both these countries, although supposedly socialist, had less tough labour protection regulations than Indonesia after 2003 (Manning and Roesad 2006: 167). Unsurprisingly, the newly empowered trade union movement in Indonesia was reluctant to modify the 2003 legislation, even after Megawati left office.

Given the rapid inflation which occurred in 1997/1998, the collapse of investment expenditures, the severe drought, the shift of workers to informal employment and the rise in unemployment, it was to be expected that poverty would increase. The official estimates published by the CBS showed an increase in the headcount measure of poverty between 1996 and 1999. But the extent of the increase was a matter of considerable controversy. By 2000, it appeared that poverty levels were trending downwards, although there was some dispute about the extent of the decline. These controversies will be reviewed in more detail in Chapter 8.

Lingering problems: re-capitalising the banks and corporate governance

By the early years of the twenty-first century, Indonesian policy-makers and commentators were well aware that Indonesia's economic performance was being compared unfavourably with that of China, India and Vietnam. These three countries all had lower per capita GDP than Indonesia in 1990, and at that time were not included among the Asian 'miracle economies'. But their growth rates had accelerated over the 1990s and into the new century, while both Indonesia and Thailand appeared to be struggling to recover from the 1997/1998 crisis. Among many sections of Indonesian public opinion, both secular and Islamic, it was felt that in spite of the successful transition to a more democratic system of government, many of the Suharto-era problems still plagued the country. In addition, new problems had emerged, not least the huge cost of recapitalising the banking system.

These costs had three main elements: compensation to Bank Indonesia for the liquidity support extended in 1997/1998, compensation to those banks which took over the liabilities of banks that were closed, and recapitalisation of those banks which were permitted to continue to trade. In all these cases finance was provided through the recapitalisation bonds, interest payments on which were charged to the government budget (Enoch, Frecaut and Kovanen 2003: 84). By late 2000, it was clear that the cost of servicing the additional public debt would amount to at least 4 per cent of GDP in that fiscal year, and would increase in subsequent years as the government would have to start retiring some of the bonds issued (Ramstetter 2000: 19). This additional burden on the budget meant that other categories of expenditure including health, education and public works would have to be squeezed. By 2004, the total costs to the government of financial support to the banks (liquidity support and costs of the bonds issued for bank recapitalisation) was estimated to be Rp.431 trillion or 50 per cent of GDP in 2004. This was a higher cost, relative to GDP, than incurred in Chile and

Uruguay in 1981, or in Thailand, South Korea and Malaysia in 1997 (Djiwandono 2004: 69). As Frecaut (2004: 55) pointed out, these losses did not represent money lost to the economy, but rather transfers from the banks to other parts of the economy, especially to the corporate sector. 'Ultimately the crisis was mainly a large-scale wealth redistribution exercise, neutral for the banks, beneficial for the corporations and, to a lesser extent, for household borrowers and depositors, but disastrous for the general public.'

After the Indonesian Bank Restructuring Agency (IBRA) was established in 1998, it took over, in effect nationalised, most of the private banks. Thus on behalf of the government it gained ownership of these banks and of the assets transferred by the banks, and by their former shareholders 'as part of settlement arrangements in compensation for central bank liquidity support' (Frecaut 2004: 41). But it rapidly became clear that the pledged assets were far less valuable than originally claimed. IBRA's task was to extract as much value as it could from these assets, thus reducing the final cost of bank restructuring to the public as a whole. But its success rate was poor; by 2005 it was estimated that it had only managed to extract less than 30 per cent of the face value of the assets.

Most of the large conglomerates which had grown mighty during the Suharto era were forced to divest themselves of at least some of their assets to settle outstanding loans with banks. But the divestment process was often far from transparent, and there were a number of examples of businesses being purchased from IBRA by groups which were hardly arms-length from the old conglomerate. In addition, several conglomerates leveraged their assets to obtain new loans abroad. Perhaps the most egregious example of this was the Sinar Mas conglomerate, which through an affiliated company, APP, borrowed heavily in the USA and Asia to finance the expansion of its pulp and paper businesses in China and elsewhere. This continued after 1997, in spite of the fact that the bank linked to Sinar Mas had granted large loans to APP which APP refused to pay back once the bank had been taken over by IBRA. It became clear that IBRA itself was hardly acting as an independent honest broker in the Sinar Mas–APP affair, but permitted the sale of assets at discounted prices to entities suspected of being linked to Sinar Mas.[4]

The Sinar Mas–APP case, and others like it, raised broader problems of corporate governance which were taken up after the crisis by international agencies, both in Indonesia and Thailand. Before 1997 this was not an

[4] The Sinar Mas story has attracted several analyses; see Studwell (2007), Matsumoto (2007: Chapter 8), Pirard and Rokhim (2005) and Brown (2004: 392–401).

issue which was given much attention; most commentators believed that even if firms were badly managed and ran into cash flow difficulties, their problems could be sorted out in a context of dense business networks, and of rapid economic growth.[5] Bankruptcy legislation existed in Indonesia, as in most parts of Asia, often based on legislation in the former colonial power. But given the corruption and inefficiencies in the legal system in Indonesia, there was little incentive to use it. Faced with widespread corporate collapse in 1998/1999, it was clear that more effective procedures would have to be put in place, but there was little agreement on how this should be done. The Bretton Woods institutions tended to blame the problems in the corporate sector in Indonesia, as well as in Thailand and Malaysia, on the ownership structure of many large firms, where even in publicly listed companies, families retained control over most key decisions and minority shareholders had little power. Although there was some evidence that the structure of ownership was changing after the crisis, particularly in Indonesia, there was considerable debate about the effect of these changes on firm performance.

In an analysis of how six large conglomerates in Indonesia dealt with the aftermath of the crisis, Sato (2004) drew a number of conclusions, not all of which supported the view that concentrated ownership led to poor management. She pointed to the example of the Gudang Garam Group, whose core business was the manufacture of clove cigarettes. In spite of the fact that the founding family remained in control, the firm survived the crisis with little damage. She also argued that the cases of Sinar Mas, together with the Astra and Gajah Tunggal groups, showed that foreign creditors did not play a constructive role in monitoring the basic health of the conglomerate. Neither did public listing on the stock exchange lead to better corporate governance in several of the cases she examined, especially if the owner-managers had good links to key figures in the government. She also found that the presence of professional managers in conglomerates such as Sinar Mas and Gajah Tunggal with no close ties to the founding families did not exercise a check on the rights of owner-managers to have a final say in group decision-making.

The ongoing problems with corporate restructuring in Indonesia and the publicity given to the activities of IBRA led many Indonesians to suspect that, in spite of the political changes which took place in the wake of Suharto's departure from office, the problems of 'corruption, collusion and nepotism', which had provoked student protests in 1998, had not gone away. Certainly there were important changes in the banking system, with many of the private banks being either sold to foreign banks,

[5] See the quotation from Larry Lang in Suehiro (2001: 22).

or forced to hire in consultants to advise on bringing them into line with international best practice. But the state sector, although undergoing considerable restructuring, had little contact with foreign banks, and successfully resisted demands from the IMF for divestment of a majority of their shares (Sato 2005: 115–17). More broadly, it was clear that powerful groups within the parliament, and in the governments of the three presidents who succeeded Suharto in quick succession between 1998 and 2001, were apparently able to influence the decisions of IBRA and other government agencies, including the courts, in favour of business groups associated with the Suharto era. These perceptions were shared by domestic and foreign business groups, and were confirmed by Indonesia's ranking in international league tables of corruption and governance. The governance league table constructed by World Bank economists showed that the control of corruption in Indonesia had actually deteriorated between 1996 and 2005. This was in spite of the improvement in 'voice and accountability' which had occurred (Table 5.2). There was also some deterioration in Malaysia, the Philippines and Vietnam over these years, although in 2005 Indonesia was ranked lower in terms of control of corruption, and in terms of government effectiveness, than any other ASEAN country except Laos, Cambodia and Myanmar.

Table 5.2 *Governance scores for Asian countries, 1996 and 2005*

	Voice/accountability		Government effectiveness		Control of corruption	
	1996	2005	1996	2005	1996	2005
Country:						
Singapore	0.35	−0.29	2.31	2.41	2.38	2.24
Malaysia	−0.11	−0.41	0.75	1.01	0.57	0.27
Brunei	−1.04	−1.04	1.09	0.56	0.41	0.25
Thailand	−0.05	0.07	0.58	0.40	−0.33	−0.25
India	0.23	0.35	−0.45	−0.11	−0.32	−0.31
Philippines	0.11	0.01	0.22	−0.07	−0.41	−0.58
China	−1.36	−1.66	0.15	−0.11	0.00	−0.69
Vietnam	−1.39	−1.60	−0.28	−0.31	−0.68	−0.76
Indonesia	−1.22	−0.21	0.08	−0.47	−0.49	−0.86
Laos	−1.18	−1.54	−0.07	−1.09	−1.00	−1.10
Cambodia	−0.76	−0.94	−0.66	−0.94	−1.00	−1.12
Myanmar	−1.80	−2.16	−1.20	−1.61	−1.25	−1.44

Note: Countries are scored for each indicator on a scale ranging from −2.5 to +2.5. For example on the control of corruption indicator, the worst country in 2005 (Equatorial Guinea) had a score of −1.79 and the best (Iceland) has a score of 2.49.
Source: Kaufmann, Kraay and Mastruzzi (2006), Appendix C.

These league tables were widely consulted by potential investors in many parts of the world, and they certainly contributed to the perception, both in Indonesia and abroad, that greater political freedom had not been sufficient to solve some of the deep-seated problems in the country. Some academic commentators went further and argued that it was 'crucial to the post-Suharto trajectory that *reformasi* did not sweep aside the predatory and illiberal social and political forces nurtured by the New Order' (Hadiz and Robison 2005: 231). These authors argued that over the three decades of Suharto's New Order, a 'rigid state-corporatist system' was imposed which was able to co-opt much of the middle class who were happy to trade political freedom for greater economic security. While many of the new middle class were damaged by the crisis, Hadiz and Robison suggested that, at least up to 2004, there was little sign that they wanted the kind of sweeping changes which would be required to tackle the problems inherited from the Suharto era.

In his review of the process of democratic reform set in train after Suharto left office, Horowitz (2013: 1–2) argued that the reform process was 'insider dominated', and important roles were played by leaders who were prominent during the Suharto years. He also pointed out that there was little consultation with civil society however defined, or with the wider public. This might seem to support the arguments of Hadiz and Robison that the changes were cosmetic rather than fundamental. But Horowitz also argued that the process was successful in moderating the role of the military, and steering Indonesia away from the dangers of ethnic and religious violence. It was the expectation of those involved in the reform process that a more open and accountable political system would make it easier to achieve the elusive goal of a 'just and prosperous society'. Political and constitutional reform would lead to greater economic reform. To what extent did this happen after 2004?

6 The SBY years
Building a new Indonesia?

Promise of a new dawn

The disenchantment which many Indonesians felt with the reform process, and with the leadership of President Megawati Soekarnoputri, was reflected in the results of the parliamentary elections held in April 2004. The political party which emerged with the largest number of votes, 21.6 per cent of the total, was Golkar, which had dominated the political scene through the Suharto years. The Indonesian Democratic Party of Struggle (PDIP), the party of Megawati, managed to come second with 18.6 per cent of the votes, but this was a sharp decline from 1999 when the party gained one-third of the total vote. The remaining votes were spread among a number of parties, some of them Islamic in orientation and some secular (Marks 2004: 152). These results reflected growing frustration on the part of many Indonesians with the slow economic recovery since the crisis of 1997/1998, and a nostalgia for the greater economic progress during the Suharto years.

The presidential election which was held in July 2004 marked a historic shift away from the past practice of indirect presidential elections through an augmented parliament, the Peoples' Representative Council (MPR). For the first time, Indonesia would have a directly elected president and vice-president. The strongest ticket was widely considered to be that of Susilo Bambang Yudhoyono (SBY), a retired general and former cabinet minister under Megawati, and Jusuf Kalla, a businessman from South Sulawesi and member of Golkar. SBY had come up through the military under Suharto; he had graduated from the Magelang Officers' Academy in the 1970s and had also studied in the USA. He was widely considered to represent the moderate, secular wing of the armed forces, which had opposed the spread of Islamic views in the military in the last years of the Suharto regime. Fluent in English and well travelled (he had commanded the Indonesian contingent to the UN Peacekeeping Force in Bosnia in the 1990s), he presented himself with considerable success as a 'thinking general', who was well informed about world events and also capable of implementing much-needed reforms at home. Even while he was a cabinet minister, he had continued to study economics at the Bogor Agricultural University, and had set up his own think tank (the Brighten Institute) to advise him on policy issues[1].

In a speech in Singapore in May 2004, Yudhoyono (2004) set out his 'vision, hopes and aspiration' for Indonesia's future for an international audience. He acknowledged that, in spite of the improving macroeconomic indicators, the 1997/1998 crisis had left deep scars on Indonesian society and that many Indonesians were still not benefiting from the recovery. He argued that faster economic growth, of at least 7 per cent per annum, was necessary to improve living standards and reduce unemployment. He also stressed the need for better education, infrastructure and business-friendly policies. More effort must be made to build local communities, and encourage them to take responsibility for their development needs. On foreign policy, he emphasised the importance of ASEAN, which would remain 'the anchor for Indonesia's foreign policy'. Above all, he claimed that he was committed to a 'modern, democratic, outward-looking, open and tolerant Indonesia', a claim that he was to repeat to audiences in many parts of the world over the next ten years. It was a message which resonated with many Indonesians; in the first round of voting the SBY–Kalla ticket secured 41 per cent of the vote. In a run-off election held in September against Megawati and her running mate, Hasyim Muzadi, the SBY–Kalla ticket won by a convincing majority.

Most of the economic targets set out by Yudhoyono during his campaign were included in the draft of the medium-term national development plan released by *Bappenas* (the national planning agency) at the end of 2004. The targets included in the plan were a return to economic growth of 7.6 per cent per annum by 2009, an increase in investment/GDP ratio to 28 per cent (most of which was to come from the private sector), a reduction in the stock of government debt to around one-third of GDP, together with a decline in open unemployment to 5.1 per cent of the labour force and a reduction in the proportion of the population below the official poverty line to 8.2 per cent. The draft plan emphasised the need to revitalise the agricultural sector, rehabilitate and extend infrastructure, improve the business climate and restructure and privatise state enterprises (Booth 2005: 211). Budgetary revenues were to be increased relative to GDP; tax collections were to rise by 0.5 per cent per annum. Soon after his election, Yudhoyono presided over an 'infrastructure

---

[1] Under the auspices of the Brighten Institute, he published several monographs which examined fiscal and poverty alleviation policies; among others see Yudhoyono (2003), and Yudhoyono and Harniati (2004).

summit' designed to attract foreign investment into large-scale infrastructure projects including toll roads, bridges and energy projects.

By 2009, when he was running for re-election, few of these targets had
been met, and many Indonesian and foreign commentators were expressing concern with Yudhoyono's economic management. The infrastructure summit held in early 2005 generated much optimism about the
potential for public–private partnerships in Indonesia, but four years
later there were few visible results. True, Yudhoyono was hardly the first
politician in history to find that, having achieved power, delivering on
economic promises was much more difficult than making them. The
economic crisis which hit the USA and other Western economies in
2008, together with obstruction from an often hostile parliament, could
plausibly be blamed for some of the difficulties his government experienced in meeting economic targets. But to many observers he often
seemed indecisive and rather weak. The emergence of two new parties
in 2009, each led by former generals, might have been expected to shake
up the political system and open the way for serious challengers in the
2009 parliamentary and presidential elections.

But in fact that did not happen. Yudhoyono's own party, the
Democratic Party (PD), emerged as the largest single party in the
parliamentary elections, and in the presidential election Yudhoyono
and his new running mate, Dr Boediono, a respected economist, gained
almost 61 per cent of the popular vote, making a run-off election
unnecessary. Many Indonesians apparently thought that this pair was
a safer choice than either Megawati, this time teamed with the controversial former general Prabowo Subianto, who only managed to get
27 per cent of the vote, or the vice-president, Jusuf Kalla, now running
with another former general, Wiranto. Given the uncertainties in the
global economy, a majority of the electorate thought it was better to stick
with the incumbent, and hope that the country's economic performance
would continue to improve.

These hopes were not disappointed, at least at the macroeconomic
level. Indonesia managed to escape the global economic crisis of 2008/
2009 with only a slowdown in growth in 2009; in several neighbouring
countries, growth was either much slower, or negative (Table 6.1).
Between 2010 and 2013, growth rates in Indonesia appeared quite
robust. In the decade from 2003 to 2013, real GDP grew by almost
76 per cent, which on an annualised basis was slightly lower than the rate
projected by *Bappenas* in 2004, but much better than many observers
had expected when Yudhoyono took office. Unemployment rates also
trended downwards; by 2014 open unemployment had fallen to under
6 per cent of the labour force. The percentage of the population below

Table 6.1 *Growth in GDP: Indonesia, Vietnam, Philippines, Malaysia and Thailand (2007 = 100)*

	Indonesia	Vietnam	Philippines	Malaysia	Thailand
2007	100	100	100	100	100
2008	106	106	104	105	102
2009	111	111	105	103	101
2010	118	119	113	111	108
2011	125	126	118	117	109
2012	133	133	126	123	117
2013	141	140	135	129	120

Sources: Indonesia: www.bps.go.id; Other countries from Asian Development Bank, *Key Indicators for Asia and the Pacific, 2014* (www.abd.org).

the official poverty line was also falling, according to the figures prepared by the Central Statistics Agency. There was also mounting evidence that Indonesia's international reputation as a location for foreign investment was improving; inward investment flows accelerated sharply from 2005 onwards, and in the years from 2008 to 2012 Indonesia received more inward flows of foreign direct investment than any other country in Southeast Asia except Singapore (Unctad 2013: 214).

Thus it was not surprising that when Yudhoyono gave his final Independence Day speech to the nation on 17 August 2014, he emphasised the economic achievements of his decade in power. Indonesia, he claimed, was now viewed as a successful and stable middle-income country, more prosperous, democratic and unified than at any time in its history. In terms of total GDP it was the sixteenth largest global economy and, as a member of the G-20 group of nations, was playing an increasingly important role in global economic policy discussions. He stressed the country's success in improving access to education and health care, and in reducing poverty. The middle class was growing in size, and confidence; in an oblique criticism of the Suharto era, he expressed the hope that in the course of the twenty-first century, progress in Indonesia would be measured not in terms of the number of large conglomerates but in terms of the size of the middle class.

Most politicians on leaving office tend to stress their achievements and downplay their failures. Critics claimed that while the macroeconomic achievements of the Yudhoyono era were clear enough, they were based on favourable external circumstances which were unlikely to continue. Indonesia like other resource-based economies had performed well in the decade up to 2013 because of increased global demand for a range of

Table 6.2 *Changes in the terms of trade and GDP growth rates, 2005–2014*

Year	Terms of trade (2000 = 100)	GDP growth rates (%)	
		Constant prices	ToT corrected
2005	91.8	5.7	4.6
2006	96.7	5.5	8.0
2007	93.2	6.3	4.4
2008	83.7	6.0	0.7
2009	86.0	4.6	7.0
2010	83.0	6.2	4.1
2011	81.5	6.5	5.0
2012	75.8	6.3	3.5
2013	71.6	5.7	3.4
2014	70.8	5.1	5.6
GDP growth (2000=100)		209.3	182.1

Note: The correction for the terms of trade follows the methodology set out in Bank Indonesia (1987: 101).
Source: www.bps.go.id.

minerals, including coal and natural gas, as well as for agricultural commodities including natural rubber and vegetable oils. This increased demand was fuelled by rapid growth in the major Asian economies, especially China. But in fact the external environment facing Indonesia in the years after 2006 was not as favourable as was often assumed. The commodity terms of trade declined quite sharply between 2000 and 2005; after a recovery in 2006 the decline continued until 2014. Although export prices did increase, import prices including those of petroleum products were increasing faster. Indonesia had become a net importer of petroleum products in the early twenty-first century, and was thus highly vulnerable to increases in world prices. As a result, growth rates in GDP corrected for the terms of trade decline were lower in most years than those estimated from the constant price data (Table 6.2).

In addition, critics of the Yudhoyono years pointed to the government's failure to reform the large state enterprise sector, to reduce budgetary subsidies for fuel and electricity, or to tackle the growing crisis in infrastructure. Even the apparent achievements in reducing poverty were called into question, for reasons which will be discussed further in Chapter 8. It was also argued that, although GDP growth was quite strong in the decade to 2013, much of it was derived from construction and the service sector. The sectors producing traded goods (goods whose

Table 6.3 *Sectoral breakdown of GDP, 2003 and 2013*

Sector	Percentage breakdown		Percentage of increment
	2003	2013	
Agriculture	15.2	12.3	8.3
Mining	10.6	7.1	2.4
Manufacturing	28.0	25.5	22.3
Utilities	0.7	0.8	0.9
Construction	5.7	6.6	7.8
Trade	16.3	18.1	20.5
Transport/Communications	5.4	10.6	17.3
Finance	8.9	9.8	11.0
Other Services	9.2	9.3	9.5
Total	100.0	100.0	100.0

Source: www.bps.go.id.

prices are determined by international markets), agriculture, mining and manufacturing, only accounted for around a third of total growth in this decade, and the share of these sectors in total output fell from over 50 per cent in 2003 to 45 per cent in 2013 (Table 6.3). These three sectors together only accounted for a small part of the growth in the employed labour force between 2003 and 2013; the agriculture sector shed labour while manufacturing industry accounted for less than 20 per cent of the total growth in employment (Table 6.4). Much of the growth in employment took place in trade and other services. The rest of this chapter will examine in more detail the reasons for the rather slow output growth in both agriculture and manufacturing industry, compared with other parts of the economy. It will also look at the growth in both output and employment in services.

The changing role of agriculture

In his early pronouncements on economic policy, Yudhoyono stressed the importance of the agricultural sector in promoting economic development, through supplying food and raw materials for industry, as well as generating foreign exchange (Yudhoyono 2003: 58). But during his decade in power, the share of agriculture in total output fell, and its contribution to employment growth was negative. The results of the 2013 Agricultural Census showed that there had been a decline in the total number of agricultural households since 2003, from 31.2 million

Table 6.4 *Sectoral breakdown labour force growth, 2003 and 2013*

Sector	Percentage breakdown		Percentage of increment
	2003	2013	
Agriculture	46.3	34.8	−12.7
Mining/Utilities	1.0	1.4	3.6
Manufacturing	12.0	13.3	18.4
Construction	4.5	5.6	10.2
Trade	18.6	21.4	33.0
Transport/Communications	5.5	4.5	0.6
Finance	1.4	2.6	7.3
Other services	10.7	16.4	39.6
Total	100.0	100.0	100.0

Source: www.bps.go.id.

Table 6.5 *Percentage breakdown of farm household incomes, 2004 and 2013*

Income source	2004	2013
Agricultural enterprise	44.1	46.7
Other enterprises	16.5	13.5
Other receipts	15.0	12.3
Agricultural labour	7.4	6.9
Other labour	17.0	20.7
Total	100.0	100.0
Numbers of holdings (millions)		
Java	17.956	13.429
Sumatra	6.616	6.287
Sulawesi	2.417	2.261
Bali/Nusatenggara	1.942	1.788
Kalimantan	1.631	1.556
Maluku/Papua	0.670	0.814
Total	31.232	26.135

Source: CBS: ***Laporan Bulanan Data Sosial Ekonomi,
edisi 54,*** November 2014, p. 116 (www.bps.go.id).

households to 26.1 million. Most of this decline occurred in Java, although only in Maluku and Papua was there an increase (Table 6.5). The survey of sources of income of agricultural households carried out in 2013 showed that 46.7 per cent of total income of agricultural households was derived from the agricultural holding, and a further 13.5 per cent from non-agricultural enterprises. Much of the rest came from labouring jobs both on and off the farm, although non-agricultural labour was a more important source (Table 6.5). There was an increase in the percentage of households engaged in growing tree crops, especially palm oil and rubber.

These trends can be interpreted in several ways. The decline in the numbers employed in agriculture, together with a decline in the number of agricultural households, might suggest that numbers employed in the agricultural sector were inflated after 1997 as a result of the fact that many Indonesians moved back into agriculture when they lost jobs elsewhere. As the economy improved, they moved back out of agriculture towards more productive employment in other parts of the economy. In a report published in 2014, the World Bank (2014: 6) took the view that labour productivity in the agricultural sector in 2009–2012 was still much lower than in other parts of the economy, so the fall in the size of the population dependent on agriculture was to be welcomed. But given the evidence of multiple sources of income for most agricultural households, it is clear that many of those 'employed in agriculture' according to the census and survey data are in fact getting a part, in many cases quite a large part, of their income in other sectors.

Whether a decline in numbers of agricultural households, and in the agricultural labour force, does represent an improvement in labour productivity and incomes depends on whether the move out of full or partial agricultural employment is voluntary or whether people are being pushed. The push mechanisms could include compulsory purchase of land for non-agricultural purposes, or the termination of rental agreements giving people without ownership rights access to agricultural land. In addition, increased mechanisation could have been reducing demand for wage labour in many agricultural tasks. The available census and survey data provide few clues on what mechanisms are in fact causing the observed declines. It seems probable that many people who are leaving agriculture, especially young people with some post-primary education, are doing so out of a belief that more lucrative employment is available in other sectors, especially in urban areas.

In Java, and in some parts of Sumatra and Sulawesi, some migrants may be able to find employment in the urban service sector, but often jobseekers are frustrated in their search. Some may return to their rural homes and find employment in small enterprises. There would seem to be an argument for government policies to support further household income diversification in rural areas, but the evidence indicates that those policies which have been implemented have not been very successful. The favoured vehicle in the Suharto era was cooperatives, which

Table 6.6 *Percentage of agricultural households receiving government assistance, 2003*

Regions	Own resources for purchasing inputs	Percentage with government assistance		
		Credit	Extension	Other
Sumatra	85.2	2.1	10.0	3.7
Java	85.2	2.5	15.5	4.6
Bali/Nusatenggara	83.2	3.1	13.6	10.4
Kalimantan	90.3	2.9	13.6	5.7
Sulawesi	85.9	2.7	14.4	4.4
Maluku/Papua	85.4	1.2	6.5	5.9
Indonesia	85.4	2.5	13.7	4.9

Source: CBS: **Sensus Pertanian** 2003: **Buku C: Hasil Pencacahan Survei Pendapatan Rumahtangga Pertanian**, Tables 30, 31, 32, 34.

supplied credit and other support to farm households. But few agricultural households belonged to cooperatives, and many of those who did belong received no services. The 2003 Agricultural Census found that the great majority of agricultural households were using their own resources to purchase inputs and fewer than 3 per cent were using government-provided credit (Table 6.6).

Another explanation for the slow growth of agricultural output since the end of the Suharto era, and the growing importance of non-food agriculture, is that most government assistances to the sector, whether in the form of import controls or input subsidies, were removed. This occurred in step with a gradual reduction in protection to manufacturing industry, so that in the years from 2000 to 2009, relative rates of assistance to agriculture and industry were only slightly negative. This contrasted with the years from 1970 to 2000 when industry received much more government assistance (Anderson, Rausser and Swinnen 2013: 439), although the food crop sector was given more assistance compared with tree crops. A similar trend has been noted in other parts of Asia including China, India, Thailand and Vietnam. By 2008, effective rates of protection on agricultural products were slightly higher than on manufactures (Marks and Rahardja 2012: 80).

Since the late 1990s, food imports have increased rapidly in Indonesia. The country is once again importing considerable quantities of rice, and has become one of the largest importers of wheat in the world. There have also been substantial increases in imports of corn, soybean, meat and dairy products (Table 6.7). To some economists this trend was welcome as evidence of increasing household incomes, leading to a more

Table 6.7 *Imports and exports of foodgrains in Southeast Asia:* (×*1,000 metric tons: annual average: 2010/2011 to 2013/2014*)

	Rice	Corn	Wheat
Net importers			
Indonesia	1,777	2,646	6,902
Philippines	1,288	NA	3,611
Malaysia	1,018	3,092	NA
Net exporters*			
Thailand	8,329	NA	−2,034
Vietnam	6,979	−1,625	−2,248
Myanmar	1,224	NA	NA
Cambodia	959	NA	NA

* Minus sign denotes imports.
Source: USDA, **Grain: World Markets and Trade**, August 2014.

diversified diet. But increased food imports have been unwelcome to many domestic producers, and from 2010 onwards the government reintroduced import quotas on a range of agricultural products, with a view to achieving self-sufficiency. In 2012, the parliament passed a new food law which included a range of measures including quotas and even bans on food imports, restrictions on exports of unprocessed farm products and greater government involvement in food procurement and processing. Doubts have been expressed as to whether the targets of self-sufficiency can be met, given continuing growth in domestic demand for food (Nehru 2013a: 155). To the extent that import controls will lead to higher domestic prices for basic foods such as rice, sugar and soybean, this will negatively affect incomes of the poorer groups who devote a higher part of their expenditures to food. Thus policies intended to assist food producers could have serious implications for poverty. These issues are examined further in Chapter 8.

In the immediate post-independence years, there was considerable hostility towards foreign owned estates, and even after the nationalisation of Dutch properties in the late 1950s, estates continued to struggle with labour problems, an over-valued exchange rate and adverse trends in global prices. By 1975, the amount of land controlled by large estates had fallen to around 752,000 hectares, which was only about 63 per cent of the 1940 figure. Land under smallholder producers of tree crops was estimated to be around 5.4 million hectares in 1975, which was probably an understatement. Smallholders had proved to be far more resilient in the face of the economic turmoil of the post-independence years, and by the 1960s smallholder producers dominated output of crops such as

Table 6.8 *Planted area controlled by large estates and smallholder producers of tree crops (×1,000 hectares)*

Year	Large estates	Large estates (Palm oil)	Smallholders	Smallholders (Palm oil)
1940	1,197.7	109.6	NA	NA
1960	841.8	104.3	NA	NA
1975	752.1	170.9	5,385.2	..
1991	2,114.4	779.3	9,336.8	384.6
2000	4,246.3	2,991.3	11,549.6	1,190.2
2008	5,647.3	4,451.8	14,451.4	2,903.3

Source: 1940 and 1960: CBS (1963: 81); 1975: CBS (1979: 242–3); 1991: CBS (1997: 211–12); 2003: CBS (2004: 211–12); 2008: CBS (2010: 242–5).

rubber and coffee. But in the last quarter of the twentieth century, area controlled by large estates once again grew rapidly, mainly as a result of increased production of palm oil (Table 6.8). The rapid growth of palm oil cultivation was the result of favourable global market trends and policies which favoured land acquisition by Indonesian and foreign investors. The Suharto government pursued a policy of encouraging smallholder cultivation through the establishment of nucleus estates which were located around large estates, and could utilise their processing facilities. This policy was continued under subsequent administrations and by 2008, area under both smallholder and estate cultivation of palm oil had expanded to over seven million hectares (Table 6.8).

The rapid expansion of palm oil cultivation was not without controversy, and became entwined with the larger issue of deforestation. By the early twenty-first century, as world concern about global warming and climate change grew, the problem of rapid deforestation in Indonesia was attracting both national and international attention. Estimates of the rate of deforestation from 1985 to 1997 were put as high as 1.7 million hectares per year (World Bank 2001:7). Comparative data published by the FAO showed that Indonesia's rate of deforestation between 1990 and 2000 was higher than that of Brazil, the Congo and most other developing countries, although there was a decline after 2000 (Resosudarmo et al. 2012: table 3.1). An audit of the management of Indonesia's forests carried out by the National Audit Board in 2008 showed that, of Indonesia's total forest area of 133.7 million hectares (70 per cent of the land area of the country), only 85.6 million hectares was in 'good condition'. An estimated 38.8 million hectares were in poor condition, and much of this land was partially or completely denuded of forest cover.

This figure is supported by other estimates which put the loss of forest cover in Indonesia over the past four decades at around 40 million hectares (Wicke et al. 2011).

What were the processes driving forest loss? What was the economic impact of the expansion of agricultural land outside Java, especially for palm oil, compared to commercial exploitation of forests? The official view in Indonesia for many years was that forest loss was mainly due to shifting cultivators, who were encroaching on the land controlled by the Department of Forestry. By the early 1990s, some studies were pointing out that commercial logging and smallholder encroachment were two sides of the same coin. The commercial exploitation of forests made it much easier for small farmers to encroach on land which had been difficult for them to access. As more sophisticated satellite imaging technology became available, it became clear that large plantation companies and forest conglomerates were the main actors driving forest loss. Small cultivators, including those displaced by large estates, and spontaneous transmigrants also played some role, but these farmers were not, by and large, swidden cultivators (World Bank 2001: 13).

By the time Yudhoyono took office in 2004, pressure was building on the Indonesian government to conserve what remained of the country's pristine forests, and give more attention to the consequences of agricultural growth for forest conservation. Many national and international researchers and environmental activists placed the blame for deforestation squarely on commercial developers, both logging companies and those involved in palm oil cultivation, although it was argued that mining companies also played a role (Resosudarmo et al. 2012: 31–7). It was clear the growth in area under palm oil, although substantial, could only have accounted for a small part of the loss of forest cover of around 40 million hectares since the 1970s. To quote one study, 'palm oil alone cannot explain the large loss in forest cover but ... rather a web of interrelated direct causes (including palm oil production expansion) and underlying drivers are responsible' (Wicke et al. 2008: 1). Among the underlying drivers have been population growth, increasing prices for many agricultural and forest products, and policy failures.

The evidence indicates that at the end of the first decade of the twenty-first century, there is more than 20 million hectares of land in Indonesia which was formerly under forest cover but is now denuded of trees. Some estimates go even higher. While forest concessionaires were legally obliged to reforest this land, in many cases they have not done so. Until the early twenty-first century, this land was still under the control of the Department of Forests, with the result that an estimated 40 million Indonesians are living in degraded areas with few trees left but which are still classified as forest, and which they cannot legally cultivate (Elson 2011:5). The government has since 2005 made it easier for local communities to take over this land on a lease-hold basis and use it for a range of purposes including the planting of tree crops, although some observers think the progress has been disappointingly slow.

Some studies have suggested that Indonesia could bring as much as 28 million hectares of new land under palm oil without further encroachment on those forest areas still in good condition, if the currently degraded land is used for new plantations and smallholdings (Wicke et al. 2011). Such estimates may be exaggerated, but there is certainly scope for increasing production of both food crops and tree crops on this land. The challenge for government will be to accelerate the pace of community control, so that degraded land can be used in ways which will raise the income of millions of rural households, without causing further environmental damage. Some NGOs and advocacy groups expressed disappointment that the Yudhoyono government had not achieved more in facilitating community control, although much of the responsibility lies with provincial and district governments, who have not always sided with community groups. The impact of the decentralisation reforms on the environment will be examined further in Chapter 9.

Slow industrial growth

After the very steep nominal devaluation of the rupiah in 1997/1998, it was hoped that the traded goods sectors of the economy, especially agriculture and manufacturing industry, would benefit from increased income, and expand their enterprises. In fact, as is clear from Table 6.3, any benefit was short-lived. The effect of the devaluation was at least partly eroded by inflation. In addition, tariff and non-tariff protection to the manufacturing sector was reduced, to meet obligations imposed by the WTO and by various regional trading arrangements. By 2008, trade policies were much less protectionist than in the Suharto era (Marks and Rahardja 2012: 82). Other reasons for the slow growth performance of the large-scale manufacturing sector included minimum wage and other employment legislation introduced in 2003 which led to very high severance pay entitlements in Indonesia compared with other parts of Asia, poor human capital, and the continuing failure of the government to tackle the problems of inadequate infrastructure. These problems were not unique to Indonesia; India also experienced a decline in the share of manufacturing in GDP between 2001 and 2011, when it was only 14 per cent of GDP (Nehru 2013b: table 2). But their adverse impact on rates of growth in the manufacturing sector in Indonesia attracted considerable critical attention over the decade from 2004 to 2014.

Increasingly Indonesia was unfavourably compared with other countries in Asia, which were participating more actively in the growth of 'Factory Asia', where 'billions of different parts and components from plants spread across a dozen nations' are assembled and dispatched to markets all over the world (Baldwin 2006). By the early twenty-first century trade in parts, components and accessories (intermediate goods) had become the most dynamic part of international trade; in 2009 it accounted for more than half of non-fuel commodity trade. According to one analysis, trade in intermediate products encourages specialisation of different economies, leading to a 'trade in tasks' that adds value along the production chain (World Trade Organization 2011: 4). As early as 2001, parts and components accounted for as much as half of total trade in the Philippines, and a lower but still significant component in Malaysia, Thailand and Vietnam. Indonesia was criticised for 'not participating vigorously' in the new regional production networks which were evolving across East and Southeast Asia (Gill and Kharas 2007: 29; Lipsey and Sjoholm 2011: 56–7). Although Indonesia's share of world manufactured exports increased between 1994/1995 and 2006/2007, its share of several categories was below Malaysia and Thailand, both much smaller economies (Athukorala and Hill 2010: table 7).

The blame for Indonesia's supposedly poor performance was placed on the factors already mentioned, especially inadequate infrastructure and a shortage of workers with appropriate skills. In addition there was a widespread feeling that Indonesia was failing to benefit from the rise of China as a regional and global power. China had become an important market for some Indonesian commodities, including coal, LNG, palm oil and rubber, but most Indonesian imports from China were manufactures. To some observers, this seemed a re-imposition of a colonial pattern of trade. Critics contrasted the Indonesian experience with that of Thailand where exports of primary products had accounted for around 40 per cent of all Thai exports to China in 1995, but had dropped to just over 20 per cent in 2012 (Lee 2013: 4). Manufactured goods dominated Thai exports to China, and manufactures also accounted for most Chinese exports to Thailand. This 'intra-industry' trade in parts and components also accounted for a growing share of Chinese trade with the Philippines, Malaysia and Vietnam. Indonesia appeared to some commentators to be missing out.

An alternative argument is that, in the early decades of the twenty-first century, Indonesia's comparative advantage continues to be in resource-based exports, and that the country's strong export performance in agriculture and minerals inevitably places pressures on other traded goods sectors, including labour-intensive manufactures. This of course is the familiar 'Dutch Disease' argument which was much discussed in Indonesia over the 1970s; discussions of the Indonesian case can be found in McCawley (1980) and Warr (1984). Given the country's resource endowments, it is unrealistic to expect Indonesia to produce the same exports as other Asian countries. In addition, the supposed advantages of greater involvement in 'Factory Asia' networks were called into question after the onset of the global economic crisis in 2008. Many of the products made in Asia were sold in the markets of Europe and North America, and production contracted as these economies entered a deep recession. Indonesia's relatively robust performance after 2008 indicated that continued reliance on resource-based exports was not necessarily damaging to the country's economic performance. The real challenge must be to foster growth across the economy by improving infrastructure and skills, and by tackling the problems in markets for land, labour and capital.

The development of the service sector

For several decades it has been clear to economists studying long-term processes of economic development that employment patterns in late-developing countries are very different from those in Europe or Japan in the nineteenth and early twentieth centuries. While the share of the agricultural sector in total employment tends to fall as GDP rises, for any given share of agriculture in the total labour force, the tendency has been for the proportion of the labour force in services to be higher in countries of Asia, Latin America and Africa than in Japan, Germany, France or the United Kingdom in the nineteenth and early twentieth centuries (Berry 1978). Within Asia, there were also significant differences since 1970 between Korea and Taiwan on the one hand and Southeast Asia on the other. If we look at the distribution of the labour force in these countries for years when per capita GDP was broadly similar, it is striking that the percentage of the labour force in manufacturing, and in the industrial sector, was higher in Taiwan and Korea, and the share of the service sector lower than in Indonesia or the Philippines (Table 6.9).

This trend towards more service sector employment in Indonesia has been attributed to a number of factors (Alexander and Booth 1992: 287–90). The country's resource endowments have encouraged the development of a capital-intensive mining sector, which has generated little employment. It has also been argued that many industrial processes used in Indonesia today are more capital-intensive than in the

Table 6.9 *Percentage breakdown of the labour force in Asian countries,
1971–2012**

	Agriculture	Manufacturing	Industry**	Services
Taiwan (1971)	35.2	21.6	30.2	34.6
Korea (1974)	48.8	16.2	21.5	29.6
Malaysia (1978)	43.9	13.1	20.1	36.0
Thailand (1989)	66.6	9.0	11.9	21.5
Indonesia (2010)	40.5	10.8	17.5	42.0
Philippines(2012)	32.3	8.3	15.1	52.6

* Per capita GDP in the years shown was between $3,700 and $3,900 except the
Philippines which was lower (from Penn World Tables, v. 7.1, 2005 constant
prices; data are derived from the growth rates of domestic absorption).
** Includes mining, manufacturing, utilities and construction.
Sources: GDP data: Heston, Summers and Aten (2012); Labour force data:
Taiwan: ***Taiwan Statistical Data Book, 1974*** (Taipei, Executive Yuan); Korea:
1974 Special Labor Force Survey Report (Seoul: Bureau of Statistics);
Malaysia: ***Mid-Term Review of the Third Malaysia Plan, 1976–1980*** (Kuala
Lumpur: Government Printer); Thailand: ***Statistical Yearbook of Thailand
No. 39, 1992*** (Bangkok: National Statistical Yearbook); Indonesia: CBS (2012a);
Philippines: ***Philippine Statistical Yearbook 2013*** (Makati: National Statistical
Coordination Board).

early twentieth century. This is the result of a century of technological
progress in Europe and the USA with a strong bias towards substituting
capital for labour. While several Asian countries, including Indonesia
before the 1997/1998 crisis, were successful in building up labour-
intensive manufacturing industries in sectors such as garments, footwear and electrical assembling, these industries were often footloose and
moved to new sites when labour and other costs rose, or when the
general economic environment deteriorated. This seems to have happened in both Indonesia and Thailand after 1998.

In addition, patterns of domestic demand have shifted to services such
as health, education, transport and communications at an earlier stage of
development in many parts of Asia than in Europe or Japan in the first
part of the twentieth century. This reflects the fact that technological
progress has made these services cheaper. The most spectacular example
is probably the mobile phone revolution, which has spread across most of
Asia with amazing rapidity. Indonesians have embraced this technology
with great enthusiasm, and the country is now one of the largest markets
in the world for companies such as Facebook and Twitter. But at the same
time, the service sector remains the employment sector of last resort for

many who cannot find employment in agriculture and industry. They tend to gravitate to small-scale trading and transport occupations and a range of community and personal services where entry barriers are low. The 2010 Population Census found that over 40 per cent of the total labour force of 104.9 million people was employed in services, and of these the majority, over 28 million, were in trade and personal and community services (excluding education and health). Much of this was likely to be low productivity work, with poor remuneration.

Budgetary policies

Three years after assuming office, the Yudhoyono government ran into serious problems with the national budget. While the tax/GDP ratio did increase slightly compared with the 2003 figure, the sharp increase in world oil prices in 2007/2008 led to a substantial jump in budgetary subsidies as a proportion of total expenditures. In 2008 subsidies were 5.6 per cent of GDP, more than double the proportion in 2003 (Table 6.10). This forced the government to take the unpopular step of increasing the domestic prices of gasoline, diesel and kerosene, by between one-quarter and one-third (McLeod 2008a: 193). Public opinion accepted the increases in part at least because the government tried to minimise the impact on poorer households through targeted cash transfers. After 2008, subsidies fell as a proportion of total government expenditures, and of GDP, but the government did not increase budgetary expenditures in other areas, so that by 2010 total government expenditures were only 16.2 per cent of GDP

Table 6.10 *Government revenues and expenditures as percentage of GDP, 2003, 2008, 2010 and 2014*

	2003	2008	2010	2014
Tax/GDP	11.5	13.3	11.2	11.3
TGR/GDP	16.9	19.8	15.4	15.2
TGEx/GDP	18.4	19.9	16.2	17.5
Debt/GDP	3.4	1.8	1.4	1.3
Subsidies/GDP	2.2	5.6	3.0	3.9
Regional/GDP	6.0	5.9	5.3	5.7

Note: TGR is total government revenues; TGEx is total government expenditures; debt is all debt service payments; subsidies refers to energy and other subsidies; regional refers to all transfers to regions.
Source: 2003: Kenwood (2004: 15); 2008 and 2010: www.bps.go.id; 2014: Damuri and Day (2015: 13).

compared with almost 20 per cent in 2008. This proportion increased only slightly in later budgets; by 2014 expenditures amounted to 17.5 per cent of GDP, while tax receipts changed little from the 2003 percentage (Table 6.10).

This cautious approach to fiscal policy met with approval by those who advocated small government on ideological grounds but it created several problems. Critics pointed out that both the tax/GDP ratio in Indonesia and tax revenues per capita terms were low compared with many other Asian countries. Expenditures per capita were also low (McCawley 2014: 205). While some progress had been made with reforming the public sector, and improving the pay and incentives for senior managers, many civil servants lacked both the skills and the capacity to take more responsible tasks in line ministries, or in the state enterprises (McLeod 2008a: 197–201). In addition, a large share of the budget, amounting to almost 6 per cent of GDP through the Yudhoyono years, was transferred to local governments, mainly to rural and urban districts. While guidelines were laid down for the use of funds, monitoring was often inadequate and it was far from clear in many cases how the money was being used. The problems relating to the decentralisation legislation will be discussed in greater detail in Chapter 9.

Those who advocated large-scale reform, or outright privatisation, of state enterprises were also disappointed with progress after 2004. Between 1998 and 2004, there was some divestment of minority stakes in some government enterprises but in only two cases did the government retain less than 50 per cent of the total value of the asset (McLeod 2005: 143). Resistance to privatisation both in the parliament and in the bureaucracy was considerable, and the three presidents who succeeded Suharto had little appetite for confronting it. Although Yudhoyono appeared to be more supportive of measures to reform and restructure the state enterprise sector, little was achieved after 2004. As will be argued in the following section, the lack of progress on privatisation sent conflicting messages to those investors which the government was trying to encourage to enter public–private partnerships on infrastructure development.

Infrastructure problems

Probably no single issue has generated more discussion in the post-Suharto era, both in policy circles and among the general public, than the state of the nation's infrastructure. Congestion in ports became more severe as the economy recovered from the 1997/1998 crisis, while traffic congestion was a growing problem in most urban areas across the country. While there has

Table 6.11 *Length of roads and vehicle numbers, 1965–1966, 1989–1990 and 2012 (×1,000 km; ×1,000 vehicles)*

	1966	1989/1990	2012
Roads	83.3	271.2	504.2 (25)
Cars	179.5	1,320.6	10,432.3 (60)
Trucks	92.9	1,124.2	5,286.1 (51)
Buses	19.6	371.6	2,273.8 (41)
Motorcycles	281.8	6,857.9	76,381.2 (55)

Note: Figures in brackets refer to the percentage in Java.
Sources: 1966: CBS (1971: 270–2); 1989/1990: Department of Information; ***Lampiran Pidato Kenegaraan 1994****: p. X/12; CBS (2014: 360–1).

been some improvement in inter-city highways, such as the motorway between Jakarta and Bandung, many of the roads in Java and in other parts of the country have changed little since they were constructed in the colonial era. The trans-Java expressway, which has been under discussion since the 1970s, was still incomplete in 2010, although progress was made in the final phase of the Yudhoyono presidency (Davidson 2015: 234). There have been some improvements in road systems outside Java, especially in Sumatra, but much work remains to be done, both in new road construction and in maintenance of the existing network.

The deficiencies in the national road network have become more obvious as numbers of vehicles grew far more rapidly than road capacity in the 1990s and 2000s (Table 6.11). Many people living in urban areas have been forced to use cars for commuting journeys because of the lack of modern mass rapid transport systems; in most cities there are still only crowded buses. The inter-city railway system in Java was upgraded in the 1970s and 1980s but since then there has been little progress in building new high-speed track or in installing new carriages. Electricity generation per capita in the early twenty-first century was still only around one-third of the average for middle-income countries (McCawley 2010a: table 1). Even the irrigation network in Java, originally built in the colonial period and rehabilitated and extended in the Suharto era, is once again in need of substantial improvement. Outside Java, some new projects have been initiated, but much agricultural land is still rain-fed.

Given all these problems, it was hardly surprising that both presidential candidates in the 2014 election made a number of promises about building new infrastructure across the country, although neither gave much detail on how the ambitious goals they set out were to be funded. There had in fact been considerable debate within government circles on the state of the nation's infrastructure since the beginning of the Yudhoyono presidency. In 2004, the economics coordinating minister formed a team to study the financing of infrastructure development, which came up with an estimate which in rupiah terms amounted to 10 per cent of GDP. Some observers found this amount unrealistic and it was certainly much higher than World Bank estimates, which amounted to 5 per cent of GDP (Soesastro and Atje 2005: 23). But these World Bank estimates were much lower than those contained in an earlier World Bank study, published in 1992, which suggested that average levels of public investment in Indonesia should be maintained at around 10 per cent of GDP, with much of that directed to infrastructure (McCawley 2010b: 7).

For much of the 1970s and 1980s, government investment programmes had amounted to almost 10 per cent of GDP, much of which was devoted to rehabilitation of existing infrastructure, as well as new projects. The Indonesian government, often through state enterprises, was able to access loans from the World Bank, the Asian Development Bank and other foreign donors for major projects in sectors including electric power, roads and irrigation. But by the end of the 1980s the major multilateral and bilateral agencies had largely stopped lending for infrastructure. This reflected the ideological climate of the times; it was argued that most projects should be carried out by the private sector, either alone or in partnership with governments. In Indonesia during the 1990s there was particular concern about shortage of capacity in the power generation sector. Between 1990 and 1997 the state-owned electric power company in Indonesia (PLN) signed twenty-six agreements with private investors to bring on stream substantial new capacity using gas, geothermal and coal-fired plants (Wells 2007: 342). After the crisis hit, there was growing concern about the economic viability of many of these projects, and about the conditions attached to the original contracts. All twenty-six agreements had to be renegotiated, or terminated. The resulting disputes with the foreign investors, some of which continued until 2007, attracted widespread international attention, and damaged Indonesia's reputation in global business circles.

As Wells (2007: 359) pointed out, by the time Yudhoyono took office and tried to attract foreign investors into infrastructure projects, it was far from clear that Indonesian officials had learnt the lessons from the power projects of the 1990s:

The causes of the unfavourable terms and the damaging disputes did not lie in inadequate regulations, unfriendly legislation or lack of guarantees. Rather, they arose because officials did not have or rejected information from elsewhere, because the personal interests of officials and their relatives dominated negotiations, and because the organisation and procedures for negotiations were both vague and complex. The negotiations did not follow the required tendering process, they ignored available economic expertise, advisers were not used effectively, and the decision-making process was unclear, leaving openings for extensive official 'entrepreneurship'. The resulting agreements were characterised by returns to investors that were out of proportion to the risks they carried.

It was well known even before Suharto left office that most of the Indonesian partners involved in the projects were either members of the Suharto family, his close business associates or relatives of other key ministers (Wells 2007: table 3). They had little expertise in the complex business of building and running power plants; that was to be provided by the foreign partners. The role of the domestic partners was simply to cream off part of the profits. While the foreign companies might have been able to run the plants more efficiently than the PLN had they been given a free hand, they were forced by their Indonesian partners, and by the government, to follow pricing and other conditions which either would have penalised Indonesian consumers, or would have led to high budget subsidies, or some combination of both. The entire experience not only damaged Indonesia's reputation among potential foreign investors in infrastructure projects but also created a climate of opinion within Indonesia which was hostile to private investment in infrastructure. These factors influenced the decision of the constitutional court in December 2004 to annul the electricity law passed two years earlier on the grounds that it allocated too much control to the private sector.

Thus the legacy of the Suharto-era projects cast a long shadow over debates on infrastructure, and goes some way to explaining the confused nature of the debate over infrastructure development down to the end of the Yudhoyono era. On the one hand, some policy-makers in Jakarta were prone to argue that 'finance was not the problem' and instead claimed that problems over land acquisition, project design and legal and regulatory uncertainty were the main problems (McCawley 2010b: 11; Suleman and Iqbal 2012: 262–70). The World Bank has claimed that 'the lengthy and complex land acquisition process is the main constraint during the implementation stage' for many projects (World Bank 2012: 28). This report also drew attention to the problem of delays at the budget preparation stage. While there can be little doubt that these problems have hampered the implementation of many projects, there has also been a reluctance to tackle head-on the issue of where the finance is to come from. Suleman and Iqbal (2012: 270–1) argued that short-term and domestic financing was not a major constraint; both the central government and many provincial and district governments were not spending all their budgetary allocations for infrastructure because of capacity constraints.

But at the same time, the private sector has experienced difficulties in obtaining long-term finance for infrastructure projects. According to Suleman and Iqbal, most domestic banks were unwilling to lend for longer than twelve years, and the reluctance of local banks to fund projects has affected the attitude of international financial institutions including sovereign wealth funds. Other possible approaches could include using the retained earnings of state enterprises, and bond flotations by state enterprises, perhaps in partnership with the domestic private sector or with foreign firms. But experience both in Indonesia and elsewhere suggests that, outside the telecommunications sector, private investors are usually reluctant to support large projects without guarantees of support from government (McCawley 2010a: 17).

In addition, many in the parliament, the civil service, the media and the NGOs continue to be suspicious of private involvement in infrastructure building, especially if it is foreign in origin. The reasons for this suspicion of the private sector are discussed further in Chapter 7. There is also a widespread conviction in Indonesia, as in many other low- and middle-income countries, that prices for public utilities, including irrigation, electricity and rail transport, should be low enough to make them affordable to all users. Unsurprisingly, few private investors will become involved in infrastructure development unless prices can be charged which are high enough to give a reasonable return on their investment. Resolving these issues in the Indonesian context, where many users have been accustomed to low prices for decades, will not be easy.

Trends in population growth and education since Suharto

As was pointed out in Chapter 4, the Suharto era witnessed a remarkable decline in fertility in many parts of the country, together with a rapid expansion of the educational system, although from the late 1980s onwards, post-primary enrolments stagnated, and the government goal of universal school attendance for all children in the six to fifteen age groups was not achieved by 1998. It was feared that the severe economic downturn in 1998 would cause many families to withdraw their children from the school system, but in fact this did not happen. Government aid to schools to prevent large-scale dropouts appeared to have been effective; crude participation rates at all levels of schooling actually increased between 1996 and 1999. They continued to increase between 1999 and 2013, although in that year the goal of universal enrolments up to the lower secondary level had still not been achieved (Table 6.12). The data on school attendance from the 2010 Population census confirmed

Table 6.12 *Crude participation rates in primary and secondary schools, 1993–2013*

Year	Primary	Lower secondary	Upper secondary
1993	105.1	61.1	40.1
1996	107.2	70.5	44.9
1999	108.0	76.0	48.4
2003	105.8	81.1	50.9
2006	110.0	81.9	56.7
2009	110.4	81.3	62.6
2013	107.7	86.0	66.6

Note: Crude participation rates refer to total enrolments in the age groups 6–12, 13–15 and 16–18. Figures greater than 100 mean that over-age students are enrolled in primary schools.
Source: www.bps.go.id.

previous studies which had shown little difference in school attendance by gender, or by urban and rural areas in the seven to twelve age groups, although urban–rural differences increased in the thirteen to eighteen age groups (CBS 2012: 348–56).

While the enrolment figures in the early years of the new century were broadly encouraging, there was growing concern about the quality of education. The achievement of Indonesian children in international tests in science and mathematics was very low in comparison with other parts of Asia. Indonesian students were ranked second to bottom in the international PISA tests in student achievement in maths, science and reading. These tests are administered by the OECD, and in 2013 tested over half a million students aged fifteen to sixteen across countries in Europe, the Americas and Asia. Indonesia was ranked lower than in the previous PISA tests in 2010, and the poor result triggered considerable debate in the national press, especially as the Yudhoyono government had increased funding for schools, including higher salaries for teachers. What had gone wrong? Commentators blamed short school hours; at the primary level most students get only three hours per day, which is much lower than the Asian average. In addition it was argued that many teachers were poorly trained, and often not competent to teach maths and science subjects.

By 2014, there was also widespread concern about access to family planning, which was triggered by evidence that the fertility decline had apparently halted after Suharto left power. Demographic and Health Surveys (DHS) which have been carried out in Indonesia for several decades showed that the total fertility rate had declined to 2.6 in 2002/2003 but not changed since then. Although some demographers have argued that the DHS overstate fertility rates, there does appear to be agreement that the rate of decline has slowed if not stalled, and that fertility rates in Indonesia are now among the highest in Asia, with the exception of the Philippines. United Nations data show that in 2010 fertility rates were higher in Indonesia than in India, Malaysia, Vietnam and Bangladesh, all countries which had higher rates than Indonesia in the 1990s (McDonald 2014: 42). Based on these findings, the Minister of Health stated in April 2013 that the family planning programme had been a failure over the decade from 2003. Some commentators blamed the decentralisation policies for disrupting the activities of National Family Planning Agency; it was also argued that the greater influence of Islamic parties since 1999 led to more conservative attitudes to family planning.

The evidence that fertility is rather higher in Indonesia than previously thought has led to higher projections of population in coming decades. The Population Reference Bureau estimated in 2014 that Indonesia's population would reach 306.7 million in 2030 and 365.3 million in 2050, when it would be the fifth largest country in the world. These projections raise a number of issues about education and employment, food supply and energy use. If they are broadly correct, it appears that Indonesian imports of food and petroleum products will continue to increase, while the problem of matching the output of the education system with the needs of the labour market will not get any easier. On the other hand, the fact that fertility is declining more slowly than in countries such as China or Thailand means that the ageing problem will be less serious in coming decades, and a large proportion of the population will continue to be in the working age groups. The challenge for policy will be to ensure that young people graduating from schools and institutions of higher learning will be equipped with the skills they will need to find productive employment.

7 Economic nationalism, economic rationalism and the development of private business after 1950

Economic nationalism after 1945

It was argued in Chapter 3 that the terms of the financial agreement finally agreed in 1949 were considerably harsher than those negotiated with the former colonial powers by other newly independent governments in Asia, including India, Pakistan and the Philippines. An Indian economist pointed out that, along with an impoverished economy, newly independent India 'also inherited some useful assets, in the form of a national transport system, an administrative apparatus in working order, a shelf of concrete development projects and substantial reserves of foreign exchange' (Vaidyanathan 1983: 948). Independent Indonesia had few such assets after almost four years of Japanese occupation followed by four more years of war against the Dutch army. The terms under which power was transferred caused bitterness among even the more moderate leaders, and after 1950 the continuing Dutch economic presence fuelled nationalist sentiments in the parliament and in the business community. An issue which was bound up with resentment against the Dutch was the position of the Chinese, whose economic role seemed to many nationalists to be way out of proportion to their relatively small numbers compared with the indigenous population.

The 1930 Population Census had enumerated 1.233 million Chinese in the whole country, which was only about two per cent of the population of 60 million. The percentage was probably slightly higher after 1950, as in-migration from China, although restricted, did continue until 1940. In addition, the Chinese tended to have large families and lower rates of infant and child mortality than most indigenous Indonesians. Mackie (2005: 98) suggested that the ethnic Chinese could have numbered around two million, or 2.5 per cent of the total population, in the early 1950s. As a result of their better access to education in the late colonial era, and the emphasis that many assimilated, Dutch-speaking Chinese families placed on professional qualifications, the Chinese were over-represented in occupations such as medicine and law. It was also widely

believed that Chinese owned many of the medium- and large-scale businesses not controlled by the Dutch or other foreign interests. Those
Chinese who had migrated to Indonesia in the 1920s and 1930s often
went into business using contacts with other members of their extended
families or dialect groups. Although they often started as small traders or
money lenders, they seized the opportunities offered by the independence
struggle, not least in smuggling arms and materials from Singapore, and
in some cases had built up significant businesses by the time power was
transferred in 1949.[1]

Many of the nationalist leaders had, to a greater or lesser extent, been
influenced by the views of Dutch colonial officials on the entrepreneurial
abilities of indigenous Indonesians, especially the Javanese. In the nineteenth century, most Dutch and other foreign observers tended to dis-
miss the Javanese as lacking thrift, or any capacity for entrepreneurial
activities. Alexander and Alexander (1991: 377) argued that these attitudes affected the official statistics collected by the Dutch, which concentrated on output of food crops and export crops, and largely ignored
small-scale trade and handicraft industries. But by the early decades of
the twentieth century, views were changing on the capacities of the
indigenous population (Booth 1998: 290–3). Fasseur (1999) quoted
one Dutch writer who pointed out in 1908 that several centuries earlier,
the Javanese had been successful merchants in areas far beyond their
own island. He asked why they were now considered by most Europeans
to be incompetent at any task outside small-scale agriculture. Just how
many Dutch or other foreign observers, were asking such questions in
the early twentieth century is difficult to judge. But whether as a result of
the ethical policies, or because of population growth, many Javanese,
and other indigenous Indonesians, were beginning to seek new employment opportunities outside the traditional rural economy.

The work of Boeke, referred to in Chapter 2, was influential in shaping
views both within Indonesia, and in the wider community of scholars
studying the problem of 'underdevelopment' which was emerging in the
1950s. Boeke had become rather disillusioned with the results of the
ethical policies, and by the 1920s was calling for a rather different set of
policies which were oriented to building up a class of indigenous entrepreneurs, able to compete not just with immigrant Chinese but also with
Western capitalists. In his most influential work, published in English in

[1] Twang (1998) gives a detailed analysis of the impact of the Japanese occupation and the
independence struggle on Chinese business groups in Indonesia. He argues that smuggling was particularly important in encouraging the emergence of 'new Chinese businessmen' most of whom were recent migrants to Indonesia, rather than assimilated,
Dutch-speaking Chinese.

1953, he depicted the 'eastern pre-capitalist' economies as characterised by limited needs, little market-based exchange, few professional traders and certainly little division of labour along Smithian lines (Boeke 1953: 12–14). He also argued that non-economic motives, both cultural and religious, prevented many Indonesians from grasping the economic opportunities available to them. Unsurprisingly, his views were criticised by several economists in the post-independence era; if Indonesians really were impervious to economic incentives, how could their widespread involvement in the cultivation of cash crops such as coffee and rubber be explained? Surely their economic backwardness was more the result of repressive colonial policies than an innate reluctance to engage with the market economy?

The 1930 Population Census collected valuable data on employment patterns among indigenous Indonesians, which made clear that many Indonesians, both in Java and elsewhere, were involved in non-agricultural activities including manufacturing and trade. Indigenous workers comprised over 90 per cent of all workers in manufacturing and government service, and over 80 per cent of those in trade (Table 2.4). In some parts of the country, especially Central Java, many women were involved in trading activities. The problem was not that indigenous Indonesians were trapped in subsistence agriculture and could not move into other occupations. Rather it was that most of the employment they found outside agriculture was either in the lower grades of government services, or in enterprises which were small-scale, mainly using family labour. The barriers to business growth among the indigenous population seemed almost insuperable.

How were these barriers to be overcome? The leading economist among the early nationalist leaders, Sumitro Djojohadikusomo, had been trained at the Netherlands School of Economics in Rotterdam, and reacted against what he saw as the majority view among Dutch officials trained at Leiden University 'that Indonesia could never develop into a modern economy because the people's values were different' (Sumitro 2003: 54). This criticism was to some extent unfair; not only were official views changing by the late colonial era, but innovative new policies were being adopted in credit provision which were having an impact on business development, especially in Java (Booth 1998: 301–7). Many indigenous Indonesians were employed in the rural banks and pawnshops, including Sumitro's own father who rose to a senior position in the 1930s. The newly empowered nationalist leadership which took power in late 1949 was well aware that they had to prove their legitimacy by building on, and greatly expanding Dutch policies, not just in the provision of credit, but more broadly in the development of a robust class of indigenous businesses which could compete with both Dutch and Chinese enterprises.

The first cabinet, formed in December 1949, was led by Mohammad Hatta, the co-signatory with Sukarno of the declaration of independence in 1945. Several members were 'non-party' while most of the others were from the Nationalist Party (PNI) and the Masjumi, considered to represent modernist Moslems, many of whom had business interests outside the agricultural sector. Hatta had also studied in the Netherlands, but was more suspicious of capitalism. He thought that cooperatives were a more suitable vehicle for developing both agricultural and non-agricultural enterprises in the new republic, although this view was not universally shared.[2] Pressured by groups outside the cabinet, the Hatta cabinet moved quickly to dismantle the federal state inherited from the Dutch, and on 17 August 1950, the new unitary republic of Indonesia came into existence. The first cabinet of the unitary state was inaugurated in September 1950 and was headed by Mohammad Natsir, from the Masjumi party. Several members were carried over from the Hatta cabinet, including Sjafruddin Prawiranegara, also from Masjumi and a close ally of Natsir, who continued as Minister of Finance.

Sjafruddin had studied law in Batavia, and had joined the Ministry of Finance as a tax official in the 1930s. Like other Indonesian civil servants, he was quickly promoted under the Japanese, and became chief of the tax office in Kediri, East Java, before moving to Bandung (Sjafruddin 2003: 78). He was close to Natsir and probably drafted the passages concerning economic policy in the statement of government policy read by Natsir to the parliament in September 1950. As was noted in Chapter 3, the statement stressed the need to retain the services of foreign nationals in the economy. 'The expulsion of foreign manpower and personnel from Indonesia will not bring about a sound national economy but, on the contrary, will mean killing the hen that lays the golden eggs' (Natsir 1951: 54). The statement also emphasised the continuing importance of foreign capital in the economy, and listed a number of priority industrial sectors essential for popular welfare. Cooperatives were also to be given an important role particularly in the provision of rural credit and in marketing commodities such as rubber and copra. Foreign trade was to be encouraged, and while it was acknowledged that trade with the Netherlands and other Western powers would continue to be important, the need for closer economic ties with other parts of Asia and with Australia was also mentioned.

As was argued in Chapter 3, the Natsir statement can be seen as encapsulating the views of the 'administrators' within the nationalist

---

[2] Sjafruddin (2003: 83) thought that while cooperatives might play a useful role in agriculture, they were unlikely to succeed in other sectors of the economy.

movement. These were the politicians who, while fully grasping the problems which Indonesia had inherited from the Dutch colonial era, advocated a cautious, pragmatic approach to economic policy-making. Most in this group were sympathetic to private enterprise, and not overtly hostile to foreign capital. They were well aware that the attainment of political independence had opened up a much greater range of business opportunities for Indonesians, but some government assistance would be necessary (Feith 1962: 88–9). One obvious example was the provision of credit from the state-owned banks and import licences to domestic firms. In addition, in the private sector, many Dutch and Eurasian businesses were being sold as their owners decided to return to the Netherlands or to third countries. Almost all the political parties agreed that it was desirable that indigenous businesspeople should purchase these companies, if necessary with government help.

The conflicts arose between those who argued for more active 'hot-house' policies which would rapidly develop an indigenous business class, and those who saw the dangers of such policies, and advocated a more cautious approach. In April 1950, the non-party Minister of Welfare in the Hatta cabinet, Ir Djuanda, had established what became known as the *benteng* programme, whose purpose was to develop a strong indigenous class of businesspeople in Indonesia. To begin with, the focus was on securing indigenous control of the import trade, although the regulations did not exclude Chinese who had acquired Indonesian citizenship (Mackie 1971: 47–8). The Minister of Trade and Industry in the Natsir cabinet, Dr Sumitro, broadened the policy to include credit and other support for indigenous businesses. Mackie argued that the Small Scale Industrialisation Plan was a 'well conceived attempt to provide simple pieces of equipment to backyard manufac-turers on a loan basis with easy repayments'. But it was discredited by poor administration and many loans were never paid back. Other poli-cies adopted in the early 1950s were aimed at demobilised soldiers who were encouraged to set up small business along cooperative lines, although many of these ventures failed because the soldiers lacked business skills.

But in spite of the policy failures in the early 1950s, the evidence suggests that a number of large enterprises owned by indigenous Indonesians were established, as well as a number owned by Chinese. Lindblad (2010: 106–8) has argued that the problems surrounding the *benteng* programme have overshadowed the fact that a number of successful indigenous Indonesian firms were formed in the 1950s, some of which have survived to the present day. He cited a survey of some 4,200 incorporated firms in 1953, which showed that at least 40 per cent of trading firms and

33 per cent of manufacturing firms were under the control of indigenous Indonesians. These figures refute the widely held view that the Chinese completely dominated that part of industry and commerce which was not in foreign hands. Lindblad stressed that 'in the 1950s a genuine new vitality in indigenous entrepreneurship' emerged that had little to do with the positive discrimination favoured by many politicians. It was true that some ethnic groups from outside Java, especially Sumatrans, were over-represented in the firms enumerated, but there were also firms controlled by Javanese, and businesspeople from other parts of the country.

Lindblad (2008: 93) also estimated that around one in five of the 200 largest business groups in Indonesia in 1990 had in fact been established in the early post-independence years, and that this group 'of old-timers consisted of just as many firms owned by indigenous Indonesians as by ethnic Chinese'. He argued that the early post-independence period was probably more conducive to the establishment of indigenous businesses than the Suharto era, an issue to which I will return later. But in spite of this apparent progress, many politicians began to lose patience with government policies which they viewed as too timid in scope and largely irrelevant in their results. They felt that something more dramatic was needed. As world prices for exports fell and a serious foreign exchange crisis developed, a more comprehensive system of import licences was introduced in 1953 by the first cabinet led by Ali Sastroamidjojo. Many of the beneficiaries of the expanded licensing system were well-connected Indonesian 'briefcase importers' operating with Chinese traders, although the dominant role of the Big Five Dutch firms was not greatly affected (Mackie 1971: 48; Lindblad 2008: 130–5).

It is difficult to dissent from Lindblad's judgement that the *benteng* policy has been seen by most subsequent historians as a failure, and indeed as a case study of how policies designed to build up indigenous business groups in newly independent countries can easily go wrong. But what were the alternatives for Indonesia in the 1950s? One option would have been to proceed more slowly, to have screened the applicants for foreign exchange licences and credit from government banks more carefully and to have encouraged both foreign and Chinese enterprises to employ more indigenous Indonesians in managerial capacities. This is probably what politicians such as Hatta, Sjafruddin and Sumitro would have wanted. But they were swimming against strong currents of economic nationalism, and of hostility to all forms of capitalism, which they could not resist. Sumitro and Sjafruddin both left the cabinet in 1952, after which they debated their views on economic policy in a series of articles mainly published in the Dutch-language paper *Nieuwsgier*.

Sumitro advocated policies which were more protectionist, and less tolerant of the continuing Dutch presence, while Sjafruddin was more gradualist in his thinking. Probably as Thee (2010: 54) pointed out in his review of the debate, Sumitro was more realistic in his grasp of the problems facing the newly independent nation. But both men were ultimately swept aside as more extreme nationalist and socialist views took hold after 1956.

Other debates in the 1950s centred around the desirability of an economy based on mutual self help and the 'family principle', versus one based on economic liberalism. In a symposium at the University of Indonesia in 1955, Wilopo, a nationalist leader who had been prime minister in the early 1950s, argued that it was necessary for Indonesia to reject the liberal model of the colonial era which had 'produced misery and injustice among the great mass of the Indonesian people' (Wilopo 1955: 380). Widjojo Nitisastro, then a young lecturer at the University of Indonesia, who was to become the leading economic adviser to Suharto, pointed out that the private sector comprised not just the large Dutch concerns which were nationalised later in the 1950s, but also millions of small enterprises in agriculture and trade. Policies would have to be devised which boosted the productivity of these enterprises (Widjojo 1955: 384). Like Sjafruddin, he argued that greater attention must be given to increasing output in the economy, even if that meant tolerating the continuing presence of foreign capital. While the redistribution of income might be a desirable goal, redistributive policies should not be allowed to hamper the goal of faster economic growth.

But these views had little support in the face of more aggressive anti-Chinese actions and anti-Dutch attitudes. In March 1956, at a convention of national importers in Surabaya, a respected politician, Assaat, launched a bitter attack on the role of the Chinese (Feith 1962: 481–2). For the first time, a leading political figure called for specifically racial policies to favour ethnic Indonesians. He called into question the loyalty of the Chinese to the Indonesian state, whether or not they had acquired Indonesian nationality. As Feith pointed out, the Assaat movement had most support among indigenous business groups, but it affected policies in other sectors as well. Quotas were imposed on Chinese students in schools and universities, especially in the prestigious faculties such as medicine and law. Perhaps what was most surprising in the Indonesian context was that these anti-Chinese demands had not become explicit sooner after the transfer of power in 1949. One reason was that key cabinet members in the early cabinets were well aware of anti-Chinese resentment but felt that legal steps, in particular the granting of citizenship, together with the emergence of indigenous business groups, would gradually defuse the problem. By the mid-1950s, it was clear that they had underestimated the extent to which anti-Chinese feeling would be used by a growing number of politicians to call for far more aggressive policies against both Chinese and foreign, especially Dutch, enterprises.

The sequence of events from 1956 onwards which led to the expropriation of all Dutch assets in Indonesia has been extensively documented by Lindblad (2008: Chapter VIII). The continuing resentment over Dutch enterprises in the estates sector and in banking and trade was reinforced by what was seen as Dutch intransigence over the province of West New Guinea (Irian Barat), which was still controlled by the Netherlands. The military, which was playing an important role in fighting rebellions in both Sulawesi and Sumatra, also began to realise that it could benefit from nationalisation of Dutch assets. Whether the governments of the day took an active role in the takeovers of Dutch assets, or whether they were pushed along by the angry masses, egged on by the military, has been debated, but the final outcome was beyond dispute. Over 700 Dutch-owned enterprises were expropriated. Some found their way into private ownership, either indigenous or Chinese. Many became state enterprises, managed by people from a range of backgrounds, most of whom lacked appropriate managerial experience.

The military certainly benefited. They grabbed valuable residential property vacated by departing Dutch managers, and placed retired officers in management positions in the estates sector and elsewhere. There appears to have been very little discussion about alternative futures for the expropriated assets. Could they have been turned into worker-owned cooperatives, which is probably what Hatta would have wanted, or, in the case of estates, sold off to smallholders? These options do not seem to have been considered. Most of the Dutch companies in manufacturing, trade and banking became state enterprises. Firms in the estates sector and the petroleum sector owned by non-Dutch companies continued to operate, although some British and American firms were taken over during the 'Crush Malaysia' campaign launched in the early 1960s. The Anglo-Dutch oil giant, Shell, exited from Indonesia in 1965, but the other great Anglo-Dutch conglomerate, Unilever, continued to operate. Only after Suharto assumed control in 1966 was compensation discussed, although as Lindblad (2008: 208) pointed out, the compensation paid was more than outweighed by the aid which Indonesia received from the Netherlands and other Western countries after 1966.

The guided democracy era: economic nationalism triumphant?

The second cabinet of Ali Sastroamidjojo fell in March 1957. By then it was clear that Indonesia's brief experiment with constitutional democracy was at an end, although it was far from obvious what sort of political and economic system would replace it. The politicians who had supported pragmatic economic policies in the immediate aftermath of independence had been defeated. In December 1956, Hatta resigned as vice-president; in that same month, army-led rebellions erupted in both Sumatra and Sulawesi. Sjafruddin Prawiranegara and Burhanuddin Harahap left Jakarta in early December 1957 and met early the following month with some of the dissident military leaders. In January 1958, Natsir and Roem went to Medan to attend a ceremony at the Islamic University in that city. From there they went to Padang, which had become a rallying point for those politicians, including Sumitro, who were opposed to the concept of 'guided democracy' put forward by Sukarno (Kahin 2012: 109–13). The fact that so many of the moderate pragmatists of the 1950–1957 era threw in their lot with the rebels discredited them with many military and civilian leaders who, while not always sympathetic to Sukarno, remained loyal to the concept of the unitary state.

That the years from 1958 onwards were characterised by economic stagnation and mounting inflation is clear, but what were the consequences for the distribution of national output between government, foreign enterprises, indigenous Indonesians and resident minorities, especially the Chinese? The expropriation of Dutch assets obviously reduced the share of output accruing to businesses owned by foreigners, but by how much? Anspach (1969: 182–30) argued that while the large estates, trading houses and banks taken from the Dutch passed into government hands, many smaller enterprises had been bought out by Chinese. My own estimates for 1960 suggested that around half of total output was accounted for by smallholder agricultural producers, almost all of whom were indigenous Indonesians, who also must have accounted for at least part of the output of the trade sector, and also a part of output of small-scale industry and construction (Booth 1998: 175). Indigenous Indonesians probably accounted for almost all the output of personal and community services. Altogether it seems reasonable to argue that indigenous Indonesians accounted for over 60 per cent of total output in 1960, and the government sector a further 20 per cent. Of the remaining 20 per cent probably around half remained under foreign control in sectors such as large estates and mining. That leaves at most ten per cent of output accruing from private businesses controlled by the Chinese, mainly in manufacturing, transport, wholesale and retail trade. In fact the Chinese share was probably rather lower than this. But many indigenous Indonesians in both government and the military, as well as those engaged in private business, seem to have been convinced that the proportion was much larger, and this conviction influenced policies after 1966.

Much of the literature on business development in the 1950s and 1960s has focused on the *benteng* programme, and the impact of the nationalisation of Dutch assets after 1957. But these events, dramatic as they were, only affected a small part of the population, very often those living in the main cities with good connections to political parties. What was going on in the hundreds of small towns across the country, in the capitals of the districts (*kabupaten*) and sub-districts (*kecamatan*), where thousands of Indonesians were trying to establish enterprises in sectors such as manufacturing, trade and transport? Did a genuine class of small-scale entrepreneurs develop, at least some of whom had the potential to build up modern firms? To answer such a question it was necessary to examine what was going on in those urban areas more remote from the larger cities which were less influenced by government policies.

An important study was carried out by an American anthropologist, Clifford Geertz, who studied two towns in East Java and Bali in the 1950s. His analysis of Moslem businesses in the town of Pare (which he called Modjokuto) in East Java concluded that

What the entrepreneurial group of Islamic small businessmen most lacks is not capital, for in terms of the realistic opportunities for innovation which they actually have, their resources are not inadequate; not drive, for they display the typically 'Protestant' virtues of industry, frugality, independence, and determination in almost excessive abundance; certainly not a sufficient market, for the possibilities for significant expansion of both trade and industry stand apparent in Modjokuto on all sides. What they lack is the power to mobilize their capital and channel their drive in such a way as to exploit the existing market possibilities. They lack the capacity to form efficient economic institutions; they are entrepreneurs without enterprises. (Geertz 1963: 28)

Geertz viewed most of the small businessmen in Pare as trapped in the small-scale bazaar or '*pasar*' economy, unable to move to the 'firm-type' economy which was characterised by larger enterprises run along capitalist lines (*perusahaan*), hiring in labour and selling output at a profit. He argued that several factors held the Moslem businesses back. One was intense competition from Chinese enterprises, 'long entrenched as the most developed elements within the traditional economy' (Geertz 1963: 48). He also admitted that the economic stagnation and political disorder which characterised Indonesia from the early 1950s through to the late

1960s was hardly conducive to the development of successful firms, whether owned by Indonesians, Chinese or foreigners. Some policies would have benefited indigenous businesses by removing Chinese competitors. Coppel (1983: 36–8) discussed the series of anti-Chinese measures implemented from the mid-1950s onwards, which included restrictions on university places, the head tax on aliens introduced in 1957, and the ban on retail trade by aliens outside provincial and district capitals. This ban would have affected Pare, along with many other sub-district towns. An estimated 100,000 Chinese left the country in the wake of these policies, which severely disrupted wholesale and retail trade networks.

The Geertzian analysis of the *pasar* economy has attracted some criticism over the years. Geertz depicted an economy in rural Java dominated by peasants and peddlers, whose enterprises were small-scale. They were certainly involved in the market economy, but they produced, purchased and sold small quantities of goods. Historians of the bazaar economy in other parts of Asia, particularly India and China, have argued that the Geertzian argument did not fit with the historical experience of these countries where large-scale indigenous enterprises developed using the 'crucial skills of long-distance trade' including marine experience, account-keeping and the handling of credit transactions (Ray 1995: 454). Indonesians might have been able to develop these skills before European colonialism became entrenched, but they were hampered by the arbitrary whims of sovereigns, and the lack of an indigenous system of banking and credit which could serve the needs of long-distance trade. Neither did they possess accounting skills (Ray 1995: 456). Increasingly from the seventeenth century onwards large-scale trade was dominated by foreign, especially Chinese, merchants, and in spite of the new opportunities which political independence provided, very few indigenous Indonesians were able to build successful and durable large-scale enterprises.

By the early 1960s the remaining Chinese in Indonesia had reached an accommodation with the government, and overt attacks ceased. The movement set in train by Assaat had been silenced, and the Masjumi Party, which was supported by many Moslem businessmen, had been banned after the regional rebellions. The political rhetoric of the early 1960s became increasingly anti-capitalist and more in favour of socialism, which tended to mean in practice breaking the remaining grip of foreign capital in the plantation and industrial sectors, and establishing more cooperatives in all sectors of the economy (Mackie 1971: 44–5). But rhetoric was translated into reality only to a very limited extent, and the remaining Chinese businesses found ways to operate in the larger cities, often working with the 'new class' of managers in the state enterprise sector. In particular the more aggressive Hokkien and Hokchia business groups rose to dominant positions, using their networks with Singapore and Hong Kong to smuggle exports and bring in imports of luxury products.

The New Order: economic nationalism in new (and old) bottles

The bloody elimination of the Indonesian Communist Party in 1965/1966, and the rise to power of a 'New Order' dominated by the military and non-communist civilians, gave rise to expectations, both in Indonesia and abroad, that economic policy would change in ways which would be far more supportive of the private sector. The technocrats who were recruited by Suharto were trained as economists and had worked as university teachers. They had little or no business experience. Although most had been educated in the USA, they were by no means advocates of Chicago-style free market economics; they were well aware of the resistance to what was often described as 'free-fight liberalism' in Indonesian society. But at the same time they did realise that the vast majority of Indonesians were working in the private sector and were confronting the harsh realities of the market economy on a daily basis. Wishful thinking about an economic system based on mutual self help (*gotong royong*) could not disguise this fact. The immediate task was to bring down inflation, bring some order to the public finances and introduce a market-determined exchange rate which would end smuggling and give greater incentives to producers of traded goods. The expectation was that these macroeconomic reforms would in turn create a more supportive climate for the development of private business, whether owned by indigenous Indonesians, the Chinese or foreign capital.

Attracting foreign capital was given high priority. The technocrat most involved with foreign investment policy during the late 1960s was M. Sadli, who later claimed that it was 'not a difficult time to attract foreign investment, because Indonesia did not face much competition' (Sadli 2003: 130). The governments of China and India were at that time hostile to private foreign investment from any part of the world, while Thailand and the Philippines imposed conditions which some foreign investors found unacceptable. Investors were attracted to Indonesia by the lack of foreign exchange controls, tax holidays, and the possibility of 100 per cent ownership of equity. Most of all they were attracted by the lure of abundant natural resources, and in the first few years most investment went into the mining sector, although multinationals, especially from Japan, also began to invest in import-substituting manufacturing. They realised that there was already considerable unsatisfied demand among the urban middle classes for consumer durables, and this demand was set to grow as economic growth accelerated.

Sadli was aware that by the early 1970s, opposition to both foreign aid and foreign investment was growing among politicians, civil servants and some in the private sector. The student groups which had been 'the standard-bearers of the New Order' in 1965/1966 had by the early 1970s become more critical of the government open door policy to foreign investors. This was true not just in Jakarta, but also in Bandung and Yogyakarta, both cities with large student populations. But the critical attitudes were not just confined to students. The interviews conducted by Weinstein (1976: table 7.9) found that concern about foreign investment was also expressed by many older Indonesians and these worries increased between 1970 and 1973. Many officials remembered the debates of the 1950s, and were far from happy with the post-1966 policy changes. They feared a return to the colonial model where foreign capitalists exploited Indonesia's resources for their own profit, with few benefits accruing to the domestic economy.

The increasing availability of consumer durables made in foreign-owned, especially Japanese, factories also attracted unfavourable comment in some parts of the media. The catalyst for change in government policy towards foreign investment was the anti-Japanese riot provoked by the visit to Indonesia of the Japanese prime minister, Kakuei Tanaka, in January 1974. At least eleven people were killed and there was considerable destruction of Japanese cars and property. Public anger was also vented against the so-called 'financial generals' who were thought to be selling Indonesia out to foreign, especially Japanese, interests. These included Sujono Humardhani and Ali Murtopo, both closely connected with the Centre for Strategic and International Studies in Jakarta. Other grievances were centred on the rise in prices of rice and other staples in 1972/1973. The apparent success of Thai students in bringing about political change in 1973 was a further factor, although the Indonesian protests were more focused on foreign control of the economy than those in Thailand.

The 1974 (Malari) riots brought about a number of changes in policy, in the direction of greater economic nationalism, which lasted until the mid-1980s. More controls were placed on inward investment flows, and more sectors were placed on the closed list after 1979. In the five years from 1976 to 1980, foreign investment accounted for 2.4 per cent of total domestic capital formation, but only 1 per cent in 1981–1985, which was a lower proportion than any other Asian country except the Philippines,

China and South Korea (Yoshida et al. 1994: 72). Indonesia's share of all foreign investment in Southeast Asia also fell sharply in the 1980s compared with the previous decade (Sjoholm 2015: 164). Of concern to some economists was the fact that all the foreign investment in manufacturing went into import-substituting industries, which were given considerable protection through tariffs and quantitative restrictions. In the case of the domestic automobile industry, there were bans on all imports of fully built-up vehicles. The result was that most domestic producers were producing small numbers of vehicles and were unable to reap economies of scale (Aswicahyono, Basri and Hill 2000).

Policy-making from the early 1970s onwards was also influenced by challenges to Suharto's position from within the military. Rising oil prices were increasing the amount of revenues available to the government but to the extent that they were being channelled through the state oil enterprise, Pertamina, they also fuelled the ambitions of its powerful head, Ibnu Sutowo. Sutowo was older than the president and senior to him in military rank, and appeared to be using the oil revenues to build up his own political base. He often used Pertamina funds to support regional development projects when budgetary support was not available. He sat on the board of Golkar, and was rumoured to have been a crucial source of funds for the party in the 1971 election. He no doubt believed that it was entirely legitimate for him to build up a 'state within a state', using the oil revenues to build new enterprises in, for example, the iron and steel sector. If that meant bypassing the technocrats who were trying to impose some discipline on government spending, including that of the state enterprises, so be it. Under Sutowo's leadership, Pertamina ran up large international debts, and it was only when it defaulted on payments in early 1975 that the government realised that it was ultimately responsible for these debts. At that point technocrats in the planning agency and the Ministry of Finance had to take responsibility for the negotiations with foreign and domestic creditors.

It is often claimed that the Pertamina rescue strengthened the position of the technocrats and weakened economic nationalists in the military and elsewhere. To some extent that was true, in that officials in the Planning Board and the Ministry of Finance were able to assert more control over the use of oil revenues and over other parts of the state enterprise sector. But it also made Suharto more dependent on a small number of Chinese businessmen who were able to use their international links to sort out complicated problems which the technocrats and their allies found difficult to tackle. Liem Sioe Liong was a Hokchia businessman who from the late 1960s onwards was using his links with Suharto and other key generals to build up a powerful conglomerate. He proved useful in negotiations with the Swiss-based tanker magnate, Bruce Rappaport, over contracts which Pertamina had signed but could no longer honour. Thanks to Liem, a deal was reached out of court and a damaging legal case was avoided (Borsuk and Chng 2014: 153–9). Suharto did not forget these favours and Liem's companies were to benefit from further lucrative monopoly deals. In return, Liem gave shares to Suharto family members, and helped Suharto in further rescue operations in the 1980s and 1990s.

Suharto was shrewd enough to realise that granting favours to a small number of Chinese business groups was only going to swell the growing chorus of criticism from indigenous business groups who thought that they were being cut out of lucrative government contracts, and other government favours including import monopolies. As global oil prices started to rise again in the latter part of the 1970s, the increase in government revenues gave the government more funds to use for both current and capital expenditures. In 1979 and 1980, Presidential Decisions (*Keppres*) 14 and 14A were issued which purported to grant incentives to the 'weak economic groups', a term which came to mean well-connected indigenous business groups. The so-called Team-10 was established as a centralised government procurement agency in the State Secretariat (*Sekneg*). The team's remit extended to all government departments and state enterprises including Pertamina, and in 1984 a regulation gave it sole authority to approve procurements involving the use of foreign credits (Winters 1996: 131–3).

The location of Team 10 in the state secretariat, rather than in the Ministry of Finance or the planning agency (*Bappenas*) greatly increased the patronage powers of the head of *Sekneg*, Sudharmono. During the 1980s, many lucrative contracts for procurement of equipment were granted to companies controlled by the children of Suharto and other senior officials. In his analysis of the workings of *Sekneg* through the 1980s, Winters (1996: 141) argued that in centralising almost all government procurement in one office, the result was to draw 'patronage power upward and into the center'. This concentration of power drew criticism from technocrats and others who wanted to see a more open and transparent tendering system for government contracts. While it is difficult to estimate how many indigenous business groups benefited directly or indirectly from these patronage powers it would appear that many did not, and those who were excluded for religious or political reasons were resentful. At the same time it was clear that the economic power of business conglomerates controlled by Chinese was growing. Team 10 was terminated in the latter part of the 1980s, but resentment on the part of many businesses over the blatant favours granted by the president to a small number of companies with the right political connections increased over the last decade of Suharto's presidency.

To some observers, it seemed that, by the early 1990s, the economic nationalism of the *benteng* era had been replaced 'by an economy of entrenched monopolies and privileges with lucrative shares absorbed by a well-connected elite of Chinese capitalists and a tiny *pribumi* elite sustained by ties to Soeharto and the state' (Brown 2006: 955). Ironically these changes were taking place at the same time as the technocrats, now located mainly in the Ministry of Finance, were garnering international praise for the economic reforms of the 1980s which had led to an impressive growth in non-oil exports, a far-reaching reform of the taxation system and a liberalisation of the financial system which had increased the market share of domestic private banks. It was frequently asserted that the fall in Indonesia's growth rate in the early 1980s had increased the power and authority of the technocrats to implement 'good policies'. But as in the period from 1966 to 1974, the reforms were largely confined to monetary, fiscal and trade policy. The technocrats were either unwilling or unable to venture far into the murky world of government–business relations. They had no solution to the problem so clearly identified by Geertz in Pare in the 1950s. Rather than promoting the rise of a new group of small- and medium-scale entrepreneurs, the economic growth of the Suharto era had led to the inexorable rise of an economy dominated by a few powerful and well-connected business groups.

Lists of names, and estimates of the size of these groups featured frequently in business magazines in the final phase of the Suharto era. The list produced by Habir (1999: 174–5), taken from *Warta Ekonomi*, a leading business journal, found that in 1996, the total sales of the top twenty-five conglomerates amounted to Rp. 171,853 billion, which was almost twice the size of total government domestic revenues in the financial year 1996/1997. The conglomerate which was at the top of his list was that of Liem Sioe Liong, which alone accounted for sales of Rp. 53,117 billion. The top five conglomerates, all owned by Indonesians of Chinese descent, accounted for over 65 per cent of the sales of the top twenty-five groups. Even within the group of powerful business conglomerates, sales were skewed towards a small number at the very top. Total employment of the top twenty-five was estimated to be 776,000 in 1995, or about 1 per cent of the total labour force in that year. Habir (1999: 185) pointed out that most of the conglomerates were involved in more than one business. Liem Sioe Liong's empire was built on three pillars: food processing, banking and construction materials, although, like other Chinese businessmen, he had also moved into real estate (Borsuk and Chng 2014:

409). Few ventured into manufacturing industry unless they were given monopolies; Liem built up his noodle business on the back of his near-monopoly in flour milling. The surge in manufactured exports after 1986 came mainly from smaller firms in textiles, garments, footwear and electronics, often joint ventures with foreign firms. The obvious conclusion was that most conglomerates in Indonesia, as in other parts of Southeast Asia prior to 1997, grew fat on exploiting protected markets in the non-traded goods sectors, and saw little advantage in venturing into production for global markets.

The resurgence of the plural economy?

One of the ironies of the Suharto era is that in spite of the official rhetoric in favour of promoting businesses owned by the weaker economic groups (*golongan ekonomi lemah*), it is almost certain that the proportion of total GDP originating from business groups owned by the Chinese, and by foreign investors, increased compared with the early post-independence years. In contrast to neighbouring Malaysia, post-independence Indonesia has never published estimates of ownership of assets by ethnic group, and it was only after Suharto left office that population censuses began to ask questions about ethnicity, with results that have attracted some criticism.[3] Thus all estimates of the role of the Chinese in the economy are speculative. But over the years when Suharto was in power, those economic sectors where the Chinese were largely absent since the 1950s, including agriculture and personal services, shrunk in importance relative to mining, manufacturing industry, construction, transport, wholesale and retail trade and financial services.

In all these sectors Chinese enterprises played an important role, and probably dominated among those business groups employing more than twenty people which were not foreign-owned. Indonesians of Chinese descent were also very often selected as the joint venture partners of foreign investors, particularly those from Northeast Asia. Thus the assets of foreign firms were often owned in part by Indonesian Chinese. With the liberalisation of regulations on foreign investment in the latter part of the 1980s, the share of firms with some foreign equity

---

[3] The 2000 Population Census reported that 1.83 million Indonesians identified themselves as ethnic Chinese, which was less than one per cent of the total population. Mackie (2005: 98) thought this was an underestimate. The 2010 census found that 2.8 million Indonesians gave their ethnicity as Chinese which was a little over one per cent of the total population. At the very least, it would appear that some Indonesians of mixed descent preferred not to classify themselves as Chinese.

in all large and medium enterprises had increased in non-oil and gas manufacturing to 31 per cent by 1996. It was 49 per cent in the electronics sector (Aswicahyono, Hill and Narjoko 2012: 192). These percentages increased further between 1996 and 2005.

An early study of business development since independence, which compared the *benteng* era with the early Suharto years, was carried out by Muhaimin (1982). He presented data from the Management Information Foundation which claimed that in 1980 there were 12,474 large businesses (employing more than fifty people) owned by indigenous groups and 8,923 owned by Chinese. Of the roughly 100,000 medium businesses (employing between five and fifty workers) about half were owned by indigenous groups. This source also estimated that there were around 180,000 small businesses of which 56 per cent were owned by indigenous Indonesians and 44 per cent by Chinese. Muhaimin (1982: 354–5) argued that in reality, Chinese businesses accounted for a higher share of the total than these figures might suggest, as many were established under Ali-Baba arrangements with Chinese partners usually supplying management expertise and capital.

Muhaimin (1982: 359) argued that the intense involvement of Indonesian leaders, both civilian and military, in business enterprises inhibited the development of '*bona-fide pribumi* entrepreneurs'. The essentially patrimonial nature of the Indonesian political system as it had developed since independence meant that those sectors of the economy which were generating, or had the potential to generate, large surpluses were used by the leadership to confer favours on business groups who were in turn expected to return favours to their civilian or military protectors. These practices were combined with a distrust of 'free market capitalism' and a conviction on the part of many political leaders that most Indonesians would be better off working in cooperatives, and practising some form of mutual aid (*gotong royong*).

Suharto himself, and most of his close associates, had grown up in the late colonial era, and probably shared the view of many colonial officials that most Indonesians were unsuited to the competitive world of market capitalism. He certainly seems to have agreed with Hatta and others in the early post-independence cabinets that cooperatives were a suitable form of business institution for most Indonesians, and continued to think this in the face of mounting evidence of their very limited success, even in the agricultural sector let alone other parts of the economy. By the 1990s, this emphasis on cooperatives was assuming ever more bizarre forms, as when Suharto conducted a televised meeting with a number of wealthy Chinese at his ranch south of Jakarta, and urged them to place at least 25 per cent of their assets in cooperatives. It was unclear to what extent such a policy would help small-scale indigenous businesses, let alone the poor. Many observers felt that in fact the cooperatives would be taken over by foundations (*yayasan*) controlled by Suharto and his close associates, whose assets were a closely guarded secret.

Suharto also found that Chinese businessmen such as Liem Sioe Liong could be useful in sorting out crises from the Pertamina collapse in the mid-1970s to the problems in the banking sector in the early 1990s, and he was happy to extend favours in return for their aid. Increasingly he also came under the influence of his own family who were determined to build up their own business empires, but needed the favours he could grant, as well as the support of the Chinese, to do so. An important reason for his continued support of the Chinese was that, as Schwarz (1999: 127) argued, he knew that ethnic Chinese, however rich, could never be a serious political challenge. 'But economically powerful *pribumi* businessmen, freed from reliance on government largesse, would be a different story.' Ascher (1999: 74–5) makes a similar point in discussing Suharto's approach to forest policies, especially in the latter part of the 1980s, where he often favoured joint ventures between military officers and business groups run by Chinese.[4] He knew that the Chinese lacked an independent power base, and would be happy to work with military groups in return for their protection.

Another possible reason for Suharto's apparent lack of support for *pribumi* businesses was that many were owned by Indonesians from outside Java, who often did not conform to the Javanese cultural practices which Suharto valued. He may also have feared that the development of a strong private enterprise sector in Sumatra or Sulawesi would have rekindled the unrest of the 1950s, and might even have encouraged separatist movements. His motives in blocking many *pribumi* firms from the most lucrative government contracts are perhaps understandable. But in ignoring the very real grievances of the great majority of Indonesian business people who felt they were excluded from the rich pickings scooped up by the privileged few, Suharto was sowing the seeds of his own downfall.

---

[4] Ascher (1999: 82) claimed that many Indonesians, in both government and elsewhere, did not realise the losses to the economy following the log export ban and the rapid growth of the domestic wood processing industry in the 1980s. But it seems likely that the technocrats and their advisers did understand the issues, but could do little about them, or prioritised other reforms and did not want to risk these reforms by antagonising Suharto on the logging issues. A detailed discussion of the cost of Indonesia's forest policies can be found in Gillis (1988); Gillis was a key adviser to the Minister of Finance over the 1980s.

Changing business structures after Suharto

The students who mounted protests against Suharto in the early months of 1998 were vocal in their condemnation of the corruption, cronyism and nepotism which they claimed were rampant in the government. They received considerable support from both the business community and parts of the military. Once Suharto left office, it was expected that there would be major changes in government–business relations, and that a 'level playing field' would be established on which businesses could compete, regardless of their size, or the ethnic origin of their owners and managers. But in fact many of the Suharto-era conglomerates managed not only to survive the change of regime but to maintain, or even improve their rankings in the top twenty conglomerates, measured by total sales (Table 7.1). The Salim group, now managed by Anthony Salim, Liem's son, had slipped only one place from first to second between 1996 and 2010, while several other conglomerates owned by Indonesians of Chinese descent maintained their place in the top twenty, including Sinar Mas,

Table 7.1 *Top twenty firms in Indonesia ranked by sales revenues, 2010*

Firm	Sales ($ billion)	Ranking, 1996
Jardine/Astra	10.6	2
Salim Group	8.6	1
Sinar Mas	4.9	3
Djarum	4.5	9
Bakrie	4.2	17
Gudang Garam	4.1	4
Lippo	4.0	5
Raja Garuda Mas	3.2	25
Triputra	2.5	131
CT Corporation	2.3	NA
Adaro Energy	2.0	70
Barito Pacific	1.9	15
Sampoerna	1.7	24
Ometraco	1.5	29
Gajah Tunggal	1.3	7
Panasonic Gobel	1.3	32
Wings	1.3	94
Panin	1.2	21
Aneka Kimia Raya	1.1	79
Trakindo	1.0	113

Source: Globe Asia.

Djarum, Gudang Garam, Lippo, Barito Pacific, Sampoerna, Ometraco and Gadjah Tunggal.

Some of the heavily indebted conglomerates managed to survive the 1997/1998 crisis by selling off their banks and some other businesses and bargaining hard with the Indonesian Bank Restructuring Agency to maintain control over the rest.[5] Borsuk and Chng (2014: 462–6) discuss the process through which Anthony Salim was 'cleared to carry on'. They point out that there was a widespread feeling that he had been let off too lightly, although Salim claimed that the fact that the sales of the assets he pledged to IBRA raised only about 40 per cent of their assessed value reflected the fact that the sales took place when the economy was still weak, and demand was depressed. The bargain which the Salim group, and several other conglomerates, made with IBRA was certainly facilitated by the fact that two economics ministers who took a tough line against them, Kwik Kian Gie and Rizal Ramli, had left office by the time the deals were done. Another beneficiary of favourable treatment from IBRA was Abdulrizal Bakrie, the most powerful *pribumi* businessman, whose conglomerate rose in the rankings from 17 to 5 between 1996 and 2010 (Table 7.1). The most conspicuous losers from the post-1998 settlements were the conglomerates owned by members of the Suharto family. The Bimantara Group, owned by Suharto's second son, was ranked sixth by sales in 1996; by 2010 most of its assets had been taken over by other firms. The Humpuss Group, owned by Suharto's youngest son, still survived, but had also vanished from the list of the top fifty firms ranked by sales in 2010.

To the extent that many of the large, Chinese-owned conglomerates which were established during the Suharto era have survived, and indeed prospered since 1998, does this mean that they have sound management structures and business models which suited well a more liberal era? In some cases this is probably true. Although there are a few newcomers which have risen from relatively small beginnings prior to 1998, most conglomerates listed in Table 7.1 were building on past success, which was in part at least the result of favourable treatment during the Suharto era. But to many Indonesians, not just extreme nationalists, their survival does indicate a continuation of business structures which emerged over the decades from the 1970s to the 1990s. While overt hostility to Chinese business groups might have abated, compared with the last years of the Suharto era, the evidence of their continuing importance gives rise to troubling questions. Why, twelve years after the resignation of Suharto,

---

[5] Several of the banks owned by large conglomerates prior to the crisis have been taken over by Malaysian and Singaporean banks (Carney and Hamilton-Hart 2015: table 8).

were there still so few businesses run by indigenous Indonesians which had developed into large, successful companies, able to compete in both national and international markets? Why are the great majority of Indonesian businesses still small-scale, and still concentrated in sectors such as agriculture and trade?

It was frequently argued that small enterprises weathered the 1997/1998 crisis better than larger ones, and provided an important safety net when larger enterprises were contracting in number and cutting staff. Figures from the economic censuses held in 1996 and 2006 showed that the share of manufacturing employment in firms employing between five and nineteen workers jumped from 35 to 53 per cent between 1996 and 2006 (Aswicahyono, Hill and Narjoko 2012: table 6.9). The data on all establishments outside the agricultural sector surveyed in the economic censuses of 1986 to 2006 showed that numbers increased from 16.4 million to 22.7 million between 1996 and 2006 (Table 7.2). This was a slower rate of growth than in the previous decade but still substantial given the severity of the economic downturn, and the slow recovery. The figures in Table 7.2 refer to all establishments, but the great majority would be in the small and household category, employing less than five people. In the agricultural sector, numbers of farm households increased by almost five million between 1993 and 2003 to 25 million (Booth 2012a: 63). Almost thirty per cent of these households were deriving

Table 7.2 *Number of establishments (excluding agricultural holdings) and percentage breakdown by sector, 1986, 1996 and 2006*

	1986	1996*	2006
Numbers of establishments (million)	9.28	16.40	22.71
Percentage breakdown by sector			
Mining/quarrying	1.4	1.2 (86.9)	1.2
Manufacturing	16.5	16.8 (90.7)	14.2
Utilities	0.2	0.1 (82.8)	0.1
Construction	0.9	1.3 (68.1)	0.7
Trade, restaurants, etc.	55.0	57.6 (96.1)	58.8
Transport	9.5	10.6 (91.2)	11.8
Finance/other	16.4	12.5 (91.2)	13.3
Total	100.0	100.0 (93.4)	100.0

* Figures in brackets show the percentage of all establishments with fixed premises employing five people or less. In 1996, establishments with fixed premises comprised 66.5 per cent of all establishments outside agriculture.

Sources: CBS (1998: Tables A and C); 2006 data from **Berita Resmi Statistik**, No 48/14, September 2006.

most of their incomes from non-agricultural activities including manu-facturing industry, trade and transport. Of those who gave agriculture as their main source of income, many were deriving at least part of their incomes from off-farm activity. This diversity in income sources has led some analysts to claim that rural households in many parts of Asia, Africa and Latin America have increasingly come to resemble miniature, highly diversified conglomerates, many of them with a foothold in the urban sector (Cain and McNicoll 1988: 105).

But how many of these miniature conglomerates in Indonesia have been able to develop into modern businesses? To what extent is the problem identified by Geertz in Pare in the 1950s of entrepreneurs without enterprises still the case in Indonesia? Certainly by the 1980s it was possible to find examples of successful *pribumi* enterprises which could reasonably be called medium or large scale. A study of a chilli marketing depot in Central Java found that one woman trader and her partners dealt in large quantities of perishable product in a business which had been developed over a number of years. Prices were not set by bargaining but were fixed to reflect supply and demand conditions in the market (Alexander 1986: 110). But Alexander also found that there were very few firms in rural Java which could be called capitalist in the sense that they generated surpluses through hiring in labour and selling the output at a profit, and reinvested profits in expanding the business. She argued that scaling up production often required considerable resources to finance the purchase of equipment and a distribution net-work. Many small businesses which had generated some profits found that there were more profitable investment opportunities in other sec-tors, such as transport or retail trade, which did not involve employing labour from outside the family (Alexander 1987: 108–9).

It is difficult to determine to what extent these constraints still operate to prevent the expansion of small and household enterprises in Java, or in other parts of the country. Many such enterprises have identified difficulty in getting access to credit as one factor preventing them from expanding. From the 1970s onwards the government's approach to the perceived problem of lack of credit was to develop programmes which channelled credit through government banks, often at subsidised inter-est rates. These attracted criticism from many economists, who were more impressed by the unsubsidised microfinance schemes implemen-ted at the subdistrict and village levels. These expanded rapidly in parts of Java and Bali during the 1980s and 1990s, and to a lesser extent in other provinces. They led to Indonesia becoming recognised as a world leader in commercial microfinance (Rosengard et al. 2007). But after the 1997/1998 crisis, there have been worrying signs: some of these schemes have fallen victim to pressures to amalgamate small financial institutions into larger ones. Rosengard et al. (2007) argued that innovative microfinance services have tended to be viewed with suspicion and hostility. Although such services still flourish in some provinces such as Bali, in others they have been cut back or abolished.

The people's economy, Article 33 and the new role of the courts in economic policy

The evidence that many of the large, Chinese-owned conglomerates have continued to flourish in the post-Suharto era, together with growing concern over credit and other support for small and household enterprises, has led to a resurgence in demands for a 'people's economy' (*ekonomi kerakyatan*). In many respects these demands echo those for an economy based on the principles of *Pancasila*, which were made in the 1980s. The 1980s debates were triggered by several publications by economists based at Gadjah Mada University in Yogyakarta, who expressed concern with the policies favoured by Jakarta-based technocrats based in the Planning Board and the Ministry of Finance. These policies were seen to be too favourable to foreign investors and insufficiently concerned with small-scale enterprises. Reviewing the debate, McCawley (1981: 103) found that the *Pancasila* system as outlined in Mubyarto and Boediono (1981) was based on five major points. First, the role of both state enterprises and cooperatives would be important, and these would be expected to cooperate, rather than compete with private enterprises. Second, incentives would not be based on profit maximisation, but should reflect religious and social values. Third, policies supporting greater equality would be given priority. Fourth, the creation of a strong national economy would be encouraged, which would probably involve support for firms owned by indigenous (*pribumi*) entrepreneurs. And last, economic planning would be more decentralised, allowing for greater participation of local people in decisions involving their future.

Clearly, the debates in the 1950s about appropriate economic policies, including the role of cooperatives, had an impact on these arguments. In addition, the affirmative action policies adopted in neighbouring Malaysia as part of the New Economic Policy in that country probably also had some influence. Critics pointed out that the advocates of *Pancasila* economics were vague about how their ideas should be implemented, but at least some of their views appear to have influenced Suharto-era thinking on rural and regional development policies. Professor Mubyarto was appointed as an adviser to the National Planning Board and was instrumental in setting up the *Inpres Desa Tertinggal* programme in the 1990s, which was intended to accelerate the development of remote villages, especially in Eastern Indonesia. He continued to be active in policy debates after Suharto's resignation; in a development manifesto published in 2005, he claimed that the debate over *Pancasila* economics in the 1980s was terminated by the power of what he termed 'economism', which placed too much emphasis on physical development targets, and ignored the spirit of the 1945 constitution. He went on to argue that:

> Whereas in business, economic efficiency can only be achieved through competition, this will of course not be in line with the brotherhood principle stipulated in Article 33 of the 1945 Constitution. Because the principle of brotherhood has been 'misused' by many leaders in the New Order government, some people including economists want to replace the brotherhood principle with some other principle such as the market mechanism. (Mubyarto 2005: 188)

Mubyarto went on to point out that the fight among nationalist, populist and liberal (or orthodox) economists led to the breakdown of the Expert Team of the working group of the MPR, appointed in 2001 to set out new guidelines for state policy in the post-Suharto era. This impasse meant that key decisions on the appropriate role of the state and private enterprise had to be made not in the parliament but elsewhere. Increasingly after 2002 it was the courts that took on the responsibility.

Although it had difficulty in agreeing guidelines for economic policy in the post-Suharto era, the MPR did manage to complete four major constitutional amendments by August 2002. Together, they made several fundamental changes to Indonesia's political and legal system. The third and fourth amendments required that Indonesia's first constitutional court be established, which would have the power to make final, and binding, decisions in the review of statutes (*undang-undang*), and to settle disputes concerning state organs whose power is derived from the Constitution (Butt and Lindsey 2008: 240–1). These authors pointed out that several cases brought to the court, often by NGOs, concerned attempts to dilute government involvement in key economic sectors. Some NGOs were especially hostile to initiatives which appeared to encourage more private sector investment in infrastructure. One case, discussed in Chapter 6, concerned electric power; others have looked at water resources, forestry, and the oil and gas sector.

> These cases have become a lightning rod for a wide range of popular grievances, including mistrust of entrepreneurs; allegations of widespread collusion between government and business; and a sense among NGOs that *reformasi* (post-Suharto reform) has not materially improved the circumstances of ordinary Indonesians. The cases have also become the forum for a revival of a long-standing and

persistent – if until recently frequently marginalised – ideological debate about the economic and regulatory relationship between state and subjects in Indonesia which dates back to the years before independence in 1945, and which invariably refers to Article 33. (Butt and Lindsey 2008: 242)

The decisions made by the Constitutional Court on the cases brought to them have not always supported the views of the civil society groups who brought them to court. The work of the court has not been helped by the vague wording of the 1945 Constitution which was drawn up during the Japanese occupation and influenced by Japanese notions of the integralist state. As Lev (1996: 149) argued, Raden Supomo and others who wrote the 1945 constitution wanted a powerful state and a submissive society, while at the same time rejecting the colonial economic system based on market capitalism. Thus the provisions of Article 33 state that the economy shall be organised on a common endeavour, based on the principle of the family system, that sectors of production which are important for the country and affect the life of the people shall be under the powers of the state, and that the land waters and the natural resources within the state shall be under the powers of the state and shall be used to the greatest benefit of the people.[6]

What exactly does 'under the powers of the state' mean? What for that matter does 'greatest benefit of the people' mean? Does Article 33 actually imply that all Indonesia's natural resources should be nationalised, and that private enterprise, operating on the profit principle, should have no role in their exploitation? Many Indonesians in the post-Suharto era, including some in the parliament, appear to support this interpretation. Others might argue that these provisions really mean that the government should regulate the private sector, but not exclude it entirely from exploiting natural resources or from other sectors of the economy which produce basic needs.

There was certainly a widespread feeling in Indonesia after Suharto left office that the country's resource wealth must be harnessed in ways which benefit the entire population, rather than a small number of favoured business groups. The rapid loss of the country's forests from the late 1960s to the early twenty-first century caused huge resentment which was not confined to the environmental movement. There was considerable indignation that one of the country's most valuable natural assets had been wantonly destroyed, and the profits from this destruction had accrued almost entirely to a small group of well-connected Indonesians. How could such abuses be prevented in the future? Should the courts act

---

[6] This is the translation given at www.setneg.go.id.

as a countervailing force to predatory capitalism and collusive behaviour between government and business?

Those wanting to place stronger controls on both government and business in Indonesia have gained considerable ideological support from the anti-globalisation movement, which in turn has been based on a conviction that little of the growth which has occurred in the global economy in recent decades has benefited the majority of working people. Has this really been the case in Indonesia? The next chapter reviews the evidence.

8   Trends in poverty and income distribution
The Suharto era and beyond

Estimates of poverty and income distribution after 1965

In Chapter 3, it was argued that there was considerable evidence that poverty and malnutrition were widespread in Indonesia by the mid-1960s, although the Sukarno government appeared to be in denial about the problem. The Indonesian Communist Party had drawn support from both the rural landless and employees in the estates sector and in the urban economy, but had no clear strategy for improving living standards beyond redistribution of land. The party supported the occupation of former estate land in parts of Java, but most Indonesians, even those on the left, realised that there was insufficient land in Java to give all rural households even one hectare, let alone the two hectares which the 1960 Basic Agrarian Law stipulated should be the minimum holding size. When pressed about the problem of 'too many people and not enough land', Sukarno and his ministers tended to fall back on the old colonial solution of moving people from Java, Bali and the eastern islands to the supposedly 'empty lands' in Sumatra, Kalimantan, Sulawesi and the newly acquired West Irian, later to become Irian Jaya, and now the two provinces of Papua and Papua Barat.

After power was wrested from Sukarno in 1966, economic policy was concerned primarily with macroeconomic problems. It was expected that a reduction in inflation and a return to growth would alleviate the problem of poverty, and lead to a general improvement in living standards. The first Five Year Plan of the Suharto era placed most attention on the agricultural sector, especially on increasing rice production. The Plan also stressed the need to rehabilitate and extend rural infrastructure, especially roads and irrigation. But it was criticised for its neglect of non-rice food crops, including both corn and cassava, as well as soybean and vegetables, which are important sources of protein and vitamins for the poor. By the early 1970s, some academic commentators, worried about the evidence of widespread and persistent poverty and malnutrition in Indonesia, were arguing that economic growth alone would not be sufficient to reduce poverty in Indonesia.

157

At this time there was a growing international debate over 'redistribution with growth' encouraged by the World Bank, the International Labour Organization and by a number of well-known academics in various parts of the world. In the Indonesian context the debate was hampered, at least to begin with, by a lack of reliable statistical evidence. Apart from a small number of village-level studies, little research had been published on poverty in Indonesia until the 1970s, although many observers suspected that, given Indonesia's low per capita GDP, the problem of poverty must be worse there than in neighbouring countries such as Philippines, Thailand or Malaysia. Compared with these three countries, the Indonesian Central Bureau of Statistics was slow to implement nation-wide household income and expenditure surveys. In Chapter 3, it was pointed out that the first rounds of the National Socio-economic Surveys (*Susenas*) had only limited coverage. Those carried out in 1969/1970, 1976, 1978 and 1980 covered most of the country although Maluku and Irian Jaya were excluded in 1969/1970 and Irian Jaya in 1976. In subsequent surveys, rural areas of both Irian Jaya and East Timor were excluded; indeed the first truly national *Susenas* was not carried out until 1987 (CBS 1992: 31). The samples did not permit a breakdown by province until the early 1990s; until that point, data were only published for Java and the rest of the country.

An early analysis of the *Susenas* data for Java between 1963/1964 and 1969/1970 was carried out by King and Weldon (1977). They found little change in expenditure distribution over these years in rural Java, but found evidence of growing disparities in urban areas, especially in Jakarta. They did not attempt to estimate the changing percentage of the population below a stipulated poverty line, although they noted the estimates by Sajogyo for 1969/1970, which will be discussed later. Their estimates of weekly rice consumption by quintile group in both rural and urban areas showed a considerable increase in rural areas, especially between 1964/1965 and 1967 for the poorest 20 per cent. There was little change for the bottom quintile in urban areas. Real per capita food expenditures increased for the top 80 per cent in both urban and rural areas between 1967 and 1969/1970 but fell for the bottom 20 per cent (King and Weldon 1977: table 6). The authors concluded that the evidence indicated some decline in the real standard of living for the poorer groups and growing disparities between rich and poor in urban areas.

The first attempt to propose a poverty line for Indonesia and measure the proportion of the population below the line was made by the evaluation report of the Applied Nutrition Program (ANP), which had been initiated in 1963 in Central Java with assistance from UNICEF, the WHO and the FAO. By 1972 it covered eight provinces in Java,

Sumatra, Bali and West Nusatenggara. The evaluation study report was written by Professor Sajogyo of the Bogor Agricultural University, and suggested a poverty line in terms of 240 kg rice or equivalent food grains (Sajogyo 1975: 24).[1] Converting these poverty lines into rupiah and applying them to the 1969/1970 *Susenas* data, Sajogyo estimated that 46 per cent of the rural population in Indonesia was below the poverty line. For rural Java the figure was 57 per cent (Sajogyo 1975: 73). The ANP evaluation study stressed the sharp disparity in calorie and protein intake between those households above the poverty line and those below it. In Java, the average calorie intake per person in households above the line was 2,170 per day, while those households below the line were unable to reach a calorie intake of 1,400. There was also a wide disparity in protein intake per capita; almost 54 g per capita compared with 27 g. The ANP study also found that average annual per capita food grain intake in Java (rice, corn and cassava expressed in rice equivalents) had declined from 204 kg in 1936–1939 to 175 kg in 1956–1959 and 154 kg in 1965–1960. There had also been a decline in per capita availability of soybean and ground nut (Sajogyo 1975: 67).

Other investigations of rural poverty in Java adopted the ANP concept in one form or another. Penny and Singarimbun (1973) in their study of Sriharjo, a village in Yogyakarta, claimed that villagers had a concept of 'sufficiency' (*cukupan*) which they expressed in terms of rice, and many studies used rice prices to deflate rural wage data.[2] In fact, if it can be accepted that rice is the most 'basic' of basic needs in Indonesia, its use in determining a poverty line would seem to be close to what Lipton (1983: 6) had in mind in suggesting that poverty be defined in terms of the fulfilment of one 'key' need. Sundrum and Booth (1980: 463) extended the Sajogyo analysis to 1976. They found that the percentage of the population below the 240 kg poverty line in rural areas of both Java and the Outer Islands fell, albeit in Java the fall was not very great (from 39.5 to 33.7 per cent). The fall in numbers of destitute in rural Java was also quite small, from 20.9 to 17.5 per cent. In urban areas, both in Java and elsewhere, the fall was greater.

Other estimates, including some put forward by the World Bank, showed a greater decline in the headcount measure of poverty between 1970 and 1976, especially in rural Java. But several analysts pointed out

[1] There is a history of using rice as a standard in determining poverty lines and minimum wages in other parts of Southeast Asia; for a discussion of the rice-wage formula in the Philippines, see Abrera (1976: 232–3). In Indonesia it was used as a standard in Dutch studies carried out in the early decades of the twentieth century.

[2] This is particularly true of the numerous village studies carried out by the Agroeconomic Survey. See Collier et al. (1982) for a survey of this literature.

that using rice, or a price index heavily weighted towards rice, probably underestimated the impact of inflation over these years on the poor. It was argued that the consumption basket of the poor, especially in rural Java, contained more non-rice staples, especially corn and cassava, whose prices had risen faster than rice. Thus the rate of inflation for the bottom 40 per cent in rural areas was higher than for upper income groups (Dapice 1980: 71; Asra 1989: 107). Asra (1989: 104–5) also estimated that the Gini coefficient for household expenditures increased slightly over these six years, once corrections had been made for the differential impact of inflation on different expenditure groups. The importance of differential rates of inflation for different expenditure groups was to emerge again in the late 1990s, when estimates were made of the impact of the economic crisis on poverty and inequality.

Whatever the statistics showed, there could be no doubt that many people concerned with poverty issues in Indonesia, and especially in Java, felt disappointed that the real per capita GDP growth which had occurred in the decade from 1966 to 1976 (real per capita GDP increased by almost 70 per cent over the decade) was not having a more dramatic impact on the incomes of the poorer sections of the population, whether in Java or elsewhere. Some analysts put the blame on the impact of the oil boom which had led to a sharp increase in revenues accruing to the central government budget. This in turn led to increased expenditures on salaries for government employees, who were mainly based in urban areas and had a higher propensity to consume on luxury and semi-luxury goods and services. Certainly the evidence from the *Susenas* surveys for 1970 and 1976 showed that urban–rural disparities in per capita household expenditures had widened, although they were not as high as in Malaysia or Thailand (Sundrum and Booth 1980: 459–60).

The latter part of the 1970s saw a moderation in the rate of inflation in Indonesia, and also considerable growth in agricultural production, especially rice. Using the Sajogyo poverty line, Booth (1993: table 1) found a further decline in the percentage of the poor in Java between 1976 and 1980, to 32 per cent of the population. But by the end of the 1970s, it was argued that the changes in consumption opportunities which had occurred in Indonesia since 1965 made the Sajogyo poverty line an anachronism. This was partly because many Indonesians, especially in Java, were living in urban and peri-urban areas where the Sajogyo poverty concept was never very satisfactory.[3] But also a diminishing number of

[3] The Sajogyo poverty line in urban areas was simply the rural poverty line increased by 50 per cent, although no justification was given for such an arbitrary mark-up. In Eastern Indonesia, where rice was often not the staple food, and was a relatively expensive source

Indonesians anywhere in the country by 1980 had a concept of *cukupan* which could be expressed exclusively in terms of rice. The proportion of total consumption expenditures devoted to purchase of cereals had fallen steadily everywhere in Indonesia since 1970, and other expenditures including housing and education assumed a much greater role in both actual consumer budgets and in concepts of basic needs.

The series on poverty published by the Central Bureau of Statistics in the 1980s used a broader poverty line which showed that the population in poverty fell from 40 to 28.6 per cent between 1976 and 1980, and the absolute numbers of poor fell from 54 million to 42 million (CBS 1997: 570). But the poverty line used by the CBS met with criticism, for reasons which will be discussed in more detail later. Another prominent Indonesian economist, Professor Hendra Esmara, put forward a poverty line concept in terms of average per capita expenditure on a package of basic needs (Esmara 1986: Chapter 9). Using the household expenditure data from successive rounds of the *Susenas* for 1970, 1976, 1978 and 1980, Esmara estimated average expenditures on this basic needs package, which included cereals and tubers, nuts, fish, meat, vegetables, fruit, clothing, housing, education and health. The package for urban and rural areas was broadly similar although a few extra food items were added for rural areas.

The Esmara approach was a novel one in that it explicitly allows for the concept of 'basic needs' to change over time by using average per capita expenditure on the basic commodities rather than expenditures on a fixed basket of needs (however defined). Much of the change in per capita expenditures on the basic needs package over the 1970s reflected changes in prices. But a part also reflected a decision on the part of households to consume more food, clothing, housing, education, etc. According to the Esmara approach, this revealed a change in social attitudes to, and perceptions of, what constitutes basic needs which should be incorporated in the poverty line concept. The Esmara poverty line, like that of Sajogyo and the CBS, was higher in urban areas than in rural, and the gap widened over the decade of the 1970s. But in spite of this, Esmara found that the percentage of the population below the poverty line in rural Indonesia had consistently been higher than in urban areas.

Esmara acknowledged that his concept of the 'dynamic poverty line' as changing not just with changing prices but also with changing real consumption patterns was open to objections. Suppose that at some point all the poor become better off in terms of real per capita expenditure. The

of calories, the use of a rice-based poverty line led to overestimates in the headcount measure of poverty.

Esmara measure may not in fact indicate a decline in poverty because higher expenditure on the basic needs package may well entail a new poverty line which is so much higher that poverty measured by it stays the same or even increases. He therefore also proposed a more orthodox alternative; which derived a poverty line for the years 1976–1980 from the 1970 data simply by adjusting for changes in the Jakarta Cost of Living Index. This alternative gave results in rural areas which were not very different from the 'dynamic' poverty line except for 1980. But in urban areas the poverty line was much lower (Esmara 1986: 329). Thus the estimate of the percentage in poverty is also lower using this measure. Numbers in poverty hardly changed in urban areas and fell quite markedly in rural areas (Esmara 1986: 332). But there were obvious problems with this approach as well. Why should the Jakarta CPI be used to adjust an all-Indonesia poverty line for inflation? To the extent that the rate of inflation has not been the same in urban and rural areas, or in different regions of the country, the use of the Jakarta CPI to adjust the poverty line for changes in prices may understate or overstate changes in poverty.

Beginning in the 1970s, the World Bank also paid considerable attention to issues of poverty and income distribution in Indonesia and published a number of estimates of the proportions of the population in poverty and the changes over time. Most of these estimates were made in internal documents, but publicly available estimates were given in a country study published in 1980 (World Bank 1980: 70–93). This report argued that 'growth in average per capita consumption expenditure appears to have been accompanied by a reduction in both the proportion and absolute numbers of the population at extremely low levels of per capita consumption' between 1970 and 1976 (World Bank 1980: v). But the report also found evidence of growing inequalities. The study used a poverty line of Rp. 3,000 per month everywhere in the country although to correct for regional differences in price levels, rupiah consumption expenditures were adjusted to Jakarta prices (World Bank 1980: 84). The most striking aspect of these estimates was the very marked difference in poverty incidence in urban and rural areas; the disparity was much greater than that shown by either of Esmara's estimates. Whereas according to Esmara, 16.3 per cent of the poor were located in urban areas in 1976, the World Bank found only 7.5 per cent.

In another World Bank study, Chernichovsky and Meesook (1984: 2) tried to avoid the problem of choosing a poverty line altogether by simply defining the 'poor' as the bottom two quintiles of the population ranked by their household's level of per capita consumption expenditure. Using this approach they also found a large disparity between urban and rural poverty incidence in 1978 (14.1 per cent of urban households were considered poor compared with 41.7 per cent of rural households). By contrast, the CBS estimates for the same year found that 30.8 per cent of urban households were below the poverty line compared with 33.4 per cent of rural households. Chernichovsky and Meesok criticised absolute poverty lines for 'incorporating many arbitrary assumptions' but their method appeared just as arbitrary.

The bewildering diversity of estimates of the incidence of poverty, numbers in poverty, and the location of the poor, together with the evidence that the *Susenas* surveys seemed to be underestimating total household expenditures, encouraged other analysts to adopt different approaches to the measurement of poverty in Indonesia. Papanek (1980) compiled several series on real wages; the longest was for real wages for both temporary and permanent plantation workers in Java and Sumatra from 1951 to 1978. He found that real wages fell fairly consistently from 1953 to 1968, although the fall was steeper in Java; by 1968 wages in Java were well under half those in Sumatra. Part of the fall between the 1950s and 1963 might have been the result of increased employment; total number of workers increased in all plantations except coffee (Papanek 1980: 86). Employers could have been reacting to the economic difficulties of the late 1950s and early 1960s, as well as to increasing opposition by trade unions to laying off workers, by keeping workers on, but reducing their remuneration. From 1968 to 1972, real wages increased sharply although numbers employed fell. But after 1972, the various wage series he examined did not show much sign of real increases.

Papanek (1980: 102) attributed the improvement in real wages between 1967 and 1972 to the rebuilding of a shattered economy. He also showed that in the plantation sector, employment fell after 1967. It is probable that the reduction in trade union power made it easier for the estates to get rid of older, less productive workers. But after 1972, growth became more capital-intensive and wage jobs in both the estate sector and in other agricultural sectors did not grow rapidly. Broadly, his figures support the argument that, while there was probably some improvement in living standards in the latter part of the 1960s, the benefits of accelerated economic growth were slow to trickle down to the vast majority of the population after the early 1970s. Trends in wage rates in Indonesia were an important determinant of real living standards because, by 1971, 35 per cent of male workers were employees (CBS 1975a: 187). This was a higher percentage than in either the Philippines or Thailand. In addition, many people who were classed in the census as 'self-employed' were probably earning part of their income from wage labour.

Living standards were almost certainly lower, and poverty higher, in Indonesia than in Malaysia, Thailand and the Philippines in the

Table 8.1 *Estimated food availability in the Philippines and Indonesia, 1972 (grams per day)*

Food type	Philippines	Java	Outer Islands	Indonesia
Cereals	363	297	347	325
Roots/tubers	66	216	202	211
Sugar	51	27	45	34
Pulses/nuts	15	33	10	24
Vegetables	77	36	19	30
Fruits	99	90	100	94
Meat	43	8	10	9
Eggs	9	1	3	2
Fish	107	3	18	8
Fats/oils	10	7	16	11
Calories per day	2,047	1,850	2,208	2,020
Protein per day	53	36	42	39

Sources: Philippines: NEDA (1975); Indonesia: Nicol (1974; tables 1–4).

mid-1960s, but were they still lower in 1980? Comparisons of the national headcount measures of poverty across Southeast Asia at this time were not possible, given that the poverty lines in Indonesia were lower in dollar terms than in Malaysia, Thailand or the Philippines (Booth 1993: table 11).[4] Even allowing for differences in the purchasing power of the rupiah compared with the other Southeast Asian currencies which might not have been fully incorporated in the exchange rate, it is probable that the poverty line in Indonesia allowed for a more modest basket of goods and services than in other parts of the region.[5] In 1972, the consumption of cereals in Java was well below that in the Philippines; in spite of higher consumption of roots and tubers, the total calories intake was lower, although it was higher outside Java. Protein intake was much lower in both Java and the Outer Islands than in the Philippines (Table 8.1).

By the early 1990s, the government was using the poverty line estimated by the Central Bureau of Statistics to claim that there had been a marked decline in both the headcount measure of poverty and numbers in poverty. It was estimated that 40 per cent of the population was below the

---

[4] Mangahas (1983) compared the various poverty lines used in Southeast Asian studies in the late 1970s and early 1980s. He came to the conclusion that, once adjustments had been made for differences in purchasing power, there was not a great difference between them, although the Malaysian poverty line was higher than most of the others.

[5] It is worth noting that the effect of the rice premium and other export taxes in Thailand was to lower the domestic price of rice in Thailand in dollar terms, compared with other countries in Southeast Asia.

CBS poverty line in 1976; by 1996 this had fallen to 11.3 per cent. In spite of the increase in population, numbers below the poverty line fell from 54.2 million to 22.5 million (CBS 1997: 570). This was hailed by both government and many international observers as a considerable achievement. But the CBS estimates were criticised on a number of grounds. The official poverty line used by the Central Bureau of Statistics in Indonesia was rather low in comparison with average per capita expenditures, as reported in the consumption surveys. It was also low compared with that in other Asian economies, including neighbouring Malaysia (Booth 1993: 77). Because of the bunching of households just above the poverty line, increasing the official poverty line by even a small amount showed a greatly increased headcount measure. These criticisms of the CBS estimates were to persist after Suharto left office, and will be reviewed in greater detail later.

In spite of the criticisms of poverty measurement, other indicators did show a broad-based improvement in living standards. Consumption of foodstuffs such as rice, meat and dairy products had risen continually since the late 1960s; there was a considerable growth in the daily protein intake of the population from 43.3 g per day in 1968 to 61.8 g in 1993. Not just did the diet improve but availability of other consumer goods greatly increased. Ownership of consumer durables such as televisions, refrigerators, cars and motor cycles expanded rapidly to the point where what were seen as unattainable Western 'luxuries' in the late 1960s were within the reach of millions of Indonesian households. The main factors underlying the broad-based growth in real incomes and consequent reduction in poverty between 1976 and 1996 are usually identified as follows:

(a) Government programmes in the field of agriculture and rural development were successful in boosting rural incomes in many parts of the country but especially in the major rice-producing areas. Even those households which did not cultivate agricultural land were able to benefit from greater employment opportunities as a result of the growth in output.

(b) Government reacted to the various external shocks of the early and mid-1980s, by implementing policies which promoted private sector development and reduced overall budgetary expenditures, while at the same time protecting poverty-related expenditures.

(c) The expansion of sectors such as manufacturing industry, construction, trade and transport created new employment opportunities for many who previously had to rely largely on agriculture, with the result that many rural households were by the mid-1990s able to diversify their incomes away from complete reliance on the farm holding. The 1993 Agricultural Census found that on average farm households were obtaining half their incomes from off-farm sources. In Java and Bali the percentage was higher (Booth 2012a: 65).

As far as (b) was concerned, most noteworthy was the combination of trade and industrial liberalization measures and real exchange rate adjustments which encouraged both non-food agriculture and labour-intensive industrialisation, especially in the wake of the 1986 devaluation. A World Bank report published in 1990 argued that the government's overall expenditure reduction strategy was to cut capital-intensive expenditures while trying to preserve those expenditures which benefited the poor (World Bank 1990: 19). This was particularly the case after 1986/1987 when the combination of falling oil revenues and rising debt service obligations led to a massive squeeze on non-debt government expenditures (Asher and Booth 1992: table 2.6). Civil service compensation was frozen in nominal terms and some components of the development budget (especially the transmigration programme and projects in the industrial and energy sectors) were subjected to substantial cuts. Budgetary subsidies on basic needs were relatively modest in Indonesia by the mid-1980s. Although they were cut, the ensuing price rises did not give rise to the social resentment and political upheavals which occurred in some Latin American and African countries. In short, the sharp decline in government expenditures excluding debt service obligations which occurred in the 1980s did not have a significant impact on the poorest segments of the population, because they had benefited only marginally, if at all, from most of the government expenditure programmes which were severely pruned.

But in spite of the reduction in the incidence of poverty which occurred in the 1970s and 1980s, Indonesia in the mid-1990s still faced a poverty problem of considerable magnitude. In 1996 about 22.5 million people fell below even the CBS poverty line, which many critics thought was too low. Activists in NGOs and elsewhere were angry that government ministers and senior officials with extravagant lifestyles apparently considered that people could survive on less than twenty dollars a month. A poverty line closer to the one used in Thailand for example produced a much larger estimate of numbers of poor, and a much slower decline in the incidence of poverty over the 1980s.[6] Certainly many Indonesians

---

[6] For further details on the Indonesian poverty line see Booth (1993). When the Thai poverty line for 1990 was converted into rupiah and adjusted for differences in prices, the proportion below the poverty line in Indonesia in 1990 jumped to 50 per cent, compared with only 15 per cent if the official Indonesian poverty line is used. For a comparison of poverty levels and trends in Indonesia and Thailand, see Booth (1997).

considered that poverty was still a serious problem blighting their country, and that there should be greater emphasis on poverty alleviation programmes targeted on those regions and social groups where the incidence of poverty was highest.

The changing spatial distribution of poverty in the Suharto era

For much of the twentieth century, official concern about poverty in Indonesia was preoccupied with rural Java. In the early twentieth century, the Dutch colonial authorities' concern with problems of declining 'native welfare' in Java ushered in what was termed the ethical policy. The causes of rural poverty were seen mainly in terms of growing populations pressing on limited supplies of agricultural land. The policy solutions advocated were agricultural intensification programmes, including irrigation development, to raise output per hectare, population resettlement outside Java and educational expansion to equip a growing proportion of Javanese to take up non-agricultural employment. These policies also figured prominently in the New Order economic development strategy, at least in the decades from 1969 to 1989.

The success of the agriculture intensification programmes, combined with the growth of non-agricultural employment opportunities, especially in Java and Bali, were the main reasons for the decline in the incidence of poverty in the decades from 1976 to 1996. By 1996, the Central Bureau of Statistics estimated that Java and Bali accounted for 60 per cent of the total population of Indonesia, and 57 per cent of the poor population. In several provinces outside Java, including West and South Kalimantan, East and West Nusatenggara, Maluku, Irian Jaya and East Timor, the incidence of poverty was considerably higher than in Java and Bali in 1996 (CBS 1997: tables 3.2, 12.5). This was in spite of the fact that these provinces were favoured in terms of INPRES and other central government grants.[7] To what extent was this shift in the location of poverty towards Eastern Indonesia the result of slower growth in the availability of off-farm employment?

It was clear from 1993 Farm Household Income Survey, carried out as part of the 1993 Agricultural Census, that opportunities for off-farm and especially wage employment were particularly abundant in Java and Bali

---

[7] INPRES was an acronym for *Instruksi Presiden* (Presidential Instruction) and referred to a group of grants from the central government to regional governments. Some were given to provinces, districts and villages for general development projects while others were targeted to specific sectors such as education and health.

as a result of the rapid growth in agricultural production, which led to the creation of jobs in agricultural processing, transport and trade. In addition, there was considerable growth in sectors such as construction, manufacturing and tourism, all of which absorbed labour. Increased wage income augmented rural household incomes from more traditional sources such as farming and trade, especially for households controlling little or no land, and thus reduced numbers below the absolute poverty threshold. Outside Java, and especially in the more remote regions, there were fewer opportunities for earning off-farm income, and the opportunities which were available often earned household members less income than in Java or Bali.

The situation in some provinces outside Java was complicated by the fact that much of the provincial income accrued from sectors whose linkages with the rest of the regional economy were quite limited. When rapid output growth took place in the mining sector for example, it created few employment opportunities for local people and in fact most of the profits did not stay in the province but were 'drained' off to the central government and abroad. In 1993 the export surplus (the difference between exports and imports of goods and non-factor services) was well over 50 per cent of total GDP for Aceh and Riau and just under 50 per cent in East Kalimantan. In that year, the incidence of poverty in Aceh, Riau and East Kalimantan was not much different from the national average, although per capita GDP was much higher.

The case of Irian Jaya was particularly striking. In 1996, the province was ranked fourth in Indonesia in terms of GDP per capita, although according to the CBS estimates for 1996, the incidence of poverty was 21 per cent, the highest in the country after West Kalimantan and East Timor (CBS 1997: 572). The reason for such an outcome was that a significant proportion of the GDP produced in the province was not invested or consumed there, but remitted to other parts of the country or overseas.[8] Thus average per capita consumption expenditures were low, and poverty incidence correspondingly high. This outcome probably would not have mattered very much if the indigenous people in Irian Jaya, or indeed in the other resource-rich regions of Indonesia, were happy to acquiesce in the centre's control over their natural resource wealth. Perhaps unfortunately for the Indonesian government, it was clear in

---

[8] These data are taken from the estimates of Gross Regional Domestic Product broken down by expenditures, which have been prepared by the CBS since the 1980s. It should be noted that in more recent years, imports into Aceh, Riau and Papua have increased and the export surplus has diminished, but the increased imports have gone into investment rather than consumption. In the case of Aceh, most of the imports were for post-tsunami reconstruction. See Booth (2015; table 2.4) for details.

the early 1990s that this was not the case. In Irian Jaya, a former governor was quoted in the international press as stating that, if Indonesia is viewed as a village,

the people in the house called Irian Jaya feed those in the other houses but are themselves starving. Do you think this is fair?[9]

In spite of some attempt to boost consumption and investment in Irian Jaya in the closing years of the Suharto era, this problem remained to be tackled after 1998.

What happened to inequality?

Although there was much discussion of income inequalities and criticism of the growing 'wealth gap' in Indonesia over the New Order era, the available statistical data often seemed to indicate that the distribution of income was quite equitable. Certainly the evidence from successive Household Expenditure Surveys (*Susenas*) showed that the Gini coefficient of household per capita consumption expenditure in Indonesia between 1969/1970 and 1990 fell somewhat, although there was an increase between 1990 and 1996 (Table 8.2). But other indicators based on the *Susenas* data did suggest both growing urban–rural inequalities, and growing disparities within urban areas. Per capita consumption expenditures grew more rapidly in urban Java than in other parts of the country and more rapidly in rural Java than in rural areas in the Outer Islands over the 1970s and 1980s (Booth 1992: table 10.2). Between 1981 and 1996, urban–rural differences in per capita consumption expenditures increased only slightly, although after 1980 disparities between Jakarta and the rest of the country widened more sharply (Table 8.3).

While it is probable that the cost of living, and especially the cost of housing, in the large cities was increasing more rapidly than in rural areas, employment opportunities appeared to be more abundant in Jakarta, and the other large cities, both in Java and elsewhere. They acted as a magnet for rural migrants. But many of the migrants who went to the cities were only able to find jobs as casual labourers, often in small-scale enterprises. At the same time, urban workers with scarce skills were often able to command salaries which were high by Indonesian and even by international standards. The result was increasing inequality in urban areas, measured in terms of a growing percentage of the urban population spending less than half the urban average (Table 8.4). This trend was

[9] Adam Schwarz, 'Eastern Reproach', *Far Eastern Economic Review* (11 July 1991), p. 24.

Table 8.2 *Percentage of the population spending less than 50 per cent of* Susenas *average per capita consumption expenditures (ACE) in urban and rural areas, 1969–1970 to 2012*

	Urban	Rural	Total	Gini
1969/1970	20.7	21.4	22.2	0.35
1976	20.9	17.4	20.3	NA
1980	22.6	16.7	20.5	0.34
1984	18.8	13.5	18.9	0.33
1987	18.0	10.0	17.0	0.32
1990	20.2	10.3	16.0	0.32
1996	23.2	11.8	21.2	0.36
1999	17.8	8.3	14.9	0.31
2002	19.8	8.0	17.6	0.33
2005	25.3	10.5	24.2	0.34
2007	24.4	14.8	24.2	0.38
2009	23.8	12.4	22.0	0.37
2011 (March)	27.4	17.7	26.9	0.41
2012 (March)	31.3	17.4	30.6	0.41

Sources: **Susenas** data for years from 1969/1970 to 2007 from **Pengeluaran untuk Konsumsi Penduduk Indonesia** (Jakarta: Central Bureau of Statistics, various issues, and CBS (2008b)). Data for 2009 and 2011 from CBS website (www.bps.go.id).

especially obvious in Jakarta and West Java where by 1996 over 20 per cent of the population was spending less than half the average. Even these figures could be underestimates, as many observers argued that the *Susenas* data probably underestimated expenditure inequalities. These criticisms of the *Susenas* data are discussed in the following sections.

Household survey data were also used by Leigh and van der Eng (2008: table 1) to estimate the share of incomes accruing to the top 1, 5 and 10 per cent of income earners in Indonesia in the years from 1982 to 2004. They found that the share accruing to the top 10 per cent increased from 33 per cent in 1982 to 40 per cent in 1993. The share accruing to the top 1 per cent increased from just over 7 per cent to over 9 per cent. Given that the top 1 per cent of income earners would have been mainly located in urban areas, and especially in Jakarta, their findings confirm the estimates of relative poverty given in Table 8.4.

Other inequality indicators have also been prepared by the CBS which do not rely on the *Susenas* figures. The Social Accounting Matrices, prepared by the CBS at five-yearly intervals between 1975 and 1995, also found that the gap in disposable income between the richest and poorest household groups in Indonesia widened considerably. The

Table 8.3 *Urban–rural disparities in Indonesia, 1970–2013*

Year	Urban/rural*	Jakarta/rural*
1970	143	NA
1976	173	NA
1981	179	234
1984	189	250
1987	185	271
1990	181	275
1993	192	305
1996	191	314
1999	165	277
2002	179	315
2005	198	329
2008	175	304
2011	170	308
2013	179	302

* Average annual per capita consumption expenditures in urban areas/
Jakarta as a percentage of rural areas.
Sources: Until 1990: *Survei Sosial Ekonomi Nasional: Pengeluaran untuk Konsumsi Penduduk* (Jakarta CBS, various issues); 1993–2008: CBS (2008b); 2011 and 2013: from www.bps.go.id.

Table 8.4 *Percentage of the population spending less than 50 per cent of* Susenas *average per capita consumption expenditures (ACE) in urban and rural areas, 1984, 1996 and 2012*

Region	1984	1996	2012
Jakarta	14.2	22.1	33.3
West Java	21.6	23.9	30.2
Central Java	17.1	15.2	30.8
East Java	13.5	16.4	22.7
Urban Indonesia	18.8	23.2	31.3
Rural Indonesia	13.5	11.8	17.4
Indonesia	19.0	21.2	30.6

Sources: 1984 and 1996: *Survei Sosial Ekonomi Nasional: Pengeluaran untuk Konsumsi Penduduk per Propinsi 1984, 1996* (Jakarta CBS); 2012: from www.bps.go.id.

poorest group comprised rural households where the main source of income was agricultural labour, while the richest in rural areas were those households cultivating more than one hectare of land. In 1975, the income of these households was around twice that of the agricultural labour households while in 1995 it had increased to almost three times. In 1995, the upper income groups in urban areas were receiving over eight times the incomes of agricultural labour households, compared with around six times in 1975 (CBS 2008a: 75).

Further evidence on urban income disparities comes from the three Cost of Living Surveys carried out in 1968–1971, 1977–1978 and 1989. These surveys showed that the Gini coefficient of family income was higher in Javanese cities than elsewhere, and considerably higher than that estimated from the *Susenas* expenditure data. Perhaps surprisingly, the Cost of Living Surveys showed little change in the distribution of household income in urban Java over two decades of rapid economic growth and urbanisation. But in 1989 the Gini coefficient of household income in urban Java was already over 0.4, which is generally considered to indicate quite a skewed distribution. Broadly comparable data from similar surveys in the Philippines, a country where the distribution of income is often considered to be quite unequal, and indeed closer to Latin America than to other parts of Southeast Asia, showed a Gini coefficient of urban household incomes of 0.5 in 1965, dropping to 0.43 by 1988. This latter figure was not much higher than that found in urban Java (Booth 2000: 76).

Taken together, the statistical evidence does suggest that disparities in income were already high in urban areas in the late 1960s, and that urban–rural, and especially Jakarta–rural, disparities were growing between 1970 and 1996. Certainly, discontent over income distribution, and the urban–rural divide, on the part of civil society groups, was becoming increasingly vocal even before the crisis of 1997/1998. This discontent may have been due in part at least to changing societal tolerance towards such disparities.[10] The increasing evidence of extravagant lifestyles on the part of a small urban elite, many of whom were either Chinese or the children of senior political and bureaucratic figures, aroused anger among the much larger numbers of middle-class families who were struggling to educate their children and maintain a lifestyle based on what they perceived as 'Western' consumption norms. The fact that increasing numbers of Indonesians were aspiring to such a lifestyle by the 1990s is of course a reflection of increased disposable incomes. But the revolution of rising expectations ensured that middle-class urban dwellers, and probably some in rural areas as well, were more inclined to resent what they had not yet managed to achieve, rather than appreciate the fact that they and their families were enjoying amenities which their parents could never have imagined. The rapid

---

[10] In a classic paper Hirschman (1973) drew attention to the importance of changing perceptions of inequality in developing countries, and the implications for social stability.

growth of media advertising promoting an extravagantly 'Western' way of life only increased resentment that this way of life remained the privilege of a tiny proportion of the total population.

The 'new middle class' of upwardly mobile professionals, managers and salaried employees in clerical and administrative occupations, although the topic of much academic and media attention in the 1990s, were themselves only a small proportion of the urban labour force in Indonesia in the 1990s.[11] Under them were large and rapidly growing numbers of industrial and sales workers and self-employed people in the small-scale trade sector. Many of these were probably recent arrivals from the rural hinterland. They often worked long hours and lived in over-crowded and insanitary conditions. Exactly what they thought about their lot was difficult to determine, as little attention was paid to their views by the Indonesian government, the media or by most foreign observers. But the violent disturbances which were increasingly becoming a feature of Indonesian urban life in the 1990s, even before the events which exploded in tragic loss of life and destruction of property in May 1998 in Jakarta and other parts of the country, were a warning signal. To a considerable extent these events were fuelled by popular frustrations, frustrations which the political system, crafted by Suharto and his close associates over several decades, was increasingly unable to address.

The impact of the crisis

Once it had become clear in mid-1998 that the economic crisis in Indonesia was leading to a severe decline in real GDP, there was a flurry of activity on the part of the Indonesian government, international organisations including the World Bank, the UNDP and the ILO, and the main bilateral donors to try to estimate the impact on poverty. Unfortunately, much of the debate in the latter part of 1998 took place in a statistical vacuum, as complete GDP data for 1998 were not available, and the *Susenas* survey of household expenditures was carried out at three-year intervals, so that after 1996 the next one was scheduled for 1999. Thus in mid-1998, it was far from clear what impact the decline in GDP, however large it turned out to be, would have on consumption expenditures. Another complication was that the expenditure components of GDP were not all expected to fall at the same rate. To the extent that investment expenditures were falling

---

[11] According to the 1996 Labour Force Survey the employed labour force numbered some 85.7 million, of whom 7.65 million were in professional, technical, administrative and clerical positions. If we define the middle class as those in these occupation groups with at least junior secondary education, they comprised around 8.4 per cent of the total labour force.

faster than total GDP, the decline in consumption expenditures, which in the short run would drive poverty, was expected to be less than the fall in GDP. Nevertheless, these statistical uncertainties did not prevent the World Bank, the Indonesian government and the ILO/UNDP from publishing studies of the likely impact of the GDP decline on poverty in the latter part of 1998.

The initial World Bank estimates suggested only a minor impact on poverty, while the Indonesian government and the ILO/UNDP published estimates which suggested a much greater impact. The Indonesian government estimates predicted that the headcount measure of poverty in 1998 could jump to almost 40 per cent compared with 11.3 per cent in 1996 (Booth 2003: 123). As it turned out, the World Bank estimates were too optimistic while the other two were too pessimistic. Once the full GDP figures for 1998 and the results of a special *Susenas* conducted in late 1998 became available, it was clear that real per capita consumption expenditures had fallen by around 7.3 per cent, which was around half the decline in real per capita GDP. As would be expected, this led to an increase in poverty but the increase was not as severe as some of the initial predictions had indicated. Using the new poverty line for 1996, the CBS found that between 1996 and 1998, the headcount measure of poverty increased from 17.5 to 24.2 per cent, and numbers in poverty jumped from 34 to 49.5 million (CBS 2009: 181). Such an increase was serious, and the government adopted a number of policies to address it, which will be examined in the next chapter. But the increase in poverty was not as catastrophic as some other estimates were suggesting.

Other studies which came out over the next few years did produce evidence of a sharper increase in the headcount measure of poverty between 1996 and late 1998, and a faster decline until 2001, than the CBS figures. Suryahadi, Sumarto and Pritchett (2003: figure 2) estimated that the headcount measure of poverty was around 18.7 per cent in 1996 and fell to 15.3 per cent in mid-1997, just before the crisis began. It then jumped to 33.2 per cent in late 1998, implying that an extra 35 million people were pushed into absolute poverty as a result of the crisis. But from late 1998 to early 2002, their estimates found that the headcount measure dropped again to around 13 per cent, which was lower than before the crisis began. Certainly by 2000, both the CBS and other estimates agreed that poverty levels were trending downwards, although there was some dispute about the extent of the decline.

But these national estimates masked considerable variation by region. Before the crisis, it has been argued that the impact of economic growth on poverty decline was much greater in Java and Bali than in the more remote regions of Kalimantan, Maluku and Irian Jaya, with Sumatra and

Sulawesi falling between these two extremes (Friedman 2005: 193). The reason for this was that much better transport networks, together with faster industrial growth, allowed people to take advantage of off-farm employment opportunities without necessarily moving to urban areas. An analysis of the *Susenas* data from 1993 to 2002 across 260 districts found considerable regional variation both in the impact of the crisis and in the extent of the rebound after 1998. This study concluded that in a 'non-negligible' proportion of districts, the poverty rate in 2002 had at least doubled as a result of the crisis (Ravallion and Lokshin 2005).[12]

By 2000, another problem was drawing the attention of both the Indonesian government and foreign agencies – the rapid increase in violence, especially outside Java. According to one data base, the incidence of non-secessionist violence in Indonesia was quite low until 1996, but increased rapidly to a peak in 1999, and then fell back (Tadjoeddin 2014: 32). After 1998, violence against the Chinese minority in Java declined but there was an increase in conflict in several provinces outside Java, including Aceh, Irian Jaya (Papua), Maluku and parts of Sulawesi. In several of these regions the violence had a religious motivation: in Maluku, Papua and some parts of both Sulawesi and Kalimantan, indigenous Christian populations resented the influx of Moslem populations from Java and elsewhere. Tadjoeddin (2014: 109) argued that grievances centred on feelings of relative deprivation were crucial in triggering ethnic violence in the post-Suharto years.

To the extent that the increase in poverty which resulted from the crisis was a factor in accelerating feelings of relative deprivation in conflict-prone regions, it could be argued that the economic crisis was a causal factor in the escalation of ethnic and religious violence. One measure of relative deprivation is the proportion of the population consuming less than half the average; by this measure relative deprivation actually fell between 1996 and 1999 (Table 8.2). But it can plausibly be argued that the violence which erupted after 1997 was the result of longer-standing grievances about the impact of a range of government policies on different ethnic and religious groups across the country. The crisis thus fuelled tensions which had been simmering for years, and in several regions these

---

[12] These authors argued that it was the relatively well-integrated parts of the country which, although less poor in a steady state, were more vulnerable to an economy-wide crisis, and that the poor and isolated were less badly affected precisely because they had benefited less from the boom. But other researchers have argued that the impact of the crisis was felt 'by individuals throughout the income distribution' (Thomas et al. 2004: 82). This study focused on the impact of the crisis on educational enrolments. They found that reductions in spending on education were especially marked for poorer households, who held back younger children from attending school in order to allow older children to continue their education.

tensions boiled over into serious violence. A cross-sectional analysis of district-level data in Indonesia found that less developed districts (those with relatively low Human Development Index scores) were 'more likely to experience deadly ethno-communal conflict between 1997 and 2003' (Mancini 2008: 130). This paper also argued that those districts with high horizontal or inter-group inequalities, as proxied by high inter-group differences in child mortality rates, were more prone to serious ethnic conflict. As late as 2008, at the provincial level, many provinces which had suffered serious violence after 1996 had a higher headcount measure of poverty than the national average; this was especially the case for Papua and Maluku, but also was true for Aceh and Central Sulawesi (CBS 2009: 182). The causality probably ran both ways; the higher level of poverty, and the stronger perception of relative deprivation compared to other ethnic groups contributed to the violence, while the violence led to destruction of homes and infrastructure, the displacement of populations and the creation of an unfavourable investment climate, which in turn caused more people to fall below the poverty threshold.

Post-crisis developments

After 2001, incidents of serious violence fell; official data on poverty also showed a fall in the headcount measure (the percentage of the population below the poverty line) and a decline in numbers below the poverty line (CBS 2009: 181). But in 2006, the Central Board of Statistics announced that the headcount measure of poverty had increased to 17.8 per cent, up from 16 per cent in 2005. This was an embarrassment for the Yudhoyono government, which had set ambitious targets for a reduction in poverty by 2008 (Booth 2005: 211–12). Several commentators blamed the increase in poverty on the rise in rice prices which resulted from the rice import ban imposed in late 2005 (Basri and Patunru 2006: 309). The World Bank, in a comprehensive report on poverty issued in late 2006, supported this view, pointing out that the lower expenditure groups still spent about 25 per cent of their income on rice (World Bank 2006: 29).[13] They also argued that, without the conditional cash transfers, which were given to compensate poorer households for the rise in fuel prices which followed the reduction in fuel subsidies, the rise in poverty in 2006 would have been even higher. The impact of cash transfers and other government initiatives targeted to the poor will be examined in Chapter 9.

---

[13] Ikhsan (2005) and McCulloch (2008) discuss the impact of changes in rice prices on the poor in both urban and rural areas. Both agree that high rice prices benefit only a minority of farmers, mainly the non-poor, and hurt the rest of the population.

Between 2006 and 2013, there was a steady fall in the headcount measure of poverty as estimated by the CBS; by September 2013 it was estimated to be 11.5 per cent. This translated into 28.6 million people below the poverty line. But there was growing criticism of the CBS estimates. The official poverty line, which many had considered too low in the latter part of the Suharto era, had fallen to just over 30 per cent of average per capita consumption expenditures in urban areas by 2013, compared with 42 per cent in 1996 (Table 8.5). In rural areas it was half

Table 8.5 *Urban and rural poverty lines as percentage of* Susenas *average per capita consumption expenditures (ACE) in urban and rural areas, and ACE as percentage of consumption expenditures from national accounts (NAS)*

| | Poverty lines:% of *Susenas* ACE | | |
	Urban	Rural	ACE as % of NAS
1976	66.7	72.9	68.6 (71.0*)
1978	53.9	63.0	63.5
1980	56.0	61.6	53.7
1981	58.1	62.5	56.6
1984	54.5	58.1	57.8
1987	52.0	57.0	62.9
1990	46.8	54.7	61.3
1993	43.6	54.6	51.2
1996	38.0	52.0	50.1
Revised poverty line			
1996	41.8	59.5	50.1
1999	51.2	67.8	42.1
2002	47.8	63.2	42.4
2003	45.5	63.5	42.1
2004	44.9	63.4	41.8
2005	38.0	58.6	42.6
2007	41.0	57.6	38.4
2008	41.3	57.0	35.7
2009	40.5	56.4	36.8
2011 (March)	33.8	48.5	44.7
2012 (March)	33.2	49.7	43.5
2013 (March)	32.0	50.1	43.9

* Ratio of ACE to NAS is for 1970.

Sources: National accounts and poverty lines from *Statistical Yearbook of Indonesia*, various issues, and CBS website (www.bps.go.id). *Susenas* data from **Pengeluaran untuk Konsumsi Penduduk Indonesia** (Jakarta: Central Bureau of Statistics, various issues, and CBS (2008b)). Data for 2009 and 2010 from CBS website

of average expenditures, compared with 60 per cent in 1996. Some critics of the CBS poverty line also complained that the estimation methodology was far from transparent. In the next two sections these criticisms of the CBS estimates are addressed in more detail, and some alternative estimates discussed.

Measuring poverty in Indonesia: the CBS approach

The CBS began to publish estimates of poverty in 1984, using data from the 1976, 1978, 1980 and 1981 *Susenas* rounds. In these years, the estimates were derived from the consumption expenditure data reported in the *Susenas* consumption modules, based on samples of around 60,000 households. The estimates continued to use the module data until 1996, although the module questionnaire was frequently modified (Priebe 2014: 191–7). In 1993, the CBS implemented an extensive review of the way the poverty line was set, which led to an upward revision in both the urban and rural poverty lines and a consequent increase in the head-count measure of poverty (CBS 2009: 181). Ostensibly, these revisions were made because the concept of 'basic needs' was changing as Indonesians became on average richer, and as demand for goods and especially services, including education and health services, increased. In making these revisions to the official poverty line, the CBS was acknowledging that the poverty line should be set relative to average consumption levels in the society as a whole, as Esmara had argued in the 1980s.

The adjustments were probably intended to address the widespread claims by NGOs and others that the official line was 'too low'. The revisions made in 1996 did increase the poverty line in both urban and rural areas relative to average consumption expenditures, but since 1999 there had again been a steady fall in the poverty line relative to average per capita consumption expenditures, especially in urban areas (Table 8.5). By the early twenty-first century it was clear that the CBS poverty line was producing headcount measures of poverty which were well below those estimated by international agencies including the World Bank and the Asian Development Bank. These estimates will be reviewed in more detail later, but it is worth noting that the World Bank approach also attracted criticism for being too low.[14] In 2005 the

---

[14] Bhalla (2010: 134–7) has pointed out that although national poverty lines generally increase in line with per capita consumption data from the national accounts, a scatter diagram shows a large number of outliers. A number of Latin American countries have national poverty lines above two dollars a day, while several large Asian economies including China, India and Indonesia have poverty lines below what would be predicted given their average per capita consumption.

Table 8.6 *Percentage of the Indonesian population below poverty lines of Asian Development Bank, World Bank and CBS, 2005–2010*

Asian Development Bank and CBS, 2005	ICP PPP	Poverty line PPP	CBS
Percentage below poverty line	38.7	24.1	16.0
Numbers (million)	87.5	54.4	35.1
World Bank and CBS			
Percentages below:	**$1.25**	**$2.00**	**CBS**
2008	22.6	54.4	15.4
2009	20.4	52.7	14.2
2010	18.1	46.1	13.3

Source: Asian Development Bank (2008: 13); World Bank figures from http://data.worldbank.org/indicator/SI.POV.DDay and http://data.worldbank.org/indicator/SI.POV.2Day (Accessed 12.8. 2013); CBS figures from the *Statistical Yearbook of Indonesia*, various issues between 2005 and 2011.

ADB estimated that, using the poverty survey approach, 24 per cent of Indonesians were poor, compared with 16 per cent using the CBS approach. Using the $1.25 a day line, the WB estimates of headcount poverty were considerably higher than the CBS estimates in 2008–2010; the difference was much greater using the $2 a day measure (Table 8.6).

Another long-standing criticism of the CBS methodology was that the urban line is much higher than the rural one, the difference being far in excess of any reasonable estimate of cost of living differentials (Booth 1993: 65). In the 1980s, the much higher urban poverty line used by the CBS produced headcount measures of poverty which were higher in urban than rural areas, although many observers felt that the reverse was true. One study which used six rounds of the *Susenas* (1984, 1987, 1990, 1993, 1996, 1999) found that the headcount measure of poverty for Indonesia as a whole in all these years was consistently much lower in urban than rural areas (Friedman 2005: 170). By contrast, the CBS estimates for 1984, 1987 and 1990 found that the headcount measure was higher in urban areas, and only slightly lower in 1993 and 1996 (CBS 1997: 570). The differences can be explained by the different methodology which Friedman used to estimate the poverty lines in urban and rural areas.

After 1996, the CBS modified its methodology for estimating urban and rural poverty lines, and since 2006 the urban poverty line used by the CBS has been falling relative to the rural one; in 2012, the urban poverty line was around 17 per cent higher than in rural areas compared with

Table 8.7 *Percentage breakdown of numbers in poverty,*
urban and rural area, Java and Outer Islands, 1996 and 2012

Region	1996	2012
Urban		
Java	22.8	24.7
Outer Islands	9.3	11.8
Indonesia	32.1	36.5
Rural		
Java	33.7	30.5
Outer Islands	34.2	32.9
Indonesia	67.9	63.5
Indonesia		
Java	56.4	55.3
Outer Islands	43.6	44.7
Indonesia	100.0	100.0

Sources: CBS (1997: 570–4); CBS (2012b: 176–8).

33.5 per cent higher in 2006 (CBS 2012b: 175). The fall in the urban poverty line relative to the rural one may be the result of adjustments made by the CBS in the light of growing evidence that most of the country is urbanising rapidly, and that differences in living costs, and especially housing costs, between urban and rural areas are falling. A consequence of these narrowing differentials is that in 2012 the CBS estimates found that a high proportion of the total poor, 63.5 per cent, were in rural areas, in spite of the fact that around half the total population was living in urban areas (Table 8.7). The implications of this for policy will be examined in Chapter 9.

It has been noted that since the early 1990s, the CBS began to publish poverty estimates by province. These estimates have been widely used but some analysts have criticised them on the grounds that a different estimation technique can produce very different results. The estimates for 1999 given by Pradhan et al. (2000: table 2) using an iterative procedure to determine the poverty line by province and urban and rural areas indicate that the CBS method gives a higher headcount estimate of poverty in urban areas, and a lower estimate in rural areas, both at the national level and for individual provinces. While the aggregate estimate of poverty for the country as a whole was only slightly lower using the CBS method (23.6 per cent compared with 27.1 per cent) there were larger differences in a number of provinces. These authors argued that the iterative method chooses reference groups to reflect equivalent real incomes in urban and rural areas while the CBS method uses reference groups which reflect an assumption of higher living costs in urban areas.[15]

In his survey of changes in the CBS methodology for estimating poverty, Priebe (2014: 202) concluded that since 1984, the coverage, timing, questionnaire design and sample composition of the *Susenas* surveys have all changed many times, as has the technical procedure for estimating national and provincial poverty figures. These conclusions obviously throw doubt on the comparability of the estimates over time. Unfortunately, most of the studies which have used the *Susenas* data over the years have ignored these problems. The issue of the reliability of the *Susenas* will be taken up again later in the chapter.

Measuring poverty in Indonesia: other approaches

Given the problems with the CBS poverty line, and given the fall in the CBS poverty line relative to average per capita consumption expenditure shown in the *Susenas* surveys (which might itself be understated for reasons discussed later), there must be doubts about the official assertion that the headcount measure of poverty has been falling quite rapidly in Indonesia since 1999. An alternative approach is to estimate trends in relative poverty over time. As has been noted, this approach was adumbrated by Esmara in the 1980s, and is widely used in other parts of the world. As Atkinson (1975: 189) pointed out, the relative nature of poverty has long been recognised, going back as far as Adam Smith. In the Indonesian context, the choice of a relative poverty line of, for example, half of average per capita consumption expenditures can be criticised on the grounds that it confuses poverty measures with distributional considerations. On the other hand, it can also be argued that, as over half of all Indonesians now live in or close to urban areas, they increasingly tend to judge their living standards by comparing their situation with others living around them. Thus relative poverty measures may be more useful than estimates which use some absolute poverty line, determined using a methodology which is not always clear, and which produces results which may not be comparable over time.[16]

---

[15] Friedman (2005: 174) also produced estimates of poverty by province for 1987 and 1993. In rural areas, there was quite a high degree of correlation between his results and those of the CBS for 1993 ($r = 0.71$). But the correlation was lower in urban areas ($r = 0.52$).

[16] Ravallion (2009: 392) argues that a relative poverty measure that rises with the mean income of a country makes sense as a money metric of welfare 'if poor people experience relative deprivation – a negative externality from living in a well-off place'. He suggests that in traditional rural villages, people are less likely to experience such negative externalities, but relative poverty is likely to become more relevant in economies which are urbanising rapidly and where traditional notions of mutual assistance are disintegrating.

The evidence indicates that between 1970 and 1990, relative poverty defined in this way fell in rural Indonesia and in the country as a whole, although there was little change in urban areas. There was an increase in both urban and rural areas between 1990 and 1996 (Table 8.2). Between 1996 and 1999 relative poverty fell in both urban and rural areas as a result of the economic crisis, at the same time as the headcount measure was rising. The fall in relative poverty during the crisis reflected the faster fall in expenditures in the upper income groups relative to those in the lower deciles. But after 1999 the percentage of the population spending less than 50 per cent of the average rose again and by 2012 it was higher in urban areas than in any year since 1970 (Table 8.2). Between 1984 and 2012, the increase in urban areas appears to have been particularly rapid in Jakarta (Table 8.4). In rural areas, relative poverty also increased although had not returned to the 1970 figure by 2012.

In recent years, as panel data have become available, it is possible to estimate which households are likely to be most vulnerable to falling into poverty, especially in the face of shocks including natural disasters and economic downturns. Related to the issue of vulnerability is the distinction between chronic and transient poverty, where the chronically poor are those with incomes below the poverty line, who are likely to stay poor in future. The Indonesian evidence from the late 1990s showed that the GDP contraction in 1998 of around 13 per cent caused a sharp increase in the headcount measure of poverty. According to Suryahadi and Sumarto (2010: 59–60), not only did the headcount measure of poverty increase, but much of this was due to an increase in those classified as chronically poor. They estimated that the chronic poor made up only 20 per cent of the total poor in 1996, but 35 per cent of the much larger numbers of poor in 1999. They also argued that average vulnerability to poverty (the probability that a person will be poor in the future) also increased. Thus the total vulnerable group (the currently poor plus those likely to become poor) more than doubled as a percentage of the population over these three years.[17]

Another study examined poverty dynamics between 2005 and 2007, years which were characterised not by economic collapse but by quite robust economic growth (Dartanto and Nurkholis 2013). These authors used the CBS poverty line and found that 28 per cent of all poor households were chronically poor in the sense that they remained poor in both

---

[17] Strauss et al. (2004: 47–8) using the panel data from the Indonesian Family Life Survey found that between 1997 and 2000, there was considerable movement in and out of poverty. Over half those judged to be poor in 1997 were not poor in 2000, and over half those in poverty in 2000 were not poor in 1997. These authors argued that the Indonesian data were consistent with those from other parts of the world.

years, while 7 per cent of non-poor households became poor in the later year. They also found that raising the poverty line by 25 per cent led to an increase of over 100 per cent in the poverty rate. Rural households were more vulnerable to falling into poverty than urban ones, and those in Java-Bali were more vulnerable to negative income shocks than in other parts of the country. This study also used an ordered logit model to analyse the determinants of poverty; the results have important implications for poverty policy which will be analysed further in Chapter 9.

Post-1996 trends in inequality

The fact that the Gini coefficient estimated from household per capita consumption expenditure fell between 1970 and 1990 has often been used to support the claim that these two decades were characterised by egalitarian or pro-poor growth, although it was argued in a previous section that it is likely that disparities between urban and rural areas increased, and that the share of income accruing to the top earners also increased. The reasons for the equitable growth in rural areas are complex but have been attributed by some researchers to the rapid growth in agricultural output. Output per worker in the agricultural sector between 1968 and 1992 has been estimated to be 4.5 per cent per annum, which was high by international standards (Fuglie 2010: table 6). The increase in agricultural output provided more employment, both within agriculture and in other sectors such as trade and transport.[18] In addition in the latter part of the 1980s, there was an acceleration in growth of labour-intensive manufacturing which provided stable wage employment for a growing number of workers.

The increase in expenditure inequality which took place in the final years of the Suharto era could also have been due, in part at least to trends in agricultural output. Economic growth continued to be strong up until 1997, but after 1992 there was a sharp slowdown in growth of agricultural output per worker, from 4.5 per cent per annum to 1.5 per cent per annum, which continued through to 2001 (Fuglie 2010: table 6). This slowdown would have affected incomes in rural areas, and also would have encouraged more migration to urban areas. With the onset of the crisis in 1997, the Gini appears to have fallen quite sharply, and was still

---

[18] In their analysis of poverty reduction in Indonesia before and after the Asian Crisis, Suryahadi, Hadiwidjaja and Sumarto (2012: 223–4) found that growth in the urban service sector had the most powerful effect on poverty reduction both before and after the crisis. Agricultural growth also had an important impact on poverty decline, but after the crisis the impact was important in rural areas only.

below the 1996 level in 2005 (Table 8.2). The fall in the Gini after 1996 indicates that the better-off people in urban areas experienced a more severe downturn in nominal incomes and expenditure than the less well-off, although many Indonesians in both urban and rural areas were pushed below the poverty line between 1996 and 1999 (CBS 2009: 181).[19] Relative poverty fell sharply between 1996 and 1999 in both urban and rural areas (Table 8.2).

After 1999, there was an increase in the proportion of the population living below half average per capita consumption expenditure, especially in urban areas, which indicates that inequality was increasing in Indonesia in the first decade of the twenty-first century. This hypothesis is confirmed by the evidence that the Gini coefficient has been rising since the crisis of 1997/1998, and by 2011 was ten percentage points higher than in 1999 (Table 8.2). The increase in the Gini coefficient which occurred between 1999 and 2011 was accompanied by an increase in the share of income accruing to the top 20 per cent of the expenditure distribution, and a fall in the share of the bottom 40 per cent in both urban and rural areas. By 2011, when the Gini reached 0.41, the top 20 per cent in urban areas accounted for 49.1 per cent of total expenditures, while the bottom 20 per cent accounted for only 6.4 per cent (CBS 2011: 61).[20] In rural areas, the shares were 42.6 and 8.3 per cent. While these increases have caused alarm in some quarters, it has been argued that the level of inequality in Indonesia does not seem to be especially high compared with other parts of Asia, or indeed compared with other countries at medium levels of human development (Table 8.8). The ratio of income shares accruing to the top and bottom quintiles of the income distribution was, according to the World Bank figures, considerably lower than in Malaysia or China, and much lower than Latin American countries at similar levels of per capita GDP. But it should be noted that while income

---

[19] Skoufias, Suryahadi and Sumarto (2000) argued that inequality indicators actually increased between 1997 and 1998, using real rather than nominal expenditure data. This shows that inflation hit the poorer groups more severely. The evidence on the percentage of total income accruing to the top 1 per cent, and the top 5 per cent of the income distribution in the years between 1996 and 2001 showed an increase in both cases (Leigh and van der Eng 2008). According to these estimates, the share accruing to the top 1 per cent increased from 9.7 per cent in 1996 to 15.5 per cent in 2001, although it fell after that, and by 2004 was below the 1996 figure. This suggests that the top income earners were protected from the reduction in earnings which affected the middle groups in urban areas.

[20] Aswicahyono, Hill and Narjoko (2011: 127) have argued that there was a sharp slowdown in industrial employment growth since the crisis of the late 1990s. This slowdown was in part due to slower industrial growth but also due to a fall in the elasticity of employment growth to output growth. Manning (2012: 238–9) argued that while unemployment fell since 2006, many of the new jobs were in casual employment, with low pay'.

Table 8.8 *Countries ranked by HDI: per capita GDP, percentage share of the bottom quintile in total consumption, and ratio of top to bottom quintiles*

Country	HDI rank*	Per capita GDP*	% share bottom 20%	Ratio
Sri Lanka**	92	4,066	7.7	5.8
Tunisia**	94	6,105	6.7	6.4
Fiji	96	4,210	6.2	8.0
Jordan**	100	4,469	7.7	5.7
China	101	6,519	4.7	10.0
Thailand	103	7,578	6.7	7.0
El Salvador	107	6,083	3.7	14.4
Bolivia***	108	3,613	2.1	28.2
Paraguay	111	3,615	3.3	16.7
Egypt***	112	4,559	9.2	4.4
Moldova	113	2,476	7.3	5.7
Philippines	114	3,032	6.0	8.3
Honduras	120	3,552	2.0	30.0
Indonesia	121	3,814	7.6	5.8
South Africa	121	7,303	2.7	25.3
Kyrgyzstan	125	2,096	6.8	6.4
Tajikistan	126	1,726	8.3	4.8
Vietnam***	127	2,430	7.4	5.9
India**	136	3,477	8.5	5.0
Cambodia	138	1,878	7.9	5.6
Lao PDR	138	2,308	7.6	5.9

* HDI rank 2012; per capita GDP data from Heston, Summers and Aten (2012) and refer to 2005 PPP data; Laspeyres index derived from growth rates of C, I and G at 2005 prices. Unless otherwise noted all data refer to 2009.
** 2010 data.
*** 2008 data.
Note: Ratio refers to the ratio of the income/expenditures share of the top 20 per cent of the distribution to the bottom 20 per cent.
Sources: HDI data from http://hdr.undp.org/en/statistics; GDP data from Heston, Summers and Aten (2012). Other data from http://data.worldbank.org/indicator/SI.DST.05TH.20? countries (accessed 12.8.2013).

data are used to estimate quintile shares in many countries, in Indonesia expenditure data are used. Even if expenditures are accurately measured, they tend to show lower inequality, because richer households save more.

Much of the discussion about trends in inequality in Indonesia and in other developing countries has used data from household income and expenditure surveys. To the extent that these surveys are unreliable, for reasons further discussed later, the inequality indictors derived from them must also be suspect, as must the international comparisons shown in Table 8.8. But what other indicators are available? Very little work has been done on inequality trends in non-monetary indicators, either in Indonesia or in other parts of Asia. An exception is a study of changes in disparities in under-5 child mortality by income groups in a number of developing countries (Minujin and Delamonica 2003). It is well known that in many countries in Asia, Africa and Latin America, infant and child mortality is higher among poorer groups but on average has also been falling in recent decades. Minujin and Delamonica looked at rates of decline from the mid-1980s to the mid-1990s across quintile groups and found that in a number of countries the rate of decline was much higher in the richest quintile than in the poorest quintile. The Indonesian data were compared with ten other countries where child mortality had fallen over these years; the disparity in the percentage declines was larger than in most of the other countries. In the Philippines, under-5 mortality in the richest quintile was 24.5 per thousand in 1998 compared with 78.7 per thousand in the poorest quintile; comparable figures for Indonesia in 1997 were 28.8 and 108.2.

It is also well known that there are large disparities in post-primary enrolments by economic status in Indonesia. In 2003, the data from the *Susenas* module on education found that enrolments rates among those aged 19–24 in the top quintile of the income distribution in urban areas was 33.5 per cent; it was much the same in 2012. Among the bottom 40 per cent in rural areas the figure was 2.7 per cent in 2003 and had increased only slightly to 4.7 per cent by 2012. Even in urban areas, less than 12 per cent of young people in the nineteen to twenty-four age group from the bottom 40 per cent of the expenditure distribution were enrolled in post-secondary institutions (Table 8.9). Children from

Table 8.9 *School participation rates[a] by expenditure group and location, 2012*

	7–12	13–15	16–18	19–24
Urban				
Bottom 40%	98.2	87.0	54.1	11.6
Middle 40%	98.8	93.2	66.3	16.6
Top 20%	99.4	95.5	74.9	32.6
Rural				
Bottom 40%	96.2	84.1	45.9	4.7
Middle 40%	98.1	89.6	60.8	11.2
Top 20%	98.7	92.8	68.4	22.0

[a] Percentage of the population in the relevant age groups who are attending school.
Sources: CBS (2013).

better-off households in urban areas have a much better chance of continuing to post-secondary education than those from poor rural backgrounds, and the disparity in enrolment rates has narrowed only slightly between 2003 and 2012.

By the second decade of the twenty-first century, a consensus was emerging that economic growth was less pro-poor during the *reformasi* years than during the Suharto era. This conclusion was very disappointing to those Indonesians and foreign observers who had expected that a more open and democratic political system would widen economic opportunity and thus lead to a more egalitarian society. In fact the opposite seemed to be happening after 2001. Some analysts placed the blame on economic policies post-Suharto including the re-emergence of a commodity boom based on gas, coal and agricultural commodities, especially palm oil, changes in labour market policies which have deterred employers from hiring new workers, and the growth of budgetary subsidies on fuel and electricity which have benefited the middle classes and squeezed expenditures which might have assisted the poor (Yusuf, Sumner and Rum 2014: 251). There is probably some truth in these arguments, although past history shows that commodity booms need not lead to greater inequality in Indonesia. The oil boom of the 1970s seems not to have led to greater inequality, at least as shown by the *Susenas* data, although urban–rural expenditure inequalities did increase (Tables 8.2 and 8.3). This was in part at least because of the government's success in using the extra government revenues to assist the rural sector, and especially rice farmers, although at the same time urban incomes and expenditure were rising faster than those in rural areas. Labour market policies over the 1970s and 1980s were also flexible; minimum wages were quite low and there was less regulation of hiring and firing practices (Manning 2014). The redirection of budgetary expenditures in the post-Suharto era to recapitalise the banking system and to finance large subsidies to non-poor groups has certainly had an adverse effect on equality, although arguably longer-term factors have also played a part.

One such factor concerns access to education. It was pointed out in Chapter 4 that post-primary educational enrolments stagnated in the last decade of Suharto's rule, mainly because of the high costs of school attendance. Many young people joined the labour force over this period with poor skills and little opportunity for improving them. To the extent that most were still in the labour force after 2001, they comprised a large group of poorly paid workers in unproductive jobs. If they came from households which controlled agricultural land, they would have benefited from rising prices of agricultural commodities. But many would have come from poorer households with little or no land. They were trapped in poorly remunerated service sector employment. At the same time young people from richer households in urban areas had a much better chance of completing high school and gaining a tertiary qualification which at least gave them the opportunity of seeking a well-paid career. Improving access to education, and improving its quality is thus key to achieving a more equal society in Indonesia.

The other important factor determining overall inequality trends is access to land. Since the 1980s, the evidence indicates that access to land is a crucial factor in determining the total income of farm households. The data from the farm income survey attached to the 1983 Agricultural Census found that the monthly income of households rose by holding size. While households controlling only small amounts of land derived more from off-farm employment than households controlling larger holdings, the income from off-farm activities was not sufficient to bring their total income up to the level of those households with larger holdings (Booth 2002: 185). The households with larger holdings were apparently able to access credit and other government services which in turn enabled them to give their children better education and thus allow them to access more lucrative off-farm employment.

The evidence from agricultural censuses since 1973 indicates that average holding size appears to have been declining, and the number of micro holdings, of less than 0.1 hectares, has been growing. It appears that more and more Indonesians in rural areas are subsisting off tiny plots while a smaller but growing number are cultivating larger farms (Booth 2012a: 72). Both groups are diversifying their income sources but over time it is probable that those households controlling larger amounts of land will be more successful in increasing household incomes in absolute terms, especially if they are able to access credit. If these trends persist, it is probable that agricultural growth will contribute to greater income disparities within rural areas in future decades.

How reliable are the *Susenas* surveys?

Because they have been so widely used in the analysis of poverty and income distribution in Indonesia since the 1960s, as well as in the comparative data compiled by the World Bank and other international agencies, the *Susenas* surveys have been subject to considerable critical scrutiny over the years. In their defence, it has been argued that the CBS follows internationally approved data collection procedures in their social surveys, and the data are thus unlikely to be of lower quality than those collected by countries such as the Philippines and India, both of which have been conducting household surveys since the

1950s. But Priebe's analysis raised worrying issues about inconsistencies in the way that the *Susenas* surveys have been conducted over time, as well as changes over time in the CBS methodology for estimating the poverty line.

A frequently used check on the accuracy of household survey data is to compare them with the household expenditure component of the national accounts. Several studies have shown that successive *Susenas* surveys since the 1970s have diverged from the national accounts data by an increasing amount. Cameron (2002: 10) pointed out that over the 1990s, the *Susenas* were only about 50 per cent of the national accounts data. The proportion had fallen much further to around 36 per cent by 2008/2009 (Table 8.5). In the years from 2011 to 2013 the March quarter *Susenas* results can be compared with the quarterly national accounts data, probably a more accurate procedure. For these three years the proportion was around 44–45 per cent. It was only slightly higher for food expenditures compared with non-food expenditures (Table 8.10).

Disparities of around 50 per cent have also been found in the data in both the Philippines and India. In the Philippines, the family income and expenditure surveys (FIES) carried out in 1961, 1965 and 1971 yielded estimates of household consumption expenditure which amounted to around 70 per cent of the national accounts data, but in 1975 it fell to about half (Mangahas 1982: 133–4). Mangahas argued that the gross under-coverage revealed in the 1975 survey meant that the data should not be used to estimate inequality indicators, including decile shares and the Gini coefficient. In India, the ratio declined from around 68 per cent in 1983 to 56 per cent in 1999/2000, which means that estimates of the growth of household consumption expenditures derived from the national accounts data have been considerably more rapid than those based on the survey data (Deaton 2010: 201–2). As Deaton points out, the Indian debate on the discrepancies between the survey data and

Table 8.10 *Food and non-food expenditures:* Susenas *as percentage of private consumption expenditures, national accounts*

	Food	Non-food	Total
2011 (March)	46.2	43.3	44.7
2012 (March)	46.9	40.4	43.5
2013 (March)	46.4	41.7	43.9

Source: www.bps.go.id.

those from the national accounts has been going on for several decades, and has produced analysis which is of considerable relevance to other countries as well, including Indonesia.

The problems which plague social survey data are well known and have been widely discussed in many parts of the world (Deaton 2010: 205–12). First there are difficulties with survey coverage, and accuracy of response. To what extent are the expenditures of the better-off excluded or undercounted? Government enumerators are not infrequently denied access to the mansions of the wealthy, or if they do get access they may not get very truthful answers to their questions. Even middle class households may be reluctant to give accurate answers. A second problem is that regions where transport links are poor or where there is conflict are often excluded. These are likely to be poorer regions, so their exclusion can bias poverty estimates downwards. Another problem is that the recall period of a week for food expenditures means that responses can be affected by the fasting month in Moslem countries, or by other short-term factors. But a recall period of one year for non-food expenditures is a long one for many households and people might simply forget some expenditures.[21] There is also the problem of home-produced goods and services, which are probably under-reported or simply excluded altogether. In addition, purchases of food prepared outside the home may be under-reported. Implicit rental payments for owner-occupied housing are included in Indonesia but probably under-estimated (Priebe 2014: 193).

Some analysts have argued that the consumption data from the national accounts should also be treated with caution, and should not be uncritically used as a quality standard against which survey data must be tested (Deaton 2010: 212–6; Havinga, Kamanou and Viet 2010). While non-exchanged services are excluded from both the national accounts and survey data, non-exchanged production of goods might be included in the national accounts but excluded from surveys. Some other important consumption items which are excluded from most surveys include the imputed value of financial intermediation, and the consumption of non-profit institutions including NGOs. NGOs have been proliferating in many parts of Asia and Africa in recent decades, but it is very difficult to estimate their consumption expenditures. Last but by no

---

[21] It is sometimes argued that, given the longer recall period, non-food expenditures could be more prone to understatement than food expenditures, although the evidence in Table 8.10 suggests that food expenditures are almost as low relative to the national income data as non-food expenditures. According to Priebe (2014: 193) the recall period for food expenditures has always been one week, but for non-food expenditures it has changed since 1984, from three months to the monthly average over a twelve month period.

means least, the household consumption component in the national accounts is not infrequently estimated as a residual (GDP is estimated by the production method, and government consumption, investment and net exports are then subtracted). The resulting number may then be subject to further modification, but is likely to incorporate many of the errors in the other components.

Given all the problems with both survey and national accounts data, the researcher in Indonesia, as in many other parts of the world, has to form his or her own judgement about how to use the data. There are those who argue that the gap between the *Susenas* consumption estimates and the national accounts data has in recent years become unacceptably large and thus the *Susenas* should not be used to estimate trends in either inequality or poverty. Others argue that the data may yield misleading figures on inequality, especially when there is evidence of under-reporting on the part of the well-off households, but can be used to estimate trends in poverty. The World Bank and the Asian Development Bank appear to think that survey data can be used to generate internationally comparable numbers on both poverty and inequality, although the World Bank has, in some publications, expressed concerns about whether the inequality indicators derived from the *Susenas* surveys are accurate (World Bank 2006: 35). It is unlikely that these divergent views will be reconciled in the immediate future, either in Indonesia or elsewhere.

Indonesia's performance in international perspective

By the early twenty-first century, several different approaches were being used by international agencies to rank countries according to the headcount measure of poverty. In the early 1990s, the World Bank began to use the 'dollar a day' poverty line, where the dollar is converted into different currencies using exchange rates adjusted to allow for differences in the purchasing power of currencies In recent years, partly in response to criticisms that the dollar a day line was 'too low', the World Bank has been using two poverty lines, $1.25 and $2.00 a day.[22] Estimates of the headcount measure of poverty using these two poverty lines are available on World Bank websites. The data for Indonesia and twenty-one other countries for years between 2008 and 2010 are given in Table 8.11. The

[22] Ravallion (2010) gives an explanation and justification of the World Bank's approach to poverty measurement, and replies to the criticisms of Reddy and Pogge (2010). Pogge (2010) provides a rejoinder to Ravallion. The critics argue that the $1.25 line is arbitrary and too low, and also the World Bank's method of calculating poverty relies on questionable data on purchasing power parities (PPPs).

countries are ranked according to their Human Development Index (HDI) score in 2012; almost all were classified as medium human development countries.

What is striking is that, although these countries are all considered to have attained at least medium human development and per capita GDP within the range of $1,700–$6,500, there are wide variations in the headcount measures of poverty.[23] The estimates for Indonesia show that 20.4 per cent of the population in 2009 were below the $1.25 poverty line and 52.7 per cent were below the $2 line. These figures are higher than for the Philippines, Vietnam and Cambodia although all three countries had lower per capita GDP than Indonesia.[24] The two headcount measures are also much higher for Indonesia than for Jordan and Egypt, where per capita GDP was only slightly higher than in Indonesia. The headcount measure for Indonesia was also higher than in three countries that were formerly part of the Soviet Union (Moldova, Tajikistan, Kyrgyzstan), and for several Latin American countries whose per capita GDP was lower than Indonesia's. Only India, where per capita GDP in 2010 was 88 per cent of that in Indonesia, and Laos had higher headcount measures.

The figures in Table 8.11 can be compared with two other comparative data sets published by the Asian Development Bank (ADB) in 2008 and 2014. These figures were estimated using a methodology which was supposed to produce poverty lines which were comparable across Asian developing countries. The 2008 study argued that the estimates of consumption PPPs taken from the International Comparisons data set are not ideal for generating comparable estimates of poverty across countries as the consumption patterns of poor households are often different from average patterns for the country as a whole. The poor may also consume different types of staples bought in different quantities, and at different prices from those paid by non-poor people. In addition to estimates of poverty using poverty lines based on consumption PPP data, the 2008 ADB study produced two further estimates, including one based on the consumption shares of the poor and also on price data collected in poverty surveys. These data attempted to estimate the prices actually paid by the poor for goods in the quantities in which they were bought. In the Indonesian case, the poverty line derived from the poverty survey data produced a headcount measure of poverty of 24.1 per cent in 2005, compared with 16 per cent according to the CBS estimates (Table 8.6).

[23] The correlation coefficient between per capita GDP and poverty for the twenty-one countries, although negative, is not very high (–0.325 for the poverty headcount measure using $1.25 per day).

[24] The data on Vietnam and Cambodia have also been subject to considerable criticism; Pincus and Sender (2008) analyse the problems with the Vietnamese data.

Table 8.11 *Countries ranked by HDI index: per capita GDP and headcount poverty measures, c. 2009*

Country	HDI rank*	Per capita* GDP	% Below $1.25	% Below $2.00
Sri Lanka**	92	4,066	4.1	23.9
Tunisia**	94	6,105	1.1	4.3
Fiji	96	4,210	5.9	22.9
Jordan**	100	4,469	0.1	1.6
China	101	6,519	11.8	27.2
Thailand	103	7,578	0.4	4.6
El Salvador	107	6,083	9.0	16.9
Bolivia***	108	3,613	15.6	24.9
Paraguay	111	3,615	7.6	14.2
Egypt***	112	4,559	1.7	15.4
Moldova	113	2,476	0.4	7.1
Philippines	114	3,032	18.4	41.5
Honduras	120	3,552	17.9	29.8
Indonesia	121	3,814	20.4	52.7
South Africa	121	7,303	13.8	31.3
Kyrgyzstan	125	2,096	6.2	21.7
Tajikistan	126	1,726	6.6	27.7
Vietnam***	127	2,430	16.9	43.4
India**	136	3,477	32.7	68.8
Cambodia	138	1,878	18.6	49.5
Lao PDR	138	2,308	33.9	66.0

* HDI rank 2012; per capita GDP data from Heston, Summers and Aten (2012) and refer to 2005 PPP data (Laspeyres index derived from growth rates of c, l and g at 2005 prices). Unless otherwise noted all data refer to 2009.
** 2010 data.
*** 2008 data.
Sources: HDI data from http://hdr.undp.org/en/statistics; GDP data from Heston, Summers and Aten (2012). Poverty data from http://data.worldbank.org/indicator/SI.POV.DDay and http://data.worldbank.org/indicator/ SI.POV.2Day (Accessed 12.8. 2013).

A further study published by the Asian Development Bank in 2014 used a poverty line of $1.51 a day, instead of the $1.25 a day used by the World Bank. It was argued that this was more appropriate to Asian conditions. Using this poverty line adjusted for differences in prices, the headcount estimate for Indonesia was 33 per cent in 2005 and 28 per cent in 2010. In 2010 the headcount measure in Indonesia was higher than in any other Southeast Asian country except Laos (Table 8.12). Although there was a slight decline in the numbers of poor in Indonesia compared with other Southeast Asian countries, the rate of decline was lower than

Table 8.12 *Percentage of the population below the $1.51 poverty line and numbers in poverty: Southeast Asian countries, 2005 and 2010*

Country	2005		2010	
	Percentage	Numbers*	Percentage	Numbers*
Laos	54.1	3.1	38.1	2.4
Indonesia	32.9	74.9	28.0	67.2
Philippines	30.9	26.4	26.9	25.1
Cambodia	45.5	6.1	25.4	3.6
Vietnam	35.6	29.4	22.4	19.4
Thailand	2.5	1.7	1.1	0.8
Malaysia	0.9	0.2	0.4	0.1
Average	27.9	141.7	22.0	118.6

* Numbers in millions.
Source: Asian Development Bank (2014: 11).

the average for the region as a whole, and much lower than in Cambodia and Vietnam. These data suggest that Indonesia's achievement in reducing numbers in poverty over these five years was not very impressive in comparison with other Southeast Asian countries; only the Philippines had a lower rate of decline.

Both the World Bank and the ADB estimates measure income or expenditure poverty, that is, they attempt to measure the proportion of the population which does not have sufficient income or expenditure to purchase a basket of basic needs. Other rankings use non-monetary indicators including demographic and educational indicators. Probably the best known composite index, which includes both monetary and non-monetary indicators, is the HDI, which the UNDP has been publishing since the early 1990s.[25] This index divides countries into four groups, very high, high, medium and low human development. As is clear from Table 8.10, there are considerable variations within the medium human development group (which includes six countries in Southeast Asia) in both per capita GDP and income/expenditure poverty as estimated by the World Bank. Countries such as Vietnam and Cambodia rank more highly on the HDI than on per capita GDP alone, because they perform better on the non-monetary indicators. In recent years, Indonesia has ranked slightly higher than Vietnam, Laos and Cambodia but lower than Thailand and the Philippines.

---

[25] The HDI does not incorporate distributional data; all the figures used are averages.

A recent initiative by the Oxford Poverty and Human Development Initiative has been the construction of a Multidimensional Poverty Index (MPI). The MPI is a composite index which reflects 'deprivations in very rudimentary services and core human functionings for people across 104 countries' (Alkire and Santos 2010: 7). It has three dimensions, health, education and the standard of living. Two indicators are used for health (child mortality and nutrition) and two for education (years of schooling and child enrolment). Six indicators are used for standard of living (electricity, clean drinking water, sanitation, flooring, cooking fuel and assets). Each dimension is equally weighted in compiling the composite index. The data used are derived from surveys carried out between 2000 and 2007. Indonesia was ranked 53, lower than Thailand, China, the Philippines, Vietnam and (perhaps surprisingly) Myanmar, but higher than Laos and Cambodia, and all the South Asian countries except Sri Lanka.

Another initiative which has attracted attention in recent years is the converse of poverty estimates, the estimation of the number of people in the developing world who could be considered 'middle class'. As Birdsall (2010: 5) pointed out, there is as yet no agreement among development economists on the minimum income necessary to become 'middle class'. She suggested a minimum income/expenditure of ten dollars a day although others have argued for a lower threshold. She also argues that the top 5 per cent of households should be considered 'rich' rather than middle class. These definitions are arbitrary and in fact in a number of countries they lead to the result that there is no middle class at all. All the households with a per capita income of ten dollars a day or more are in the top 5 per cent of the income distribution and thus should be considered 'rich'. This was true of Thailand and urban China in 1990, and even as late as 2005, the numbers earning or spending more than ten dollars a day in India and Indonesia were below 5 per cent of the population (Birdsall 2010: 10).

A further set of estimates prepared by the ADB (2010) confirm the Birdsall argument that the middle class in Indonesia is small. In 2005 there were only 2.55 million Indonesians with expenditures above ten dollars a day. This number was well below that in Thailand and indeed below Malaysia and the Philippines, in spite of the fact that total population in all three countries is well below that of Indonesia. Even if a lower cut-off is used ($4 per day) the absolute numbers in Indonesia are lower than in Thailand, although higher than in Malaysia and the Philippines. However defined, the conclusion based on the household survey data is that the middle class in Indonesia is still quite tiny by Asian standards, both in absolute terms and as a percentage of the population.

Are these results plausible? Is it really the case that the absolute size of the middle class in Indonesia was less than in both Malaysia and Thailand in the early years of the twenty-first century? Or do the results confirm the argument that the *Susenas* figures understate expenditures compared with those in other parts of Asia, including Thailand and Malaysia? To the extent that consumption expenditures on the part of the better-off are under-reported in Indonesia, the estimates of numbers in the middle class could be seriously flawed. If expenditures are under-reported in the lower expenditure groups as well, then the comparative poverty estimates given in Table 8.12 are also open to question. Given the data problems, all comparative estimates of poor and non-poor in Indonesia should be treated with caution.

Conclusions

Debates about who has benefited from accelerated economic growth in Indonesia began in the early years of the Suharto era, and continued after that era came to an end in 1998. In spite of the data problems, and the problems inherent in measuring changes in poverty and living standards in a large and diverse country, some conclusions can be drawn from the many studies which have been published. It seems indisputable that most Indonesians did experience considerable improvement in living standards over the decades from 1970 to 2010, in spite of the severe decline in GDP in 1998, and the slow recovery. Non-monetary indicators including infant and child mortality rates and literacy rates showed marked improvement. Most Indonesians were consuming more calories and protein in the early twenty-first century than previous generations and were spending longer in formal education. But Indonesia is hardly unusual in these achievements; many countries have seen considerable improvement in non-monetary indicators of living standards since the 1970s, and recent international rankings show that Indonesia still scores quite badly on some indicators.

The headcount measure of poverty estimated by the CBS has also declined, although there was a sharp increase as a result of the fall in national income in 1998. The increase was temporary, and according to the CBS figures, the headcount measure of poverty had returned to the 1996 level by 2003, after which it has continued to fall with the temporary exception of 2006. But the CBS estimates of poverty are open to criticism on two counts. First the poverty line is estimated according to a methodology which is opaque, and which appears to have changed over time, both before and after 1996. The resulting poverty line has fallen relative to average per capita consumption expenditures, especially if the national accounts data are used. Second, the *Susenas* surveys themselves have not been implemented on a consistent basis, which means that their results might not be comparable over time. Their estimates of consumption expenditures have fallen over time relative to those in the national accounts. To the extent that the *Susenas* data have under-reported consumption on the part of the higher expenditure groups, the inequality indicators based on them are likely to be flawed. To the extent that they under-report consumption in the lower expenditure groups, and the extent of under-reporting has increased over time, the official poverty estimates published by the CBS could have understated the extent of poverty decline.

These problems also throw doubt on the international comparisons of poverty estimates which have been published by the World Bank and the Asian Development Bank. These estimates use the household expenditure data from the *Susenas* surveys, and apply a poverty line which is supposedly corrected for differences in purchasing power across countries. But as the Asian Development Bank showed in its 2008 estimates, not only do the poor have different consumption baskets from the non-poor, but they often face different prices. Estimating poverty lines which take these differences into account is a complex statistical exercise. What does seem clear is that when internationally comparable poverty lines are applied to the Indonesian data, the headcount measure of poverty is higher than the CBS measure. In the Southeast Asian context Indonesia has a higher headcount measure of poverty than in countries such as Vietnam and Cambodia in spite of their lower per capita GDP.

Data problems also affect most estimates of inequality which have been made over the past four decades. Gini coefficients estimated from the *Susenas* showed little change between 1970 and 1990, and only a modest increase between 1990 and 1996. But other estimates suggest that the increase in inequality might well have been higher. Certainly many Indonesians believed that inequality in incomes was increasing between 1970 and 1996. As with the poverty estimates, the uncertainties over the *Susenas* data throw doubt on the international comparisons which suggest that inequality in Indonesia is lower than in other parts of Asia, or other parts of the world. A more accurate picture of Indonesia's progress in reducing inequality can probably be derived from the non-monetary indicators such as infant and child mortality rates. Some analyses have shown that not only do mortality rates differ widely by expenditure groups in Indonesia, but that the disparities may be widening over time.

The finding that inequality in consumption expenditures has increased in the first decade of the twenty-first century seems to have been accepted by many analysts. To the extent that this finding is correct, it raises important questions about the impact of political liberalisation on economic disparities. Has greater democracy led to more populist policies, such as fuel and energy subsidies, which have benefited the middle classes more than poorer groups? Have freer trade unions led to higher minimum wages which have had a negative impact on employment opportunities for many poor jobseekers? Is the rise in inequality the result of a systematic failure over decades to provide access to good-quality education for all Indonesian children? Or is it linked to persistent inequalities in ownership of assets, including agricultural land? These questions need to be addressed in public policy debates in Indonesia if the country is to move closer to the elusive goal of a just and prosperous society.

9 The changing role of government from the colonial era to the post-Suharto years

The colonial era: towards a modern fiscal state?

As was argued in Chapter 2, the ethical policy led to a rapid growth in government expenditures on public works, including irrigation, harbour works, post and transport and railways and tramways (de Jong and Ravesteijn 2008: 66). By 1921, public works amounted to around 40 per cent of the colonial budget. The Minister of the Colonies, Idenburg, doubted that an ambitious programme of public works could be funded from current revenues, and thought that loan authorisation powers were essential if these projects were to be completed. After 1915, borrowing increased and by the early 1920s, government debt had risen relative to national income and exports. The debt service ratio (debt service charges as a ratio of export earnings) was almost 6 per cent in 1923 (Booth 1998: table 4.4). By the standards of the late twentieth century, this was hardly a high figure. But it caused concern in the Netherlands, especially in the central bank, and among critics of the ethical policy who argued that it was an extravagant welfare programme that the colony could not afford, and whose longer term benefits were unclear. Government expenditures did grow in real terms until the end of the 1920s, but fell in the first part of the 1930s.

The increased reliance on loan finance was in part due to a perception on the part of colonial officials that it would be difficult to raise more revenues from the indigenous population. Several studies were carried out over the 1920s into tax burdens in both Java and other parts of the country, and concluded that it would be difficult to squeeze much more out of even the better-off elements among the native population. Chinese businesses were often difficult to reach through the income tax, given that their records were often kept in Chinese rather than Dutch. Both the Chinese and European populations were taxed through excises and import duties, and by the end of the 1930s, personal and corporate income taxes accounted for 22 per cent of all government revenues, which was a higher percentage than in most other parts of Southeast Asia (Booth 2013a: table 4). Government borrowing increased sharply after 1930 and by 1933, the debt service ratio had increased to 20 per cent, although it fell later in the decade. In 1935, outstanding debt per capita was higher than in any other Asian colony except British Malaya. Arguably the revenue system in the late colonial era was more diversified than in many other colonial territories, although in per capita terms revenues were well below those in British Malaya or in Taiwan.

In his study of the evolution of the fiscal state in England, Japan and China, He (2013: 4) contrasted a traditional with a modern fiscal state. He argued that the latter had two closely connected institutional features. One was a centralised tax collection, which allowed the state 'to allocate spending out of a consolidated source of revenue', and thus greatly improved efficiency in managing government finance. A centralised tax system also gave the government a guaranteed source of income which in turn permitted the government to borrow from financial markets; such markets were the second pre-requisite for a modern fiscal state. He (2013: 5–18) argued that while a modern fiscal state could only evolve in the context of a commercialised economy, it did not require a high level of industrial development. England in the eighteenth century and Japan in the mid-nineteenth century were not yet industrial economies, but both had a centralised tax system and a financial system which allowed government to leverage their tax revenues to secure long-term loans from financial markets.

Arguably, Indonesia in the late colonial era also possessed these two features of a modern fiscal state. The revenue system was tightly centralised, which allowed the central government to borrow. But all the borrowing was from capital markets in the Netherlands, London and New York. The domestic capital market remained undeveloped, and this continued to be the case after 1950, which had important consequences for government finance in the post-independence era. While the Dutch colonial government had increased revenues and expenditures, the ambitious expenditure programmes had to rely increasingly on external borrowing. There was an opportunity to develop domestic capital markets after 1900 but this was not taken.

By the 1930s, the Dutch also had established a comprehensive system of regulating production and trade in the private sector. This was partly the result of the restrictions imposed by international commodity agreements, which by the 1930s affected many of Indonesia's main exports, including tin, sugar, rubber and tea (van Gelderen 1939: Chapter IV). But in addition the Dutch were worried about problems of 'over capacity' in sectors such as coffee and rubber. This resulted from the rapid growth of smallholder production, which was competing with production of the large estates. The attempt to regulate smallholder production of crops such as rubber in the 1930s met with limited success, but it left behind a tradition of government control of markets which continued in the post-independence era. This control extended beyond production of export crops to other markets for both goods and services.

Strong rhetoric, weak state? 1950–1968

In the immediate aftermath of the transfer of power in 1949, most nationalists envisaged an important, indeed dominant, role for government in the economy. The reform of the colonial fiscal system was given priority, and the Natsir cabinet was able to implement some changes to the tax system, including the introduction of a sales tax. The surge in the value of exports as a result of the Korean war boom, together with increased imports, led to rapid growth in revenues from trade taxes, which increased to over half of all government revenues. In real per capita terms, government revenues in 1951 were probably somewhat higher than in 1938, while expenditures were roughly the same (Table 3.2). Given that real per capita GDP was lower than in the late 1930s, this was an impressive achievement for the new administration. But it was based on external circumstances which could not be sustained. By 1955, revenues and expenditures per capita had fallen to well below the 1953 level. More disturbing was the evidence that budget deficits were increasing; by 1960 the deficit was around 5 per cent of GDP (Booth 1998: 165). A deficit of this magnitude need not have led to a rapid increase in inflation had it been financed through foreign aid or borrowing, or through domestic borrowing from the private sector. But increasingly the government financed the deficit by borrowing from the central bank, in effect printing money.

As Sundrum (1973: 75) pointed out, as inflation accelerated, confidence in the stability of the currency declined; rising inflationary expectations raised the velocity of circulation so that prices began to increase faster than the money supply. To secure a given percentage increase in its share of GDP through deficit finance, government needed to increase the money supply by a substantially larger percentage. This meant ever-increasing inflation, which eroded the real value of expenditures further. By 1962, the real value of expenditures per capita had fallen to under 40 per cent of their 1953 level (Table 3.2). Furthermore, routine expenditures on salaries, wages and equipment, together with defence outlays accounted for a large proportion of the total budget, while expenditures on public works, health and education never reached one-fifth of the total. This was a steep decline compared with the second decade of the twentieth century when expenditures on public works comprised almost

40 per cent of total government outlays (Booth 1998: 142). In 1957, the Economic Commission for Asia and the Far East estimated that government investment expenditures in Indonesia and the Philippines amounted to only 2.6 per cent of GNP, compared with almost 10 per cent in Japan, Burma, Taiwan and South Korea. The share of government in total investment expenditures was lower in Indonesia than in any other Asian economy in the late 1950s (Booth 1998: 167).

In spite of the weak performance of the revenue system after 1955, and the low government investment expenditures relative to national income, successive governments in both the parliamentary and guided democracy era continued to set out ambitious goals for the role of government in the economy. The nationalisation of virtually all Dutch assets in 1957/1958 meant that the size of the state enterprise sector increased considerably. The eight-year development plan launched in 1961 was expected to run until 1968. It assumed that surpluses from state-owned enterprises would play an important role in financing plan projects in food production, basic industries, education, transport and popular welfare. In fact, the poor financial performance of most of the nationalised industries meant that the petroleum sector played the key role in plan finance; one minister claimed that this sector accounted for 75 per cent of all funding for plan projects (Paauw 1963: 229). The end of the Irian campaign in 1963 did permit a reduction in defence expenditures, but by 1965, defence outlays, including the cost of the 'Crush Malaysia' campaign, amounted to 40 per cent of budget expenditures. Plan expenditures were a much smaller proportion of realised budget expenditures, and in 1965 amounted to only 1.2 per cent of GDP (Bank Indonesia 1968: 32–3).

There can be little doubt that, in spite of the efforts of government officials in the Ministry of Finance and the Planning Board to improve revenue collections, and to allocate government revenues to those expenditures intended to increase the long-term productive capacity of the economy, the decade from 1955 to 1965 saw a gradual decline in the role of government in the economy. To the extent that the last part of the colonial era had seen some progress towards a modern fiscal state, that progress was reversed after the mid-1950s. Budgetary revenues accruing to the central government fell in real per capita terms, in large part because of declining central government control over the export sector. Plans to use profits from nationalised industries to finance capital expenditures were realised only to a very limited extent; such revenues as were extracted came mainly from the petroleum sector. The domestic financial sector remained undeveloped, and the government was unable to fund the growing budget deficits through non-inflationary means, instead relying increasingly on printing money. But revenues which could be raised in this way were limited, and by 1965, government expenditures amounted to only 10.7 per cent of GDP. Almost all were devoted to routine expenditures and to the military.

The first phase of the New Order

The main challenges facing the technocrats advising Suharto after 1966 were to reduce inflation, bring order to the public finances and boost economic growth. They knew that the three goals were interlinked; if they wished to reduce inflation, it was essential to eliminate budget deficits financed by borrowing from the central bank. A return to economic growth could only take place if key actors in the private sector had more confidence in the determination of the government not just to reduce inflation but to give greater incentives to export producers, to improve infrastructure, education and health care, and to strengthen the institutions necessary to support a market economy. Given the neglect of the previous decade, these were Herculean challenges for an untried group of academics. Suharto himself was far from secure in his position, and he confronted a range of forces within both the army and civil society who were determined to pursue their own interests, and who, in most cases, had little understanding of the economic challenges facing the country.

The technocrats realised that foreign aid would be essential to supplement government savings (the difference between domestic budgetary revenues and routine expenditures), and permit a rapid growth in capital expenditures. By 1969, inflation had been brought under control, and the government was able to embark on the first of the five-year plans of the Suharto era. The emphasis was on rehabilitating infrastructure and boosting agricultural, especially food production, and on improving access to education through increased provision of schooling, especially in rural areas. The government also moved, at first cautiously, towards implementing a national family planning policy. Reducing fertility, combined with a renewed emphasis on land settlement policies outside Java, were seen as the key to easing the problem of 'over-population' in Java. To a considerable extent these policies followed on from the ethical policy of the colonial era, which had stressed irrigation, education and transmigration as the keys to improving welfare in Java. The assumption in the early years of the Suharto period was that poverty was largely a Javanese problem and that the rest of the country had an important role to play in solving that problem.

In order to achieve the goals of the first Five Year Plan, programme and project aid and export credits were crucial. Together, they accounted for

Table 9.1 *Revenues and expenditures as a percentage of GDP: Indonesia, Malaysia, Philippines and Thailand, 1972, 1980 and 1985*

Year	Indonesia	Malaysia	Philippines	Thailand
1972				
Revenues/GDP	13.5	20.3	12.5	16.1
Expenditures/GDP				
Current	8.6	22.3	11.7	15.5
Capital	7.3	7.4	2.7	4.8
1980				
Revenues/GDP	22.2	27.3	13.0	14.4
Expenditures/GDP				
Current	12.2	19.9	9.1	14.2
Capital	12.3	13.7	5.1	5.0
1985				
Revenues/GDP	22.5	29.1	11.6	16.6
Expenditures/GDP				
Current	12.6	NA	9.3	17.5
Capital	10.9	NA	4.2	4.7

Source: World Bank (1987).

between 21 and 27 per cent of realised expenditures over the five years until 1974; revenues from the oil company tax accounted for 14 per cent of total budgetary revenues in 1969/1970, increasing to 29 per cent by 1973/1974 (Booth and McCawley 1981: 128). Although the government claimed to be running a 'balanced budget', in fact the deficit before borrowing amounted to around 3 per cent of GDP over the first Plan period, but as the borrowing was entirely from foreign sources, it was much less inflationary than borrowing from the central bank. By 1972, capital expenditures had already increased to over 7 per cent of GDP, which was about the same as in Malaysia and higher than in Thailand or the Philippines (Table 9.1). Current expenditures were considerably lower relative to GDP than in these neighbouring countries. The government was able to impose tight control over recruitment and pay in both the civil service and the military.

During the first Five Year Plan the government worked closely, and on the whole harmoniously, with foreign donors to ensure that aid funds were used to implement plan projects. Although revenues from the oil tax grew rapidly, and by 1973/1974 accounted for almost 30 per cent of total budgetary revenues, non-oil domestic revenues were sufficient to fund most of the routine budget (Booth and McCawley 1981: table 5.6). When the second Plan was drawn up, it was assumed that reliance on aid finance would continue. But in fact the rapid growth in revenues from the oil company tax meant that it was possible to increase spending on development projects while at the same time reducing aid receipts as a proportion of total budgetary revenues. This defused criticism from those both inside and outside government who were worried about the influence of foreign donors, and permitted a sharp rise in both current and capital expenditures. By 1980, total government revenues amounted to almost 25 per cent of GDP, a much higher percentage than had been achieved at any time since independence. Capital expenditures were estimated to be around 12.3 per cent of GDP, only slightly less than in Malaysia, and a much higher proportion than in either Thailand or the Philippines (Table 9.1).

It was pointed out in Chapter 4 that, although the government claimed that the budget was balanced through the 1970s, the increased reliance on foreign sources of funding, either from aid, borrowing or the oil company tax, caused a rise in the domestic budgetary deficit, which was the difference between total domestic expenditures and domestic tax and non-tax revenues. This in turn gave rise to inflationary pressures as not all government expenditures were offset by a reduction in domestic aggregate demand. A further complication was that many state enterprises relied heavily on bank lending to finance both current and capital expenditures. In fact over the 1970s, this borrowing was less inflationary than it might otherwise have been because after 1976, substantial sums were remitted abroad through the central bank to pay off the large debts occurred by the state oil company, Pertamina. The problem of off-budget finance of the state enterprise sector remained a serious one until the 1990s, and certainly reinforced the view that the budgetary documents were an incomplete guide to the full impact of the government sector on the economy.

As world oil prices began to decline in the early 1980s, there was only a modest reduction in budgetary expenditures relative to GDP; the fall in oil prices was compensated by an increase in non-oil revenues, and also by increased government borrowing abroad. In 1985, government expenditures still amounted to 23.5 per cent of GDP, although current expenditures now accounted for a larger share of the total. In that year, the Indonesian government was still spending more on capital works as a percentage of GDP than either Thailand or the Philippines (Table 9.1). But the two large devaluations of 1983 and 1986, although they increased the rupiah value of the oil company tax, also led to a sharp increase in the rupiah cost of foreign debt service. The net impact of the 1986 devaluation on the budget was slightly negative as foreign expenditures were higher than foreign revenues. By 1988/1989, the final year of the fourth Five Year Plan of the Suharto era, routine budgetary expenditures

Table 9.2 *Routine expenditures, government savings and foreign aid as a percentage of development expenditures in Indonesia, 1973/1974–1998/1999*

| Year | As a percentage of development expenditures | | |
	Routine	Government savings	Foreign aid
1973/1974	158.2	56.4	45.2
1983/1984	85.0	60.8	39.2
1988/1989	169.3	18.5	81.6
1993/1994	151.2	52.5	40.4
1996/1997	174.0	69.7	33.1
1998/1999*	150.9	67.7	32.2
1998/1999**	217.7	7.5	91.8

* Sixth Plan projections.
** Actual outturns.
Source: Booth (1994: 15); Department of Information, **Lampiran Pidato Kenegaraan 1999**: (Table II.I.I).

including debt service, were much higher than development expenditures, and government savings accounted for only 18.5 per cent of the development budget, a much lower percentage than five years earlier (Table 9.2). Foreign aid and borrowing financed over 80 per cent of all development spending, a higher percentage than in 1973/1974.

During the 1980s, there had been considerable debate about the need to reform the regulatory and licensing system which had been inherited from the colonial era, and which had become more complex in the post-independence era. Hill (1996: 116) argued that, in spite of promises made in the late 1960s, the achievements of the Suharto years had been disappointing. Foreign exchange controls had been removed, but many businesses faced a bewildering range of regulations imposed by both central government departments and local government. The implementation of these regulations was often haphazard, and in the opinion of many businesses their main purpose was to enable government officials to extract bribes in return for non-compliance. This in turn reinforced an attitude of lawlessness in the business community, or at the very least a lack of respect for government officials, who were usually regarded by private business as venal and obstructive. There were some reforms over the 1980s in the customs administration and there was some simplification of the process for approving foreign investment. But many domestic businesses viewed these reforms as favouring foreign over domestic investors. In addition, many indigenous business people resented the favours granted to large conglomerates controlled by presidential cronies. At the same time, activists in the NGO sector argued that more regulation was needed to prevent the wholesale destruction of forests and the pollution of rivers that frequently resulted from mining operations. All these issues remained to be dealt with after 1998.

Fiscal policy from 1989 to 1998: the retreat of the state?

In the latter part of the 1980s, debt service expenditures accounted for over 30 per cent of total budgetary expenditures. The debt service ratio had increased to almost one-third of total export revenues by 1987 (Asher and Booth 1992: 58–65). These figures caused widespread unease among many Indonesians both inside and outside the government, and the government responded by announcing that reducing government reliance on foreign borrowing would be an important goal of the fifth Five Year Plan (1989/1990 to 1993/1994). The Plan forecast that oil revenues would continue to fall as a proportion of total revenues, but non-oil revenues would rise. Government savings would rise and borrowing would fall as a proportion of total development expenditures. In fact these targets were largely met, although routine expenditures were still 50 per cent higher than development expenditures in 1993/1994 (Table 9.2). This was partly the result of the continuing burden of debt service charges, and partly the result of increasing numbers of civil servants, together with higher salaries (Booth 1994: 14). The sixth Plan, scheduled to run from 1994/1995 to 1998/1999, projected that routine expenditures would continue to be around 50 per cent higher than development expenditures and the proportion of the development budget funded by government savings would increase to 68 per cent, a higher ratio than in 1973/1974. Foreign aid and borrowing would decline to around one-third of planned development expenditures (Table 9.2).

The sixth Plan appeared to be signalling a decline in the role of government as a source of funds for investment expenditures and a rise in the role of the private sector. Over the fifth Plan period, government funds had accounted for only 27 per cent of total investment expenditures in the economy; this percentage was expected to fall further by 1998/1999 (Booth 1994: 10). Over the sixth Plan period as a whole, total investment expenditures were estimated to be 30 per cent of GDP; only a small proportion would be funded from foreign sources, including government borrowing and foreign direct investment. These targets gave rise to some controversy, with some economists pointing out that in the fast-growing economies in other parts of Asia investment ratios were well above 30 per cent. Concerns were also expressed about the fact that the rate of return on public sector investment projects was often low. In addition, the small role accorded to foreign sources of investment funds seemed to be a concession to economic nationalism, which might disadvantage Indonesia. In neighbouring economies including Singapore, Malaysia and Thailand, by the early 1990s, foreign direct investment accounted for a considerable part of total investment, especially in the manufacturing sector.

But at the same time as the budget figures seemed to be showing a decline in the government share of total investment expenditures, other evidence indicated that off-budget funds were being used to fund projects carried out by state enterprises. In 1994, newspaper reports stated that a $174 million interest-free loan had been given by the Forestry Ministry to the government-owned aircraft plant (IPTN), a pet project of the Minister of Technology, Dr Habibie. The forestry sector appeared to be replacing the oil sector as a source of off-budget funds for those industries favoured by the president and his close associates (Ascher 1999: 78–9). At the same time, Suharto asked several Chinese businessmen who controlled large conglomerates, including Liem Sioe Liong and Prajogo Pangestu, to contribute to projects such as the Chandra Asri olefins factory, a controversial downstream processing venture in which Suharto's son was also involved. Suharto seemed determined to press ahead with these projects, using both public and private funds, regardless of the criticism which they attracted.

Most of the sixth Plan targets were thrown badly off course by the crisis of 1997/1998. There was a rapid increase in routine expenditures, especially interest payments on the government bonds used to recapitalise the collapsing banking system. Government savings financed less than 10 per cent of development expenditures in the Plan's final year, 1998/1999, and foreign aid and loans over 90 per cent (Table 9.2). Total government expenditures actually increased relative to GDP, from around 17 per cent in 1995/1996 to 21 per cent in 1998/1999. The increase was mainly the result of increased interest payments on the bank recapitalisation bonds; development expenditures were sharply reduced relative to both routine expenditures and GDP. After Suharto left office, there were many problems to be tackled concerning the role of the government sector in the economy. One set of problems related to the role of sub-national levels of government, which was addressed through the decentralisation legislation of 1999. There were also huge costs incurred in recapitalising the banking system; these were in large part borne by the budget. But behind these issues lay crucial questions concerning the size of the public sector in the post-Suharto era, the appropriate division of tasks between the public and private sectors, and the use of off-budget funding for projects of doubtful benefit to the economy as a whole.

Post-Suharto developments

Given the serious economic problems which faced Indonesia after Suharto's resignation, it might have been expected that there would be a plan holiday while ministers and officials tackled the most pressing policy challenges. In fact, after President Habibie left office, the cabinet of President A. Wahid moved quickly to draw up a new five-year plan, termed *Propenas*, which ran from 2000 to 2004. It was a considerably shorter document than the multi-volume plans which had been issued between 1969 and 1994; the chapter on economic development was by far the longest and set out twenty-eight policy initiatives. The emphasis was on establishing a people's economy (*ekonomi kerakyatan*), which would be based on a 'just market mechanism', with appropriate concern not just for economic growth but also for distributional equity, environmental protection, guaranteed rights to both workers and business people, and better protection for consumers. In contrast to the self-congratulatory tone of the *Repelita VI* document, there was sharp criticism of aspects of Indonesia's performance, and a more candid discussion of regional problems, especially in Aceh, Papua and Maluku. But sceptics pointed out that the *Propenas* document suffered from the same problems as earlier plan documents going back to the 1950s. There were plenty of targets but little discussion of the policy initiatives which would be needed to achieve them, or whether government capacity at both central and regional levels was sufficient to implement the necessary policies. There seemed to be little appreciation of the limitations of the public sector, or any indication of policy priorities.

Given the rapid changes of presidents and ministers after 1998, it was hardly surprising that little attention was given to reforming the development planning process until 2004 when a new law was passed on the national development planning system, and a draft five-year plan (2005–2009) was circulated. Both the law and the plan documents were criticised for their lack of precision, especially on the crucial issue of coordination between government agencies and between levels of government. The lack of clarity was particularly important given that the ambitious decentralisation programme, set out in legislation passed in 1999, began to be implemented from 2001 onwards. Considerable responsibility for agriculture, education and health, forestry, irrigation and environmental protection was given to the districts, although in 2002 it appeared that over half the development expenditures allocated for these sectors was still under the control of central ministries (Lewis and Chakeri 2004: table 4). The implications of the decentralisation measures for the conduct of public policy in Indonesia will be considered later.

At the central level, there were important changes made to the way the national budget documents were presented in the early 2000s. The old distinction between routine and development expenditure was dropped, and expenditures were classified according to personnel, material, subsidies, interest payments, capital works and transfers to the regions. Another important change, following the passage of Law 34, 2004, was to move all expenditures relating to the military onto the budget. According to Rieffel and Pramodhawardani (2007: 7), many analysts assumed that during the Suharto era, the military had derived well over half their income from a range of off-budget sources. These authors argued that by 2006, the proportion was much lower, but the government's intention was to move all military expenditures onto the budget by 2009, thereby making them far more transparent. While there remained some scepticism about whether the military would be either willing or able to end reliance on non-budget income sources, the reforms certainly signalled an important change in the government's approach to funding the armed forces.

In 2001, total government expenditures had increased to almost 21 per cent of GDP; this dropped to around 16 per cent in 2010 before rising again to 17.5 per cent in 2014. Interest payments dropped as the bank restructuring bonds were retired, but budget subsidies rose to over 5 per cent of GDP in 2008, although there was some decline after that (Table 6.10). On the revenue side, total government revenues were below expenditures in all years after 2001; the resulting deficits have been financed by both loans and bond sales, which are conducted in both domestic and foreign markets. The main conclusion to be drawn from the government budgets from 2001 down to 2014 is that fiscal policy has been conservative, with expenditures low relative to GDP and revenues even lower. Some observers have expressed disappointment at the failure to increase tax revenues, which reached 13 per cent of GDP in 2008, but fell to around 11 per cent by 2014 (Table 6.10). Tax outturns have tended to fall below budget targets in recent years and collection procedures are often haphazard; it has been estimated that little more than half of registered income tax payers actually submit returns (Damuri and Day 2015: 11–12). But even if revenues could be increased, still there appear to be problems on the expenditure side. In 2014 only 85 per cent of the budget funds allocated to capital expenditures were actually disbursed.

The reasons for both the low central government tax collections and the delays in disbursing funds are complex. It is frequently alleged that

Indonesians in the private sector are reluctant to pay taxes because they feel that most government revenues are used to fund a large bureaucracy which is corrupt and only interested in using its authority to impose a range of illegal charges on private business. They see little benefit from government expenditures in terms of improved infrastructure, education or other government services. To the extent that many Indonesians have to buy services including clean drinking water, education and health care from private providers because of the poor quality of public provision, this hardly increases their willingness to pay taxes. Government officials for their part have few incentives to disburse budgetary funds quickly and efficiently, especially for capital projects where various factors from difficulties in procuring land and lack of skilled workers to worries about tendering procedures can lead to project delays. Leaving project funds in interest-bearing bank accounts is a source of extra revenue for many government agencies, and often further slows disbursement.

These problems are hardly new, and have affected project implementation for decades at both central and regional levels. But given that government departments are now subject to more critical scrutiny from NGOs, press and parliament, as well as from the Corruption Prevention Commission (KPK), it is perhaps not surprising that officials are more cautious about spending funds. As a result, the ratio of government revenues and expenditures to GDP in Indonesia remains low by Asian standards; in recent years it has been lower than in Vietnam and Laos, although both these countries have lower per capita GDP than Indonesia (McCawley 2014: 205). Budgetary expenditures per capita are about half those in Thailand, and little more than one-fifth of those in Malaysia, which inevitably affects the standard of provision of public goods, and leads to much adverse comment in the press. It also affects the government's ability to provide more protection for the poor, an issue which is discussed in more detail later in the chapter.

Decentralisation of government functions and control

During its short period in power, the government of B. J. Habibie passed two laws on regional government and regional finance which contained a number of measures giving new responsibilities to sub-national levels of government, especially the districts or second-level regions (*daerah tingkat dua*), as they had been called in the Suharto era. These new powers were to be funded through a reformed system of grants from the centre. The sweeping reforms outlined in the legislation surprised many observers, and some thought that it was unlikely to be implemented after Habibie left office. The two presidents who succeeded Habibie were both Javanese, and neither seemed very committed to the legislation. Indeed Megawati and some of her ministers appeared quite hostile. But the demand for reform of the way Indonesia was governed, both in the national parliament and in the regions, was too strong to be resisted, and the legislation began to be implemented in 2001.

The changes which took place after 2001 were a reaction against the tight central control of regional governments and regional finance which had characterised the Suharto era. Resentment against what was seen as excessive control from Jakarta was widely felt both in Java and elsewhere. There was also a fear that, after the departure of East Timor, more provinces outside Java might want to secede altogether, especially those with significant natural resource wealth. The INPRES system of regional grants from the centre to the provincial, district and village levels of government had been an effective way of channelling funds to both provincial and sub-provincial governments, and in the early phase of the Suharto era had been broadly welcomed by regional governments. But as was pointed out in Chapter 4, by the early 1990s, these funds were being skewed to Eastern Indonesia and the more populous provinces, especially in Java, were getting less. This caused resentment in these provinces; their grievances could have been addressed on the revenue side if the central government had been prepared to allow some sharing of central government tax revenues. But the Ministry of Finance consistently refused to do this.

Almost as soon as the 1999 legislation was implemented, criticisms began. Several commentators pointed out that the new grant system removed most of the controls over spending which had characterised the old grant system. The two main grants, referred to as the DAU (*Dana Alokasi Umum*) and the DAK (*Dana Alokasi Khusus*) could be used for any purpose, including salaries and wages, new buildings, and purchases of equipment as well as for capital works. Most districts received some increase in real terms compared with the previous funding system but there was little to stop them spending the funds on hiring more employees, or on building new offices. Although some rules were subsequently introduced which compelled regions to spend a certain proportion of their grants on education and other services, it was, and remains, far from clear whether such rules could be enforced. The allocation procedures for both the DAU and the DAK were opaque, and there were wide disparities in revenue allocation which have persisted to the present (Booth 2010: table 6; Niazi 2012: table 11.3; Lewis 2014: 151–2). At the same time, the revenue system remained very centralised; the opportunity for introducing even a modest degree of revenue sharing of the main taxes between the centre and the regions had once again been missed.

The problems which beset the implementation of the 1999 legislation were compounded by the splitting of provinces and districts into smaller units which began in 1999 and continued, albeit at a slower rate, into Yudhoyono's second term. In fact, the process of splitting provinces had begun in the 1950s. In the immediate aftermath of the transfer of power in 1949, it was decided to continue with the provincial and sub-provincial units formed by the Dutch in Java, although the Surakarta Sultanate was absorbed into the province of Central Java. But outside Java, provinces had not been formed in colonial times, and many boundaries were contested. Sumatra was divided into three provinces, while Kalimantan, Sulawesi, the Moluccas and the Lesser Sundas (Bali, West and East Nusatenggara) each became one province. These divisions paid little attention to ethnic or linguistic divisions, and gave rise to considerable resentment, which led to further changes. By the time of the first post-independence population census in 1961, twenty-two provinces had been created, although one (Irian Barat) remained under Dutch control. Further divisions of several provinces in Sumatra, Kalimantan and Sulawesi took place in the early 1960s, and by the end of the Sukarno era, Indonesia comprised twenty-six provinces. Already in 1961, there were marked differences in population not just between provinces, but also between districts (*kabupaten* and *kota*). The average size of a district in Java in 1961 was almost 620,000 people, which was more than twice that in Sumatra and over three times that in Maluku (Booth 2010: table 2).

During the Suharto era, East Timor was the only new province added to the twenty-six already in existence. Few new rural districts were formed apart from those in East Timor, although a small number of new urban districts (*kota*) were created. The main changes were at the sub-district (*kecamatan*) and village level where large numbers of new units were created (Table 9.3). These changes were made partly for security reasons, and partly as a result of the transmigration programme. New boundaries were often drawn with little consultation with local populations; traditional local government units, especially outside Java, were often ignored. Between 1996 and 2013, one province (East Timor) voted to leave and eight new provinces were created, all but one outside Java. There were also significant increases in the numbers of districts, sub-districts and villages, again mainly outside Java (Table 9.3). Numbers of districts, both urban and rural, increased more rapidly than population over these years with the result that the average population per district was lower in 2013 than in 1996.

Several explanations can be put forward for the rapid growth in numbers of provinces, districts, sub-districts and villages after the fall of

Table 9.3 *Numbers of sub-national units and average population size, 1973, 1996, 2013*

	Province	Kabupaten	Kota	Kecamatan	Village
Numbers of government units					
1973	26	233	54	3,177	45,586
1996	27	247	63	4,022	66,158
2013	34	405	98	6,908	79,939
Numbers in Java					
1996	5	82	25	1,795	24,814
2013	6	85	34	2,140	25,301
Percentage of the increment 1996 to 2013 from Java					
	14.3	1.9	25.7	12.0	3.5
Average population per unit (×1,000)					
1973	4,850	439*		40	2.8
1996	7,345	640*		49	3.0
2013	7,318	495*		36	3.1

* Average for *kabupaten* and *kota*.
Sources: 1973: CBS (1975b: 18); 1996: CBS (1997: 6); 2013: CBS, **Perkembangan Beberapa Indikator Utama Sosial-Ekonomi Indonesia**, February 2014 (www.bps. go.id).

Suharto, especially outside Java. That many people across the archipelago felt unhappy with the provincial boundaries which had been set in the 1950s and 1960s was well-known. These boundaries had often left significant religious and ethnic minorities stranded in provinces where they felt they did not belong. Many people lived a long distance from the provincial capital, and felt neglected by the groups which dominated the provincial governments. In Java, where the provincial and sub-provincial boundaries had been set in colonial times, the various minorities had learnt to get along with one another; the only new province created after 1998 was Banten, which comprised several rapidly growing districts to the west of Jakarta. It had been a separate residency in colonial times, and had been incorporated into West Java after independence. The capital of West Java was Bandung, a city from which Banten was geographically and culturally isolated. Several other former residencies in Java also expressed some enthusiasm for becoming separate provinces, including Cirebon and Madura, but squabbles among local elites appear to have prevented their emergence as new provinces. This also prevented the emergence of new provinces in parts of Sumatra and Sulawesi (Booth 2010: 43–4).

Most of the new provinces which were created after 1999 were the result of successful campaigns by local elites who had felt marginalised under the old provincial boundaries. Many were no doubt attracted by the lure of more power, and more control over financial resources in the new provinces and districts. When direct elections for governors, mayors and *bupatis* took place in 2005, there was widespread concern at the large amounts of money many candidates were spending to gain office. It appeared that they were expecting to make significant private gains from their period in office, and that once in office there appeared to be little to prevent them from misusing the resources under their control. These resources were in many cases much larger than under the pre-1999 system, especially if the province or district was entitled to some part of the revenues accruing from the exploitation of natural resources. By 2003, central government grants to the regions amounted to around 6 per cent of GDP, and they remained at around this level over the next decade.

Some who sought office as leaders of provinces and sub-provincial levels of government were no doubt also motivated by a genuine concern to improve the economic and social well-being of local populations who had been neglected in the old provinces. But many of the new provinces and districts created after 1999 outside Java were hampered by lack of skilled workers in areas such as public works, health and education. However much a *bupati* in West Sulawesi, of whom there were five after the province split from South Sulawesi, may wish to improve the quality of education or health care in his district, or improve the irrigation systems, roads and bridges, he will be constrained by the lack of teachers, health workers and qualified engineers. Encouraging skilled workers to come from other provinces to what is still a remote region will be difficult if not impossible, and will require generous inducements in the form of higher salaries, housing and so on.

The problem of administrative capacity is particularly important because the creation of so many new provinces and districts outside Java has led not just to great differences in population size among provinces, districts and villages, but also to considerable variations in their ability to implement projects in sectors such as health, education and public works. An extreme contrast can be made between the province of East Java, considered since colonial times as having the best administrative capacity of any province in the country, and the two new provinces of Papua Barat and Gorontalo. In both these new provinces, the total population in 2013 was just over a million people, which was the same or slightly lower than the average population of a district (*kota* and *kabupaten*) in East Java. In Papua Barat, twenty-nine *kabupaten* and one *kota* were created after the province was split off from Papua. The average population size of these districts is less than that of most *kecamatan* in East Java, although the geographic area is often larger. That many districts in East Java have the administrative capacity to spend their allocations from the central government on projects which benefit their populations can hardly be doubted. But it seems unlikely that many districts in either Papua Barat or Gorontalo have that capacity.

The solution might be to give more responsibility to provincial governments in the smaller, more remote provinces and more power to sub-provincial levels of government in the more populated provinces in Java and Sumatra. Since 2004, there has been new legislation, and more regulations which have given more powers to both provinces and the central government to review tax and expenditure programmes at the district level, and to introduce obligatory expenditure functions (Niazi 2012: 402). To many in the regions, especially at the sub-provincial levels, these laws and regulations were viewed as an unwelcome attempt to reverse the original spirit of the 1999 legislation. On the other hand, officials in both the provinces and the centre stressed the need for greater monitoring and control of the way the central grants are used. This three-way tug of war over resources and responsibilities among the centre, provinces and districts seems likely to continue in the future.

Critics of the 1999 legislation have also pointed out that it offered few incentives to either provinces or district governments to enhance their efforts to raise revenues; indeed the intention appeared to be to strengthen their dependency on central government grants. In the 1980s and 1990s some provinces were in fact raising quite considerable sums through taxes which had been assigned to them such as the motor vehicle tax, while districts received most of the land tax, and also the tax on hotels and restaurants. In addition, districts levied a range of charges on use of facilities such as markets. These charges were frequently criticised as regressive, but it appears that both provinces and districts have continued to levy them. According to the figures on regional finance published by the CBS, in both 2007 and 2012, central government transfers amounted to around 65 per cent of total expenditures of provinces, districts and villages. The remaining 35 per cent must have been raised from internal sources. In 2012, total regional government expenditures amounted to 9 per cent of GDP (Table 9.4). Central government expenditures excluding transfers to the regions amounted to 12.2 per cent of GDP. This represents a considerable shift in spending responsibilities from centre to the regions compared with the Suharto years.

Yet another criticism of the 1999 legislation was that it appeared to give few functions to villages; indeed it was argued that villages had lost out in the reformed grant system. During the Suharto years, village governments were funded through the *Inpres Desa* which had been initiated in 1969. In the early 1990s, another programme which was intended to

Table 9.4 *Percentage of sub-national expenditures by level of government and as a percentage of GDP*

Percentage breakdown of sub-national expenditures		
	2007	2012
Village	2.0	2.5
Kabupaten/Kota	73.8	68.9
Province	24.2	28.6
Total	100.0	100.0
Transfers to regions as percentage of total government expenditures		
	33.4	32.2
As percentage of GDP		
Total central government expenditures	19.2	18.1
Total central government expenditures less revenues	12.8	12.2
Total regional expenditures	10.0	9.0

Source: www.bps.go.id.

support remote villages was initiated (*Inpres Desa Tertinggal*). In 1996/1997, these two programmes accounted for a little over 5 per cent of all grants from the centre to the regions. After the changes in the grant system, the share of the villages in total grants fell; by 2012 expenditures in villages amounted to only 2.5 per cent of spending by all sub-national governments (Table 9.4). To rectify what many saw as an injustice, it was announced that grants to villages would be increased to Rp. 20.8 trillion in the 2015 budget. This amounts to around $20,000 for each of the almost 80,000 villages in the country, although it is not clear whether they will all receive the same amount. While many villages in both Java and elsewhere doubtless have the capacity to spend the money sensibly (on, for example, the repair of school buildings and health facilities built more than thirty years ago), it is probable that smaller villages in remote regions may struggle to spend the money, if indeed they ever receive it.

To sum up, it is clear that the decentralisation measures initiated in 1999 are still very much work-in-progress, and that, in addressing long-standing grievances, the changes have given rise to new problems. The new funding arrangements have certainly led to a considerable shift in the fiscal balance of power between the centre and the regions, with a much higher proportion of total expenditures being made by sub-national governments. Unsurprisingly, this has led to resentment at the centre, and in many provinces as well. In creating many new provinces and districts, especially outside Java, there are now huge disparities in the capacity of both provincial and district governments to carry out projects. Central government agencies, led by the Ministry of Finance, still want to exercise tight control over both the revenue-raising powers and the spending functions of sub-national levels of government, even if they have neither the legal authority nor the administrative ability to do so. They have also successfully resisted any attempt at revenue-sharing of the major central taxes. Conflict between the centre and the regions over both the raising of resources and their use seems likely to continue for years, if not decades.

The problem of corruption

That the Indonesian government in both the Suharto era and more recently has had an international image as a very corrupt country is beyond doubt. When international rankings of corruption began to be published by various agencies in the 1980s and 1990s, Indonesia's ranking was always low. The first table of perceptions of corruption drawn up by Transparency International (TI) in 1995 placed Indonesia at forty-one out of the forty-one countries in the index (Lim and Stern 2002: table 2). Since then, the TI index has been published at regular intervals, and many more countries have been included. The list circulated in 2014 ranked Indonesia at 107 among 174 countries. This may seem an improvement, but many of the countries now included are from Africa and Central Asia where standards of public sector probity are extremely low. Indonesia in 2014 was ranked below China and India, and all ASEAN nations except Vietnam, Cambodia and Myanmar.

These international rankings have attracted criticism, as Lim and Stern have acknowledged (2002: 20–1). But they do give some idea of the problems which foreign, and to a lesser extent domestic, investors face in their attempts to do business in Indonesia. Some Indonesian economists, and a number of foreign observers familiar with Indonesia, have claimed that these problems are largely the result of a complex regulatory system whose main purpose has been to give officials the chance to demand a range of bribes and kickbacks. They would argue that the only way to improve Indonesia's ranking in the TI index, as well as other indicators including the World Bank's 'Ease of Doing Business' index, would be to get rid of most of the regulations. Others, including many NGOs, argue that the regulations are necessary to prevent foreign companies, and their domestic associates, from plundering Indonesia's resources for their short-term profit. They would argue that the real problem in Indonesia is the lack of effective sanctions against corrupt behaviour, especially on the part of senior government officials. Unlike Singapore and Hong Kong, which appear in the top decile of the TI rankings, Indonesia has had until very recently weak anti-corruption agencies and a culture which appears to accept, and even applaud, corrupt behaviour. Yet another analysis of corruption in Indonesia views it as 'only a symptom of a fundamental problem of inappropriate personnel management practices in the bureaucracy' (McLeod 2008b: 200).

Before examining these arguments, it is useful to review the history of anti-corruption efforts in Indonesia, going back to the 1950s. Many Indonesians who were active in the struggle against the Dutch probably expected to be rewarded with jobs in either the military or the civilian bureaucracies, and a standard of living equivalent to that which Dutch civil servants had enjoyed. Most were unable to get government jobs, and by the early 1950s, it was clear to those who had managed to get either military or civilian posts that their salaries and perquisites were much lower in real terms than Dutch, or indeed native civil servants had enjoyed in the 1930s. This was partly because per capita GDP was lower; in addition numbers of civil servants increased through the 1950s, while budgetary resources were falling. Evers (1987: table 1) estimated that there were 82,000 civil servants in 1940; in 1960 the number had grown to 393,000. This was not a large number in comparison with neighbouring countries; relative to population there were twice as many government employees in Thailand and five times as many in Malaysia. But in Indonesia many government employees felt angry that their remuneration was low, and was being further reduced by rising inflation. Where opportunities were available, they sought extra compensation through charging fees for the services they were supposed to provide free, especially if those requiring the services were private businesspeople. Many also took on second or third jobs, with the inevitable result that hours spent on the main job were cut back.

By the time Sukarno fell from office, corruption in government had become endemic and was the target of student protests in 1965/1966. As inflation was brought under control in the late 1960s, it was expected that corruption would be reduced, especially as the government seemed determined to reform civil service pay scales. But in fact there was considerable evidence that the problem was getting worse. The role of the 'financial generals' who controlled large state enterprises and appeared to be treating them as their personal fiefdoms attracted growing criticism in the press and from student groups (Mackie 1970: 88–9). Probably unwillingly, in early 1970 Suharto set up a 'Commission of Four' to report on the problem. It was headed by Wilopo, who had served as prime minister in 1952/1953, and was chair of the Supreme Advisory Council. The other members were also respected former politicians.

The commission completed seven reports including one on the Attorney General's department, two on the state oil enterprise (Pertamina), two more on the government procurement agency (Bulog) and the state forestry enterprise (Perhutani) and two reports addressing general issues about restructuring government administration and eradicating government corruption. According to Mackie, the reports on the state enterprises all contained valuable information about their business practices and financial conduct. The report on Bulog recommended that its operations be reduced, and should focus on operating a rice buffer stock to stabilise prices. The report on Perhutani criticised the concessions given to foreign companies, mainly on the grounds that they secured only a small share of the forest rents for the Indonesian government. The two volumes on Pertamina addressed the complex question of how to control a state enterprise that appeared to be operating outside the control of the Ministry of Finance, and was not subject to any external scrutiny. Mackie (1970: 100) concluded that the evidence presented on the three state enterprises 'provided the basis for initiating action to remedy laxities' but much would depend on the willingness of Suharto to tackle the problem.

Publication of these reports triggered more student demonstrations, and much discussion in the press. The government responded with promises to enact legislation on the management of Pertamina and the other state enterprises, and to force all government employees to register their assets. Suharto promised to take charge personally of the fight against corruption. But in the event the results were disappointing. Little was done to control the behaviour of the senior managers in Pertamina until its debts became an international news story in 1975. As was pointed out in Chapter 4, the costs of the Pertamina rescue were huge, but it was far from clear at the time, or subsequently, that the lessons had been learned. State enterprises including Bulog were given even more monopoly power in importing not just rice but other basic foodstuffs. There was little or no attempt to audit their activities and in the case of Bulog no effort was made to ascertain the costs and benefits of its activities for the food-buying public in Indonesia.

Suharto's critics have argued that he never had any interest in imposing financial discipline on state enterprises or any other arm of government, or in curbing government corruption more generally. His main aim was to build up a massive franchise system which was intended to reward close associates, including his own family (McLeod 2008b). In the final phase of his presidency, there is considerable evidence to support this view. But in the early 1970s, his vacillation over the Commission's report is understandable in terms of his own political weakness, and the strength of other senior military figures, including Ibnu Sutowo, the head of Pertamina. Almost certainly he did not have sufficient support within the military to tackle the 'financial generals' head on at that time. Later when his position was more secure, he had lost whatever appetite he might have had for reform, and was more interested in building his own dynasty.

In spite of the lack of support from the top, there were important changes in the structure of the civil service between the early 1970s and the end of the Suharto era. There was considerable growth in numbers, although by 1996/1997 there were only two civil servants per 100 population, which was a low figure by international standards (Edgren 1987: 7). In 1973/1974, the civil service was largely male, many with low levels of education; 37 per cent had at most completed primary school. Almost half were in the lowest class (*golongan 1*). By 1996/1997, women comprised around one-third of the total, and only 10.6 per cent had less than primary schooling. A much larger proportion had post-secondary qualifications. There had also been a growth in the numbers employed in education: over 46 per cent of the total increase in numbers of civil servants over these years were in the education sector, and many of them were women (Table 9.5).

In the late 1960s and early 1970s, many graduates sought employment in the civil service as a civil service job offered stability, and there were few opportunities in the private sector. Over the 1970s, remuneration in government employment grew, mainly as a result of the growth in supplementary allowances of various kinds, usually paid to staff who were working on what were classified as development projects (Gray 1979). But such payments were discretionary, and declined over the 1980s as

Table 9.5 *Size and composition of the civil service, 1973/1974 and 1996/1997 (×1,000)*

	1973/1974	1996/1997
Total	1,527	4,094
Male	1,235	2,650
Female	292	1,444
Golongan I	720	392
Primary or less	564	435
Structural employees	202	269
Education	544	1,725

Source: Department of Information, **Lampiran Pidato Pertanggungjawaban Presiden didepan MPR 1 March 1993**, Table XXII-2; Department of Information, **Lampiran Pidato Kenegaraan 1998**: Table XXV-2.

development budgets were cut in most departments. Increasingly over the 1980s and 1990s, as the private sector demand for skilled workers grew, many of the best graduates from the best universities in Indonesia in disciplines such as medicine, engineering, accountancy and law joined private firms which usually offered higher, and more stable, remuneration. While the average level of education among government employees increased, the best and the brightest among university graduates, especially in Java, often looked for employment elsewhere. Their motivation in doing so may not have been entirely to do with remuneration. Many joined the private sector because it was believed that promotion was based on merit, and there was less need, or temptation, to become involved in corrupt behaviour. Research carried out at the end of the 1990s suggested that most civil servants were not in fact underpaid, given their qualifications, compared with what they could get in the private sector (Filmer and Lindauer 2001). It was only at the highest levels that there was a disparity in earnings, and even then additional payments, some in cash and some in kind, probably made up at least some of the difference.

Echoing the earlier generation of students who had protested against corruption in the 1960s, the students who occupied government buildings in Jakarta in 1998 also protested at the corruption and nepotism of the late Suharto era. But in the immediate aftermath of the fall of Suharto many were disappointed at the slow pace of change. The Corruption Eradication Commission (KPK) was established by law in 2002, and began work the following year. Many were sceptical that it would have any impact, given its small resources and the sheer size of the problem. Indonesia's score in international league tables remained low after 1998; indeed the World Bank's governance indicators found that although there had been some improvement in 'voice and accountability' between 1996 and 2005, there had been a decline in the corruption score (Table 5.2). Some commentators blamed Indonesia's continued poor performance on the decentralisation policies which, in giving more power to subnational levels of government, had replaced a highly centralised system of corruption with a more fragmented one. Foreign business executives complained that whereas in the past payments to officials in central departments usually resulted in the necessary permissions being quickly provided, under the new system there was far less certainty, especially at the regional level (Lim and Stern 2002: 25).

Support from President Yudhoyono for the KPK at times appeared to be less than wholehearted, and up until 2008 the KPK had only been able to investigate a small proportion of the thousands of cases submitted to it. A report which compared anti-corruption agencies across Asia found that it was 'putting up a valiant effort in an uphill battle' (APEC 2009: 121).

But funding and staffing levels did improve and by the end of the Yudhoyono administration the KPK had achieved success in a number of high-profile cases, which led to the resignation of one cabinet minister and a number of senior officials. President Joko Widodo, after his election, referred all the candidates short-listed for cabinet posts to the KPK for their assessment. It was reported that some were turned down as a result of the KPK reports. The Commission has been given considerable powers to impose wiretaps and travel bans and to demand full financial information from those under investigation. It also appears to have strong support from many in the media, leading NGOs and the wider public. But its effectiveness will in the final analysis depend on its support from the top.

What can the Indonesian government do to assist the poor?

In the immediate aftermath of the transfer of power in 1949, the legitimacy of the Indonesian government depended to a large extent on its ability to improve the lot of the great majority of Indonesians who were very poor. The creation of a just and prosperous society was part of the national ideology, *Pancasila*, to which all Indonesians were expected to subscribe during the Suharto era, and beyond. In the decades from 1966 to 1996, a number of policies were put in place which were intended to benefit the poor, including subsidies to provinces and sub-provincial governments which were intended to be spent on labour-intensive public works, a range of programmes intended to boost smallholder production of food crops and cash crops, and credit schemes aimed at small and household enterprises. In most cases, these programmes were not targeted to the very poor, but to people who had at least some productive assets. The *Bimas* credit programmes were channelled mainly to those farmers who controlled irrigated rice land, while credit schemes such as *Kupedes* were only available to borrowers who could provide some collateral (Patten and Rosengard 1991). It is probable that, to the extent that they led to increased demand for labour in the rice sector and elsewhere, their secondary impact on employment was positive. But these policies were not directly targeted to the poor.

As the full effects of the crisis became clear in 1998, demands for new policies targeted specifically to the poor increased. These demands reflected a change in public expectations regarding social protection policies. In 1966, when the problem of poverty was much worse than in 1998, there were few demands placed on what was perceived as a very weak government apparatus, beyond the hope that Suharto and his advisers would stabilise prices, and provide basic necessities, especially food, at prices which people could afford. During the oil boom years it might have been fiscally possible to have initiated a public distribution system for food, or even a system of cash transfers, but the government was never willing to do this, and there was little support for such programmes from international development agencies. By 1998, both national and international opinion had changed. From 1998 onwards, the government adopted a range of 'social safety net' policies intended not just to provide rice to those households affected by falling incomes, but also to keep children in school, and to provide some assistance for medical expenses.

The price of rice had increased sharply in 1997, and by early 1998 there were fears that many poor households would no longer be able to afford adequate food, or at the very least would have to cut back on non-food expenditures including health and education in order to buy food. In July 1998, the government introduced a subsidised rice scheme, called the OPK (*Operasi Pasar Khusus*). The name was later changed to *Beras untuk Orang Miskin* (Rice for the Poor) and proved so popular that it was continued well after the immediate effects of the crisis were over. Other policies also adopted in 1998 were school subsidies and scholarships to prevent dropouts and the provision of health cards which supposedly gave poor households free access to sub-district health clinics and some hospitals.

To what extent were these policies targeted to the poor? A number of studies were carried out in the aftermath of the crisis which suggested that around 55 per cent of the subsidised rice and 69 per cent of the health cards were allocated to the bottom two quintiles in the expenditure distribution (Suryahadi et al. 2012: 360–1). Other studies found that most of the policies were mildly progressive, although many people who received some assistance were probably not below the official poverty line (Pritchett, Sumarto and Suryahadi 2012: 141). Given that many of the officials implementing the programmes had far from perfect information on which households were poor, as distinct from near-poor or not really poor at all, these results were probably as good as could have been expected. The popularity of the programmes ensured that they continued to receive political support; in 2005 the Yudhoyono administration implemented a new health insurance scheme for the poor, although it proved difficult to implement and was revised in 2008. A further initiative in 2005 (BLT) was the granting of unconditional cash transfers to compensate poor households for the reduction in the fuel subsidy. Around 19.1 million households, almost one-third of the total, were given ten dollars per month. This programme led to much criticism as the targeting was poor and the leakage was quite high; many observers thought it was timed to coincide with the 2005 round of elections. It continued until 2009, when it was replaced with a much smaller programme targeting the very poor whose children were dropping out of school (Suryahadi et al. 2012: 364–5).

Various other initiatives were adopted by the Yudhoyono administration under the umbrella of the National Program for Community Empowerment (PNPM). This programme endeavoured to coordinate a number of schemes intended to assist the poor, most of which were initiated in the latter part of the Suharto era including the *Kecamatan Development Program* (KDP), funded by the World Bank. The KDP required the active participation of local communities in selecting projects and in supervising their implementation, which in theory at least was supposed to ensure that projects were selected which benefited the majority, and corrupt practices in project implementation were kept to a minimum. Very few independent evaluations of PNPM projects are available but it would appear that in many of them participation of the poor is quite limited. Many cannot afford the time, or the travel costs, to attend meetings, which are often dominated by local officials (Sari and Widyaningrum 2012).

Most recent studies of poverty incidence in Indonesia have stressed that there are very considerable differences across provinces and districts, and that there are pockets of poverty even in the richer regions. This suggests that there is a role for sub-national poverty alleviation agencies in formulating effective programmes. In recent years there have been attempts to establish teams in districts to coordinate poverty reduction initiatives (TKPKD). In 2010, it was estimated that around 20 per cent of districts, many in Eastern Indonesia, had not set up a team, and others did not have the full support of local officials. One research project showed that teams needed to have 'a well-developed capacity to undertake program planning and budgeting' to be successful (Sumarto, Vothknecht and Wijaya 2014: 295). Unfortunately such a capacity is unlikely to be found in small, remote regions where local leaders often lack such skills.

The impact of government: 1900–2015

This chapter has argued that in the late colonial era, some progress was made towards the creation of what has been termed a 'modern fiscal state'. Certainly by the second decade of the twentieth century, the colonial government was taking on responsibilities for many functions beyond those of the classic 'nightwatchman state'. While law and order and the collection of taxes were hardly neglected, a considerable part of the budget was directed towards public works, health and education. It was undoubtedly the intention of the governments which assumed office in the 1950s to build on the colonial legacy, but the years from 1950 to 1966 in fact witnessed an attenuation of the fiscal capacity of the central government. Only after the Suharto government initiated the first of a series of five-year plans in 1969 did the central government once again have both the motivation and the resources to assume a key role in influencing the pace and direction of economic change. Government expenditures accounted for around 25 per cent of GDP by the end of the 1970s, with a substantial part being directed to public works, health and education.

The fall in the world price of oil in the early 1980s led to a period of budgetary restructuring, including a series of reforms in non-oil taxes which were intended to reduce the dependence on oil revenues. In fact the budget became increasingly dependent on foreign borrowing over the 1980s, and after two devaluations in 1983 and 1986, together with an appreciation of the Japanese yen, the rupiah costs of servicing the debt were substantial. The growth in debt servicing charges squeezed other expenditures; in addition, by the early 1990s the government appeared to have accepted that the private sector would have to provide a large share of investment resources. This led to a fall in spending on both the maintenance of existing infrastructure, and new projects.

The problem of infrastructure became more acute after economic growth picked up in the early twenty-first century. It was pointed out in Chapter 6 that attempts to get the private sector involved in electricity generation in the late Suharto era led to very favourable contracts being granted to consortia where the local counterparts were well-connected Indonesians, most of whom lacked any technical expertise. Attempts to renegotiate the contracts led to inevitable conflicts with the foreign firms, which damaged Indonesia's reputation in international investment circles. Efforts by the Yudhoyono government to seek foreign investment in infrastructure projects met with at best partial success. Given that in recent years budgetary expenditures by the central government have not exceeded 20 per cent of GDP, it is obvious that Indonesia will have to tap non-budget sources, both domestic and foreign, to develop new infrastructure. In spite of many promises made in the 2014 election campaign, it is far from clear how this will be done.

Indonesia's fiscal problems in recent years have been complicated by the growth of budgetary subsidies on the one hand and demands for more government assistance for the poor on the other. That the subsidies on petroleum products mainly benefited the non-poor is obvious; to the extent that these subsidies can be reduced in future years it will create more fiscal space for pro-poor expenditures. But what form these expenditures should take, and how rigorously they should be targeted, remain contested issues. It does seem clear that Indonesians now expect the government to provide more assistance to vulnerable groups in society, even if a consensus is still lacking on what form such assistance should take. In other parts of the world, as people become richer they seem to want their governments to do more for them, not less. There is little reason to expect that Indonesia in coming decades will be different.

10 Conclusions

Assessing Indonesia's economic progress over more than a century is fraught with pitfalls. There have been both remarkable achievements and major disappointments. Different analysts have tended to give greater weight to either the achievements or the failures with the result that their work is often criticised as being either too optimistic or too pessimistic. This study has tried to avoid both extremes, but might at times have appeared rather inconclusive. So it might be useful to summarise the progress which has undoubtedly occurred while drawing attention to the problems which remain.

This study has argued that Indonesia inherited some advantages from the Dutch colonial period, but also many disadvantages. In the early decades of the twentieth century, the Dutch built up a diversified export economy, and an effective fiscal state which promoted a range of policies in infrastructure development, education and health care, and land settlement in the less populated regions outside Java. While public expenditures were not exceptionally high on a per capita basis, there was considerable infrastructure development in Java and parts of Sumatra; some progress was also made in health and education although here the achievements were well behind Taiwan, the Philippines and British Malaya. There can be no doubt that some in the early post-1949 governments wanted to build on the Dutch legacy, but failed to mobilise the necessary resources. By 1965, the Indonesian state was far weaker than it had been in 1941, whether one looks at fiscal and monetary policy or administrative control over the vast archipelago.

That the thirty-two years when Suharto was in power saw substantial economic and social progress in Indonesia is undeniable. Admittedly he came to power after more than a decade of economic stagnation and mounting inflation, when living standards for many Indonesians had been declining. As far as we can judge from the available evidence, in the mid-1960s the great majority of the population were living below a modest poverty line, malnutrition was widespread, and infant and child mortality rates were much higher than in neighbouring countries. Over the next three decades there were considerable improvements not just in per capita GDP, but also in non-monetary indicators based on health and education. These improvements were sustained even after Suharto left office; in 2010 the *Human Development Report* published by the UNDP found that Indonesia had had the fourth fastest improvement in the world in human development from 1970 to 2010 (UNDP 2010: 29). This improvement was due not just to increases in GDP but also to increases in non-monetary indicators as well.

Whether or not the growth which occurred in Indonesia after 1968 was 'pro-poor' can be debated; it depends on how pro-poor growth is defined. But it is clear that the benefits from economic growth did not just accrue to a small minority in urban areas. Whether one looks at school enrolments in the six to fifteen age groups, infant and child mortality or food consumption, the evidence indicates that all expenditure groups benefited. The great majority of Indonesians were, in the early twenty-first century, eating more food, and better quality food, than previous generations. For staple foods such as rice, there was a rapid convergence in per capita consumption across expenditure groups (Timmer 2015: 103). Most had managed to get some formal schooling, and the great majority were literate in the national language. They could also expect to live much longer than their parents or grandparents.

These achievements have been emphasised by those economists who are on the optimistic side of the argument about growth and living standards in Indonesia over the past five decades. But there are counter-arguments. It is important to note that many countries in Asia, and indeed in other parts of the world, have seen faster per capita economic growth since the 1960s than in previous decades, and also considerable improvements in a range of non-monetary indicators. It was pointed out in Chapter 1 that over the twentieth century, per capita GDP in Indonesia fell behind several of the countries with which it might reasonably have hoped to achieve some catch up, especially after 1950. Per capita GDP in 2010 in Indonesia was a lower percentage of GDP in the Netherlands than it had been in 1900 (Table 1.2). Over these decades, Indonesia also fell further behind Japan, China and the USA. The fall relative to the Netherlands is particularly surprising because many people in the Netherlands were convinced in 1945 that the 'loss of the Indies' would have a devastating impact on the home economy, while most Indonesians were equally convinced that the economy would develop faster if it were free from colonial control. But in fact the Dutch economy grew quickly through the 1950s and 1960s while Indonesia stagnated. Between 1960 and 2010 the gap in per capita GDP widened between Indonesia and several other countries in Southeast Asia including Singapore, Thailand and Malaysia.

Indonesia also continues to rank quite low on several international rankings including the Human Development Index, the corruption index prepared by Transparency International, the Ease of Doing Business Index prepared by the World Bank and the Global Gender Gap Index prepared by the World Economic Forum. Even in those policy areas such as food production, family planning and education, where Suharto received international recognition in the 1980s, recent developments have been rather disappointing. Indonesia is once again very dependent on world markets not just for rice but also for wheat, corn, sugar, soybeans, meat and other foodstuffs. The fertility decline which began in the 1970s seems to have stalled at above replacement levels, and the goal of zero population growth seems as elusive as ever. Although infant and child mortality rates have fallen, there are large, and possibly growing disparities between income groups. Maternal mortality rates remain high in comparison with other Southeast Asian countries (National Academy of Sciences 2013: table 2–10). In most provinces over half of all births still take place at home, often without a trained midwife in attendance.

Although there was an impressive increase in primary school enrolments in the 1970s and 1980s, it has been more difficult to achieve the goal of universal nine-year enrolments. Many able students who do manage to complete the nine-year cycle cannot advance to the senior secondary and post-secondary levels, because they cannot afford the fees. Those who do manage to stay in school until eighteen receive an education of poor quality by global standards, as shown by Indonesia's weak performance in international tests. The problems in the education sector have been much discussed in the media and in academic circles in Indonesia for many years, and a number of proposals have been advanced for improving both quality and quantity. But most involve considerable increases in government expenditures, which have not been forthcoming.

Another issue which has attracted growing attention in recent years concerns the increase in expenditure inequalities, which almost certainly reflects growing disparities in income and wealth. However 'pro-poor' growth might have been in the Suharto era, evidence is mounting that it is becoming less so in the twenty-first century. The statistics on poverty published by the CBS reported that in 2013, 28.55 million Indonesians, or 11.5 per cent of the population, were below the official poverty line. But that poverty line is now very low, and has been falling relative to average per capita expenditures as reported in the *Susenas* surveys. Other studies using what purport to be internationally comparable poverty lines have shown that the incidence of poverty in Indonesia is much higher than the CBS estimates; an estimate prepared by the Asian Development Bank

found that, in 2010, 67.2 million Indonesians were poor by their definition. Poverty issues have received more attention in Indonesia since the
1997/1998 crisis, and in recent years the government has implemented a
series of programmes designed to assist the poor, but most of the initiatives have been hampered by inadequate funding and poor targeting.
While many politicians and officials at the national level and in the regions
may sincerely wish to improve access to education, health care and other
services on the part of the poor, they are frustrated by inadequate funds
and imperfect information.

A further issue which has attracted much attention in recent years is
the state of the nation's infrastructure. It is clear that there has been
serious under-investment in infrastructure since the 1980s, but there is
controversy about the reasons. Some studies have claimed that financial
resources are available, and have blamed difficulties in acquiring land,
and also shortages of skilled labour for the slow progress. But it has also
been argued that the infrastructure needs of the country over the next
decade and beyond will far exceed the fiscal capacity of the government,
even if tax and non-tax revenues could be increased. There is certainly
scope for public–private partnerships of various kinds with both domestic and foreign contractors, but such partnerships also give scope for a
range of corrupt practices. To many observers, it appears that the
capacity of the Indonesian government in recent years to implement
large-scale infrastructure projects has been weak compared with other
Asian countries, especially China. The planning process has generated
many targets but very often not much happens on the ground. The
decentralisation process may well have adversely affected the implementation of large-scale public works projects because there are now so
many sub-national units of government who think they should be
involved in project implementation, but lack the capacity to actually
do anything except delay progress. While it may well be true, as Aspinall
(2010: 27) argued, that decentralisation has 'greatly expanded the
capacity of the political structure to absorb, neutralize, and buy off
potential democratic spoilers', it is far from clear that it has improved
the capacity of the government to implement much-needed infrastructure development. In some sectors it has also had an adverse impact on
the willingness of private investors, whether Indonesian or foreign, to
become involved in new projects, given the unpredictable demands of
local authorities.

Debates about the impact of both greater democracy and decentralisation on economic growth in Indonesia will no doubt continue for many
years to come. Some analyses argue that much of the change which has
occurred since 1998 has been superficial, that old elites are still very

powerful at both the national and regional levels, and 'real change cannot be achieved so long as the social order of the previous regime and its ascendant political forces remain intact' (Hadiz and Robison 2013: 55). These authors point out that in other parts of the world, authoritarian or oligarchic rule has shown considerable resilience in the face of economic and institutional reforms. On the other hand, several studies have pointed to the regulatory and legal reforms in Indonesia since 1998 which have strengthened the role of new institutions such as the Constitutional Court and the Corruption Eradication Commission. To the extent that these institutions can become embedded within, and supported by, the political system, they have the potential to bring about further change.

The decentralisation legislation of 1999 was a reaction to what was seen as the excessive control of regions from the centre, which was a hallmark of the Suharto years. During the decade from 1956 to 1966, the central government's ability to control the national economy declined sharply and from its inception, Suharto's New Order was determined to re-establish the centre's power. In this it was remarkably successful. But the centralisation of power led to considerable resentment in many parts of the country. Those provinces with significant oil and mining sectors (Aceh, Riau, East Kalimantan and Irian Jaya) were aggrieved at the fact that most of the revenues from the mining sector were appropriated by central government agencies; indeed most provincial officials were given no information on how large the revenues were. In the forestry sector, concessions were granted with no consultation with local people, who had to cope with the environmental consequences of uncontrolled destruction of the significant part of the nation's forest resources. The central government justified their control of both minerals and forests by claiming these resources belonged to the Indonesian people as a whole, and should be used for the benefit of the entire nation. But this argument was increasingly difficult to defend as corruption at the centre increased, and environmental problems in the regions became more severe.

The 1999 legislation was intended to address these problems although critics have argued that decentralisation, by introducing 'money politics' into the regions, may well have aggravated the problems of corruption and poor governance of natural resources. In the 1950s, policymakers tended to view Indonesia's natural resources as an almost unlimited asset, which could be exploited to fund national development projects. Many Indonesians now realise that the nation's natural resources are finite, and must be conserved, rather than plundered at will by either national or regional governments. But if government expenditures on infrastructure, health, education and welfare are to increase, taxes from conventional sources will have grow. How is this to be done? If parliaments at both the centre and in the regions are dominated by people from the higher income groups, they are unlikely to support substantial increases in either income taxes or broad-based consumption taxes. There might be scope for further borrowing to finance infrastructure projects which yield reasonable rates of return but other types of expenditure will have to be financed from recurrent revenues. So far greater democracy in Indonesia does not seem to have produced a consensus on how such revenues are to be raised.

Several recent studies have emphasised that many of the policy debates in post-Suharto Indonesia are about issues which are not new but were identified in studies dating back to the early post-independence era. The problem of extreme dualism in the Indonesian economy, with a small number of large enterprises and many millions of small or household enterprises, has attracted attention since the 1950s. Chapter 7 drew attention to the observation made by Geertz regarding the inability of small-scale businesses in East Java to grow into larger, more diversified enterprises. Since the 1970s, there have been many debates about how to foster *pribumi* entrepreneurs; inevitably these debates frequently focus on what is seen as the grossly disproportionate share of Chinese-owned enterprises among medium and large firms in sectors such as manufacturing, construction, transport, wholesale and retail trade. Some Indonesians have called for Malaysian-style affirmative action policies, in spite of the obvious absurdity of trying to implement policies designed to support more than 98 per cent of the population against less than 2 per cent. The superior performance of the Chinese in business since 1950 can be attributed to several factors, including their better access to education in the Dutch era, their exclusion from almost all public sector jobs, and from political office after 1950, and the favours some Chinese businesses received from Suharto, who probably viewed indigenous businesspeople as potential threats to his own ambitions to build up a family dynasty. Over time, it is probable that the Chinese dominance in large- and medium-scale enterprises in Indonesia will decline, but it is unclear if government policies can hasten the process.

Other issues which were extensively debated in the early years of Suharto's presidency included civil service reform, the desirability or otherwise of outward-looking trade and investment policies, and the problem of poverty, which was often viewed in terms of an urban–rural divide (McCawley 2013: 281–5). These debates continued until 1998 and beyond. It was argued in the previous chapter that the composition and remuneration of the civil service changed considerably between the 1970s and the 1990s, and by the end of the 1990s most civil servants were not badly paid compared with equivalent workers in the private sector, although many probably depended on extra payments to supplement their basic salaries. Whether Indonesian public opinion in the early twenty-first century is more supportive of 'outward looking' economic policies than it was in the 1960s can be debated, but it is clear that many millions of Indonesians are now directly engaged in the global economy, either as workers in traded goods industries at home, or as migrants seeking employment in other parts of the world. Official attitudes to both these aspects of globalisation in recent decades have fluctuated, but might in the final analysis be largely irrelevant. Indonesians, like other global citizens, will increasingly seek employment wherever they can find the opportunity to maximise their earnings, either at home or abroad, whatever the attitude of their government might be.

But at the same time many Indonesians cannot, because of their inadequate skills, their poor health, their age or other reasons, join the race towards employment in what might be termed the globalised parts of the domestic economy. Neither can they migrate to seek work abroad. What can be done to improve their lot? Providing better education and health care is obviously crucial to improve the prospects of the younger generation, although this will involve more government expenditures than has occurred since 1950. Government income supplements might help, although whether they should be delivered in cash or kind remains a disputed issue. The government administrative apparatus in Indonesia remains weak, and it would be unwise to place extra demands on it, at least in the short run.

Since the crisis of the late 1990s, Indonesia's economic growth has been reasonable, but hardly spectacular. Allowing for the decline in the terms of trade, annual average growth between 2000 and 2014 was around 4.4 per cent (Table 6.2). Per capita growth was around 3 per cent per annum. This was faster than most of the OECD economies over these years, and if this growth can be maintained, Indonesia will probably have caught up with Japan by the latter part of this century, or perhaps earlier. Obviously a faster rate of growth in Indonesia relative to the high-income Asian economies will imply faster catch-up. But economic growth is a necessary, but not sufficient, solution to the economic and social challenges which Indonesia faces. In the seven decades since Sukarno and Hatta declared Indonesia's independence in the wake of the Japanese defeat in 1945, the great majority of Indonesians have seen some improvement in living standards, but serious challenges remain. Inequalities in income and wealth are substantial and probably increasing. Access to good-quality health care and education is still restricted to a small minority, while many millions have to cope with the consequences of inadequate infrastructure and environmental degradation. Governments at both the centre and in the regions together with civil society organisations will have to tackle these challenges in coming decades. If they can do so successfully, hundreds of millions of Indonesians can look forward to a better quality of life. But if they fail, the country faces a very uncertain political and economic future.

Bibliography

Abdullah, Taufik (2010), 'Nationalist Activities during the Japanese Period', in Peter Post, William H. Fredericks, Iris Heidebrink and Shigeru Sato (Editors), *The Encyclopedia of Indonesia in the Pacific War*, Leiden: Brill.

Abrera, Ma Alcestis S. (1976), 'Philippine Poverty Thresholds', in Mahar Mangahas (Editor), *Measuring Philippine Development: Report of the Social Indicators Project*, Manila: The Development Academy of the Philippines.

Ahrensdorf, Joachim (1959), 'Central Bank Policies and Inflation: A Case Study of Four Less Developed Economies, 1949–1957', *International Monetary Fund Staff Papers*, Vol VII (2), pp. 274–301.

Alexander, Jennifer (1986), 'Information and Price Setting in a Rural Javanese Market', *Bulletin of Indonesian Economic Studies*, Vol XXII (1), pp. 88–112.

Alexander, Jennifer (1987), *Trade, Traders and Trading in Rural Java*, Singapore: Oxford University Press.

Alexander, Jennifer and Paul Alexander (1971), 'Labour Demand and "Involution" of Javanese Agriculture', *Social Analysis*, No. 3, pp. 22–44.

Alexander, Jennifer and Paul Alexander (1982), 'Shared Poverty as Ideology: Agrarian Relationships in Colonial Java', *Man*, Vol 17 (4), pp. 597–619.

Alexander, Jennifer and Paul Alexander (1991), 'Protecting Peasants from Capitalism: The Subordination of Javanese Traders by the Colonial State', *Comparative Studies in Society and History*, Vol 33, pp. 370–94.

Alexander, Jennifer and Anne Booth (1992), 'The Service Sector', in Anne Booth (Editor), *The Oil Boom and After: Indonesian Economic Policy and Performance in the Soeharto Era*, Singapore: Oxford University Press.

Ali, Shamsher (1966), 'Inter-island Shipping', *Bulletin of Indonesian Economic Studies*, no 3, pp. 27–51.

Alisjahbana, Armida and Chris Manning, 'Labour Market Dimensions of Poverty in Indonesia', *Bulletin of Indonesian Economic Studies*, Vol 42 (2), pp. 236–61.

Alkire, Sabina and Maria Emma Santos (2010), 'Acute Multidimensional Poverty: A New Index for Developing Countries', *OPHI Working Paper No 38*, Oxford: Department of International Development, Queen Elizabeth House.

Anand, Sudhir, Paul Segal and Joseph E. Stiglitz (Editors), *Debates on the Measurement of Global Poverty*, Oxford: Oxford University Press.

Anderson, Kym, Gordon Rausser and Johan Swinnen (2013), 'The Political Economy of Policies: Insights from Distortions to Agricultural and Food Markets', *Journal of Economic Literature*, Vol 51 (2), 423–77.

Andrus, J.R. (1948), *Burmese Economic Life*, Stanford: Stanford University Press.

Anspach, Ralph (1969), 'Indonesia', in Ralph Anpach et al., *Underdevelopment and Economic Nationalism in Southeast Asia*, Ithaca: Cornell University Press.

APEC (2009), *Comparative Study of Anti-Corruption Measures and Procedures in Selected APEC Economies*, Singapore: APEC Secretariat.

Ark, Bart van (1988), 'The Volume and Price of Indonesian Exports, 1823–1940: The Long-Term Trend and Its Measurement', *Bulletin of Indonesian Economic Studies*, Vol 24 (3), pp. 87–120.

Arndt, H.W. (1971), 'Banking in Hyperinflation and Stabilization', in Bruce Glassburner (Editor), *The Economy of Indonesia: Selected Readings*, Ithaca: Cornell University Press.

Arndt, H.W. (1975), 'P.T. Krakatau Steel', *Bulletin of Indonesian Economic Studies*, Vol 11 (2), pp. 120–6.

Ascher, William (1999), *Why Governments Waste Natural Resources: Policy Failures in Developing Countries*, Baltimore: The Johns Hopkins University Press.

Asher, Mukul G. and Anne Booth (1992), 'Fiscal Policy', in Anne Booth (Editor), *The Oil Boom and After: Indonesian Economic Policy and Performance in the Soeharto Era*, Singapore: Oxford University Press.

Asian Development Bank (2008), 'Comparing Poverty across Countries: The Role of Purchasing Power Parities', in *Key Indicators 2008 Special Chapter*, Manila: Asian Development Bank.

Asian Development Bank (2010), 'The Rise of Asia's Middle Class', in *Key Indicators 2010 Special Chapter*, Manila: Asian Development Bank.

Asian Development Bank (2014), 'Poverty in Asia: A Deeper Look', in *Key Indicators 2014 Special Chapter*, Manila: Asian Development Bank.

Aspinall, Edward (2010), 'Indonesia: The Irony of Success', *Journal of Democracy*, Vol 21 (2), pp. 20–34.

Asra, Abuzar (1989), 'Inequality Trends in Indonesia, 1969–1981', *Bulletin of Indonesian Economic Studies*, Vol 25(2), pp. 100–110.

Aswicahyono, Haryo, M.C. Basri and Hal Hill (2000), 'How Not to Industrialise? Indonesia's Automotive Industry', *Bulletin of Indonesian Economic Studies*, Vol 36 (1), pp. 209–41.

Aswicahyono, Haryo, Hal Hill and Dionisius Narjoko (2010), 'Industrialisation after a Deep Economic Crisis: Indonesia', *Journal of Development Studies*, Vol 46 (6), pp. 1084–108.

Aswicahyono, Haryo, Hal Hill and Dionisius Narjoko (2011), 'Indonesian Industrialisation: Jobless Growth?', in Chris Manning and Sudarno Sumarto (Editors), *Employment, Living Standards and Poverty in Contemporary Indonesia*, Singapore: Institute of Southeast Asian Studies.

Aswicahyono, Haryo, Hal Hill and Dionisius Narjoko (2012), 'Industrialization: Patterns, Issues, and Constraints', in H. Hill, M.E. Khan and J. Zhuang (Editors), *Diagnosing the Indonesian Economy: Toward Inclusive and Green Growth*, London: Anthem Press for the Asian Development Bank.

Athukorala, Prema-Chandra and Hal Hill (2010), 'Asian Trade: Long-term Patterns and Key Policy Issues', *Asian-Pacific Economic Literature*, Vol 24 (2), pp. 52–82.

Atkinson, A.B.(1975), *The Economics of Inequality*, Oxford: Clarendon Press.

Bairoch, Paul (1993), *Economics and World History: Myths and Paradoxes*, Chicago: University of Chicago Press.

Baldwin, Richard (2006), 'Managing the Noodle Bowl: The Fragility of East Asian Regionalism', *Working Paper no. 5561*, London: Centre for Economic Policy Research.

Bank Indonesia (1968), *Report for the Years 1960–1965*, Jakarta: Bank Indonesia.

Bank Indonesia (1987), *Report for the Year 1986/87*, Jakarta: Bank Indonesia.

Barclay, George (1954), *Colonial Development and Population in Taiwan*, Princeton: Princeton University Press.

Basri, M. Chatib and Arianto Patunru (2006) 'Survey of Recent Developments', *Bulletin of Indonesian Economic Studies*, Vol 42 (3), pp. 295–319.

Bayly, Christopher and Tim Harper (2007), *Forgotten Wars: The End of Britain's Asian Empire*, London: Allen Lane.

Beeby, C.E. (1979), *Assessment of Indonesian Education: A Guide in Planning*, Wellington: New Zealand Council for Educational Research in association with Oxford University Press, 1979.

Berry, Albert (1978), 'A Positive Interpretation of the Expansion of Urban Services in Latin America, with Some Colombian Evidence', *Journal of Development Studies*, Vol 14 (2), pp. 210–31.

Bhalla, Surjit (2010), 'Raising the Standard: The War on Global Poverty', in Sudhir Anand, Paul Segal and Joseph E. Stiglitz (Editors), *Debates on the Measurement of Global Poverty*, Oxford: Oxford University Press.

Birdsall, Nancy (2010), 'The (Indispensable) Middle Class in Developing Countries: or, the Rich and the Rest, Not the Poor and the Rest', *Working Paper 207*, Washington: Center for Global Development.

Boediono (2002), 'The International Monetary Fund Support Program in Indonesia: Comparing Implementation under Three Presidents', *Bulletin of Indonesian Economic Studies*, Vol 38 (3), pp. 385–91.

Boeke, J.H. (1927), 'Objective and Personal Elements in Colonial Welfare Policy', as translated and reprinted in *Indonesian Economics: The Concept of Dualism in Theory and Practice*, The Hague: W. van Hoeve 1966.

Boeke, J.H. (1953), *Economics and Economic Policy of Dual Societies, as Exemplified by Indonesia*, Haarlem: H.D. Tjeenk Willink & Zoon.

Boomgaard, Peter (1986), 'The Welfare Services in Indonesia', *Itinerario*, Vol X (1), pp. 57–82.

Boomgaard, Peter (1990), 'Why Work for Wages? Free Labour in Java, 1600–1900', *Economic and Social History in the Netherlands*, Vol II, pp. 37–56.

Boomgaard, Peter (1993), 'Upliftment down the Drain? Effects of Welfare Measures in Late Colonial Indonesia', in Jan-Paul Dirkse, Frans Husken and Mario Rutten (Editors), *Development and Social Welfare: Indonesia's Experiences under the New Order*, Leiden: KITLV Press.

Boomgaard, Peter and A.J. Gooszen (1991), *Changing Economy of Indonesia: Volume 11: Population Trends, 1795–1942*, Amsterdam: Royal Tropical Institute.

Booth, Anne (1988), *Agricultural Development in Indonesia*, Sydney: Allen and Unwin.

Booth, Anne (1990), 'The Evolution of Fiscal Policy and the Role of Government in the Colonial Economy', in Anne Booth, W.J. O'Malley and Anna Weidemann

(Editors), *Indonesian Economic History in the Dutch Colonial Era*, Monograph Series 35, New Haven: Yale University Southeast Asian Studies.

Booth, Anne (1992), 'Income Distribution and Poverty', in Anne Booth (Editor), *The Oil Boom and After: Indonesian Economic Policy and Performance in the Soeharto Era*, Singapore: Oxford University Press 1992, pp, 41–76.

Booth, Anne (1993), 'Counting the Poor in Indonesia', *Bulletin of Indonesian Economic Studies*, Vol 29 (1), April 1993.

Booth, Anne (1994), 'Repelita VI and the Second Long-term Development Plan', *Bulletin of Indonesian Economic Studies*, Vol 30 (3), pp. 3–39.

Booth, Anne (1997), 'Rapid Economic Growth and Poverty Decline: A Comparison of Indonesia and Thailand 1981–1990', *Journal of International Development*, Vol 9 (2), pp. 169–87.

Booth, Anne (1998), *The Indonesian Economy in the Nineteenth and Twentieth Centuries: A History of Missed Opportunities*, Basingstoke: The Macmillan Press.

Booth, Anne (2000), 'Poverty and Inequality in the Soeharto Era: An Assessment', *Bulletin of Indonesian Studies*, Vol 36 (1), pp. 73–104.

Booth, Anne (2001), 'The Causes of South East Asia's Economic Crisis: A Sceptical Review of the Debate', *Asia Pacific Business Review*, Vol 8 (2), pp.19–48.

Booth, Anne (2002), 'The Changing Role of Non-Farm Activities in Agricultural Households in Indonesia: Some Insights from the Agricultural Censuses', *Bulletin of Indonesian Studies*, Vol 38 (2), pp. 179–200.

Booth, Anne (2003), 'The Impact of a Severe Economic Crisis on Poverty and Income Distribution: An Indonesian Case Study, 1997–1999', in Anne Booth and Paul Mosley (Editors), *The New Poverty Strategies: What Have They Achieved? What Have We Learned?* Basingstoke: Palgrave.

Booth, Anne (2005), 'The Evolving Role of the Central Government in Economic Planning and Policy Making in Indonesia', *Bulletin of Indonesian Economic Studies*, Vol 41 (2), pp. 197–219.

Booth, Anne (2007), *Colonial Legacies: Economic and Social Development in East and Southeast Asia*, Honolulu: University of Hawai'i Press.

Booth, Anne (2010), 'Splitting, Splitting and Splitting Again: A Brief History of the Development of Regional Government in Indonesia since Independence', *Bijdragen tot de Taal-Land-en Volkenkunde*, Vol 167 (1), pp. 31–60.

Booth, Anne (2012a), 'The Performance of the Indonesian Agricultural Sector: Twelve Questions and Some Tentative Answers', in Anne Booth, Chris Manning and Thee Kian Wie (Editors), *Land Livelihood, the Economy and the Environment in Indonesia*, Jakarta: Yayasan Pustaka Obor Indonesia.

Booth, Anne (2012b), 'Measuring Living Standards in Different Colonial Systems: Some Evidence from South East Asia, 1900–1942', *Modern Asian Studies*, Vol 46 (5), 1145–81.

Booth, Anne (2013a), 'Colonial Revenue Policies and the Impact of the Transition to Independence in South East Asia', *Bijdragen tot de Taal-Land-en Volkenkunde*, Vol 169, pp. 1–31.

Booth, Anne (2013b), 'Varieties of Exploitation in Colonial Settings: Dutch and Belgian Policies in Indonesia and the Congo', in Ewout Frankema and Frans Buelens (Editors), *Colonial Exploitation and Economic Development: The Belgian Congo and Indonesia Compared*, Abingdon: Routledge.

Booth, Anne (2015), 'Trade and Growth in the Colonial and Post-colonial Periods', in Alicia Schrikker and Jeroen Touwen (Editors), *Promises and Predicaments: Trade and Entrepreneurship in Colonial and Independent Indonesia in the 19ᵗʰ and 20ᵗʰ Centuries*, Singapore: NUS Press.

Booth, Anne and Peter McCawley (1981), 'Fiscal Policy', in Anne Booth and Peter McCawley (Editors), *The Indonesian Economy during the Soeharto Era*, Kuala Lumpur: Oxford University Press.

Booth, Anne and R.M. Sundsrum (1981), 'Income Distribution', in Anne Booth and Peter McCawley (Editors), *The Indonesian Economy during the Soeharto Era*, Kuala Lumpur: Oxford University Press.

Borsuk, Richard and Nancy Chng (2014), *Liem Sioe Liong's Salim Group: The Business Pillar of Suharto's Indonesia*, Singapore: Institute of Southeast Asian Studies.

Bousquet, G.H. (1940), *A French View of the Netherlands Indies*, London: Oxford University Press.

Breman, Jan (2002), 'New Thoughts on Colonial Labour in Indonesia', *Journal of Southeast Asian Studies*, Vol 33 (2), pp. 335–39.

Brown, Rajeswary A. (2004), 'Conglomerates in Contemporary Indonesia', *Southeast Asia Research*, Vol 12 (6), pp. 378–407.

Brown, Rajeswary A. (2006), 'Indonesian Corporations, Cronyism, and Corruption', *Modern Asian Studies*, Vol 40 (4), pp. 953–992.

Bruno, Michael (1994), 'Development Issues in a Changing World: New Lessons, Old Debates, Open Questions', in *Proceedings of the World Bank Annual Conference on Development Economics, Supplement to the World Bank Economic Review*, Washington: World Bank.

Bureau of Census and Statistics (1947), *Yearbook of Philippine Statistics 1946*, Manila: Bureau of Census and Statistics.

Butt, Simon and Tim Lindsey (2008), 'Economic Reform When the Constitution Matters: Indonesia's Constitutional Court and Article 33', *Bulletin of Indonesian Economic Studies*, Vol 44(2), pp. 239–61.

Cain, Mead and Geoff McNicoll (1988), 'Population Growth and Agrarian Outcomes', in Ronald Lee et al. (Editors), *Population, Food and Rural Development*, Oxford: Clarendon Press.

Cameron, Lisa (2002), 'Growth with or without Equity? The distributional impact of Indonesia Development', *Asian-Pacific Economic Literature*, Vol 16 (2), 1–17.

Carney, Richard W. and Natasha Hamilton-Hart (2015), 'What Do Changes in Corporate Ownership in Indonesia Tell Us?', *Bulletin of Indonesian Economic Studies*, Vol 51 (1), pp. 123–46.

Castles, Lance (1965), 'Socialism and Private Business: The Latest Phase', *Bulletin of Indonesian Economic Studies*, No. 1, pp. 13–46.

CBS (1947), *Statistical Pocketbook of Indonesia 1941*, Batavia: Department of Economic Affairs, Central Bureau of Statistics.

CBS (1959), *Statistical Pocketbook of Indonesia 1959*, Djakarta: Central Bureau of Statistics.

CBS (1963), *Statistical Pocketbook of Indonesia 1963*, Djakarta: Central Bureau of Statistics.

CBS (1968), *Statistical Pocketbook of Indonesia 1964–1967*, Djakarta: Central Bureau of Statistics.

CBS (1970), *Pendapatan Nasional Indonesia (National Income of Indonesia) 1960–1968*, Jakarta: Central Bureau of Statistics, Statistical Research and Development Centre.

CBS (1971), *Statistical Pocketbook of Indonesia 1968 and 1969*, Djakarta: Central Bureau of Statistics.

CBS (1974), *Statistical Pocketbook of Indonesia 1972/73*, Djakarta: Central Bureau of Statistics.

CBS (1975a), *Penduduk Indonesia (Population of Indonesia), Seri D*, Jakarta: Central Bureau of Statistics.

CBS (1975b), *Statistical Pocketbook of Indonesia 1974/75*, Djakarta: Central Bureau of Statistics.

CBS (1979), *Statistical Yearbook of Indonesia 1978*, Jakarta: Central Bureau of Statistics.

CBS (1992), *Evaluasi Metodologi Susenas 1963/1964–1992*, Jakarta: Central Bureau of Statistics.

CBS (1994), *Statistik Pendidikan; Survei Sosial Ekonomi Nasional 1992 (Education Statistics, National Socioeconomic Survey)*, Jakarta: Central Bureau of Statistics, March.

CBS (1996), *Penduduk Indonesia: Hasil Survei Penduduk Antar Sensus 1995 (Results of the 1995 Intercensal Population Survey)*, Jakarta: Central Bureau of Statistics.

CBS (1997), *Statistical Yearbook of Indonesia 1996*, Jakarta: Central Bureau of Statistics.

CBS (1998), *Sensus Ekonomi 1996: Hasil Pencacahan Lengkap*, Jakarta: Central Bureau of Statistics.

CBS (2001), *Population of Indonesia: Results of the 2000 Population Census, Series L2.2*, Jakarta: Central Board of Statistics.

CBS (2003), *Statistik Pendidikan; Survei Sosial Ekonomi Nasional (Education Statistics, National Socioeconomic Survey)*, Jakarta: Central Board of Statistics.

CBS (2004), *Statistical Yearbook of Indonesia 2003*, Jakarta: Central Board of Statistics.

CBS (2006a), *Statistical Yearbook of Indonesia 2005*, Jakarta: Central Board of Statistics.

CBS (2006b), *Estimasi Parameter Demografi: Fertilitas, Mortalitas dan Migrasi: Hasil Survei Penduduk Antar Sensus 2005*, Jakarta: Central Board of Statistics.

CBS (2007), *Selected Socioeconomic Indicators of Indonesia, March 2007*, From www.bps.go.id (accessed 1 November 2007).

CBS (2008a), *Sistem Neraca Sosial Ekonomi Indonesia 2005*, Jakarta: Central Board of Statistics.

CBS (2008b), *Perkembangan Penguluaran/Konsumsi Rumah Tangga 1993–2008*, Jakarta: Central Board of Statistics.

CBS (2009), *Statistical Yearbook of Indonesia 2009*, Jakarta: Central Board of Statistics.

CBS (2010), *Statistical Yearbook of Indonesia 2010*, Jakarta: Central Board of Statistics.

CBS (2011), *Penghitungan dan Analisis Kemiskinan Makro Indonesia, Tahun 2011*, Jakarta: Central Board of Statisics, December.

CBS (2012a), *Penduduk Indonesia: Hasil Sensus Penduduk 2010 (Population of Indonesia: Results of the Indonesia Population Census, 2010)*, Jakarta: Central Board of Statistics.

CBS (2012b), *Statistical Yearbook of Indonesia 2012*, Jakarta: Central Board of Statistics.

CBS (2013), *Statistik Pendidikan; Survei Sosial Ekonomi Nasional 2012 (Education Statistics, National Socioeconomic Survey)*, Jakarta: Central Board of Statistics.

CBS (2014), *Perkembangan Beberapa Indikator Utama Sosial-Ekonomi: Indonesia Februari 2014*, From www.bps.go.id (accessed 12 December 2014).

Chernichovsky, Dov and Oey Astra Meesok (1984), 'Poverty in Indonesia: A Profile', *World Bank Staff Working Papers, Number 671*, Washington: World Bank.

Collier, William L. et al. (1982), 'Acceleration of Rural Development in Java', *Bulletin of Indonesian Economic Studies*, Vol 18 (3), pp. 84–101.

Coppel, Charles A. (1983), *Indonesian Chinese in Crisis*, Kuala Lumpur: Oxford University Press.

Creutzberg, P. (1976), *Changing Economy of Indonesia: Volume 2: Public Finance, 1816–1940*, The Hague: M. Nijhoff.

Cribb, Robert (1993), 'Development Policy in the Early 20th Century', in Jan-Paul Dirkse, Frans Husken and Mario Rutten (Editors), *Development and Social Welfare: Indonesia's Experiences under the New Order*, Leiden: KITLV Press.

Cunningham, Clark E. (1958), 'The Postwar Migration of the Toba-Bataks to East Sumatra', Cultural Report Series No. 5, New Haven: Yale University Southeast Asia Studies.

Damuri, Yose R. and Creina Day (2015), 'Survey of Recent Developments', *Bulletin of Indonesian Economic Studies*, Vol 51 (1), pp. 3–27.

Daroesman, Ruth (1972), 'Finance of Education, Part II', *Bulletin of Indonesian Economic Studies*, Vol 8 (1), pp. 32–68.

Dartanto, Teguh and Nurkholis (2013), 'The Determinants of Poverty Dynamics in Indonesia: Evidence from Panel Data', *Bulletin of Indonesian Economic Studies*, Vol 49 (1): 61–84.

Davidson, Jamie S. (2015), *Indonesia's Changing Political Economy: Governing the Roads*, Cambridge: Cambridge University Press.

Deaton, Angus (2010), 'Measuring Poverty in a Growing World (or Measuring Growth in a Poor World', in Sudhir Anand, Paul Segal and Joseph E. Stiglitz (Editors), *Debates on the Measurement of Global Poverty*, Oxford: Oxford University Press.

Department of Statistics (1939), *Malayan Yearbook 1939*, Singapore: Government Printing Office for the Department of Statistics, Straits Settlements and Federated Malay States.

Department of Information (1994), *Lampiran Pidato Kenegaraan Presiden Republik Indonesia: Pelaksannan Repelita V* (Appendix to the State Speech of the President: implementation of the Fifth Five Year Plan), Jakarta: Department of Information.

Dick, Howard (2002), 'Formation of the Nation-state, 1930s–1966', in Howard Dick, Vincent J.H. Houben, J. Thomas Lindblad and Thee Kian Wie, *The Emergence of a National Economy*, Sydney: Allen and Unwin.

Dixon, John A. (1984), 'Consumption', in Walter P. Falcon et al., *The Cassava Economy of Java*, Stanford: Stanford University Press.

Djiwandono, J. Soedradjad (2004), 'Liquidity Support to Banks during Indonesia's Financial Crisis', *Bulletin of Indonesian Economic Studies*, Vol 40 (1), pp. 59–75.

Dowling, J. Malcolm and Yap Chin-Fang (2008), 'Indonesian Economic Development: Mirage or Miracle', *Journal of Asian Economics*, Vol 19, pp. 474–85.

ECAFE (1964), 'Review of Long-term Economic Projections for Selected Countries in the ECAFE Region', *Development Programming Techniques Series No. 5*, Bangkok: United Nations Economic Commission for Asia and the Far East.

Edgren, Gus (1987), *The Growing Sector: Studies of Public Sector Employment in Asia*, New Delhi: Asian Employment Programme, International Labour Organization.

Elson, Dominic (2011), 'An Economic Case for Tenure Reform in Indonesia's Forests', (www.rightsandresources.org/documents/files/doc-2491. Accessed 29/11/2011).

Elson, R.E. (1994), *Village Java under the Cultivation System, 1830–1870*, Sydney: Allen and Unwin for the AASA.

Elson, R.E. (2001), *Suharto: A Political Biography*, Cambridge: Cambridge University Press.

Elson, R.E. (2008), *The Idea of Indonesia: A History*, Cambridge: Cambridge University Press.

Emmer, Pieter C. (1998), 'The Economic Impact of the Dutch Expansion Overseas, 1570–1870', *Revista de Historia Economica*, XVI (1): 157–75.

Eng, Pierre van der (1998a), 'Exploring Exploitation: The Netherlands and Colonial Indonesia, 1870–1940', *Revista de Historia Economica*, XVI (1): 291–321.

Eng, Pierre van der (1998b), 'Cassava in Indonesia: A Historical Re-appraisal of an Enigmatic Crop', *Tonan Ajia Kenkyu (Southeast Asian Studies)*, Vol 36 (1), pp. 3–31.

Eng, Pierre van der (2000), 'Food for Growth: Trends in Indonesia's Food Supply, 1880–1995', *Journal of Interdisciplinary History*, Vol 30 (4), pp. 591–616.

Eng, Pierre van der (2002), 'Indonesia's Growth Performance in the Twentieth Century', in A. Maddison, D. Rao and W. Shepherd (Editors), *The Asian Economies in the Twentieth Century*, Cheltenham: Edward Elgar.

Eng, Pierre van der (2006), 'Surplus mobilisation in farm agriculture: a comparison of Java and Japan, 1870-1940', *Bulletin of Indonesian Economic Studies*, Vol. 42 (1), pp. 35–58.

Eng, Pierre van der (2013), 'Historical National Accounts Data for Indonesia, 1880–2012', mimeo, Australian National University.

Enoch, Charles, Olivier Frecaut and Arto Kovanen (2003), 'Indonesia's Banking Crisis: What Happened and What Did We Learn?', *Bulletin of Indonesian Economic Studies*, Vol 39(1), pp. 75–92.

Esmara, Hendra (1986), *Perencanaan dan Pembangunan di Indonesia*, Jakarta: Gramedia.

Evers, Hans-Dieter (1987), 'The Bureaucratization of Southeast Asia', *Comparative Studies in Society and History*, Vol 29 (4), pp. 666–685.

Fasseur, C. (1999), 'Ethical Policy and Economic Development: Some Experiences of the Colonial Past', paper presented to the Conference on the Modern Economic History of Indonesia, Gadjah Mada University Yogyakarta, July 26–28.

Feith, Herbert (1962), *The Decline of Constitutional Democracy in Indonesia*, Ithaca: Cornell University Press.

Filmer, Deon and David L. Lindauer (2001), 'Does Indonesia Have a "Low Pay" Civil Service', *Bulletin of Indonesian Economic Studies*, Vol 37 (2), pp. 189–205.

Frecaut, Olivier (2004), 'Indonesia's Banking Crisis: A New Perspective on $50 Billion of Losses', *Bulletin of Indonesian Economic Studies*, Vol 40 (1), pp. 37–57.

Friedman, Jed (2005), 'How Responsive Is Poverty to Growth? A Regional Analysis of Poverty, Inequality, and Growth in Indonesia, 1984–1999', in Ravi Kanbur and A.J. Venables (Editors), *Spatial Inequality and Development*, Oxford: Oxford University Press.

Fuglie, Keith O. (2010), 'Sources of Growth in Indonesian Agriculture', *Journal of Productivity Analysis*, Vol 33, pp. 225–240.

Fukao, Kyoji, Debin Ma and Tangjun Yuan (2007), 'Real GDP in Pre-war East Asia: A Benchmark Purchasing Power Parity Comparison with the U.S.', *Review of Income and Wealth*, Series 53. September, pp. 503–537.

Furman, Jason and Joseph Stiglitz (1998), 'Economic Crises: Evidence and Insights from East Asia', *Brookings Papers on Economic Activity*, Vol 1998 (2), pp. 1–135.

Furnivall, J.S. (1934a), 'State and Private Money Lending in Netherlands India', *Studies in the Economic and Social Development of the Netherlands East Indies*, IIIb, Rangoon: Burma Book Club.

Furnivall, J.S. (1934b), 'State Pawnshops in Netherlands India', *Studies in the Economic and Social Development of the Netherlands East Indies*, IIIc, Rangoon: Burma Book Club.

Furnivall, J.S. (1943), *Educational Progress in Southeast Asia*, New York: Institute of Pacific Relations.

Furnivall, J.S. (1944), *Netherlands India: A Study of Plural Economy*, Cambridge: Cambridge University Press.

Furnivall, J.S. (1948), *Colonial Policy and Practice, a Comparative Study of Burma and Netherlands India*, Cambridge: University Press.

Geertz, Clifford (1963), *Peddlers and Princes: Social Change and Economic Modernization in Two Indonesian Towns*, Chicago: University of Chicago Press.

Gelderen, J. van (1939), *The Recent Development of the Economic Foreign Policy of the Netherlands East Indies*, London: Longmans, Green and Co.

Gill, Indermit and Homi Kharas (2007), *An East Asian Renaissance: Ideas for Economic Growth*, Washington: World Bank.

Gillis, Malcolm (1988), 'Indonesia: public policies, resource management and the tropical forests' in Robert Repetto and Malcolm Gillis (Editors), *Public Policies and the Misuse of Forest Resources*, Cambridge: Cambridge University Press.

Glassburner, Bruce (1971) (Editor), *The Economy of Indonesia: Selected Readings*, Ithaca: Cornell University Press.

Govaars, Ming (2005), *Dutch Colonial Education: The Chinese Experience in Indonesia, 1900–42*, Singapore: Chinese Heritage Centre.

Grajdanzev, Andrew J. (1942), *Formosa Today: An Analysis of the Economic Development and Strategic Importance of Japan's Tropical Colony*, New York: Institute of Pacific Relations.

Grajdanzev, Andrew J. (1944), *Modern Korea*, New York: Institute of Pacific Relations.

Gray, Clive (1979), 'Civil Service Compensation in Indonesia', *Bulletin of Indonesian Economic Studies*, Vol 15 (1), pp. 85–113.

Grenville, Stephen (2004), 'The IMF and the Indonesia Crisis', *Bulletin of Indonesian Economic Studies*, Vol 40 (1), pp. 77–94.

Habir, Ahmad D. (1999), 'Conglomerates: All in the Family?', in Donald K. Emmerson (Editor), *Indonesia beyond Suharto*, Armonk: M.E. Sharpe.

Hadiz, Vedi and Richard Robison (2005), 'Neo-liberal Reforms and Illiberal Consolidations: The Indonesian Paradox', *Journal of Development Studies*, Vol 41(2), pp. 220–241.

Hadiz, Vedi and Richard Robison (2013), 'The Political Economy of Oligarchy and the Reorganization of Power in Indonesia', *Indonesia*, No 96, October, pp. 35–57.

Hardjono, J.M. (1977), *Transmigration in Indonesia*, Kuala Lumpur: Oxford University Press.

Havinga, Ivo, Gisele Kamanou and Vu Quang Viet (2010), 'A Note on the (Mis) Use of National Accounts for Estimation of Household Final Consumption Expenditures for Poverty Measures', in Sudhir Anand, Paul Segal and Joseph E. Stiglitz (Editors), *Debates on the Measurement of Global Poverty*, Oxford: Oxford University Press.

He, Wenkai (2013), *Paths towards the Modern Fiscal State: England, Japan and China*, Cambridge: Harvard University Press.

Henry, Yves (1926), 'Le Credit Populaire Agricole et Commercial aux Indes Neerlandaises', *Bulletin Economique de l'Indochine*, Vol 29, pp. 69–124.

Heston, Alan, Robert Summers and Bettina Aten (2012), *Penn World Tables Version 7.1*, Philadelphia: Center for International Comparisons of Production, Income and Prices at the University of Pennsylvania, November.

Higgins, Benjamin (1968), 'Indonesia: The Chronic Dropout', in *Economic Development: Principles, Problems and Policies*, London: Constable.

Hill, Hal (1996), *The Indonesian Economy since 1966*, Cambridge: Cambridge University Press.

Hirschman, Albert (1973), 'The Changing Tolerance for Income Inequality in the Course of Economic Development', *Quarterly Journal of Economics*, 87 (November 1973) reprinted in *Essays in Trespassing: Economics to Politics and Beyond*, Cambridge University Press 1981.

Hooley, Richard (2005), 'American Economic Policy in the Philippines, 1902–1940: Exploring a Dark Age in Colonial Statistics', *Journal of Asian Economics*, Vol 16, pp. 464–488.

Horowitz, Donald L. (2013), *Constitutional Change and Democracy in Indonesia*, Cambridge: Cambridge University Press.

Hugo, Graeme J. (1980), 'Population Movements in Indonesia during the Colonial Period', in James J. Fox Editor, *Indonesia: The Making of a Culture*, Canberra: Research School of Pacific Studies, Australian National University.

Hull, Terry and I. B. Mantra (1981), 'Indonesia's Changing Population', in Anne Booth and Peter McCawley (Editors), *The Indonesian Economy during the Soeharto Era*, Kuala Lumpur: Oxford University Press.

Hunter, Alex (1966a), 'The Indonesian Oil Industry', *Australian Economic Papers*, Vol 5(1), 59–106.

Hunter, Alex (1966b), 'Notes on Indonesian Population', *Bulletin of Indonesian Economic Studies*, No 4, pp. 36–49.

Husken, Frans and Benjamin White (1989), 'Java: Social Differentiation, Food Production and Agrarian Control', in Gillian Hart, Andrew Turton and Benjamin White (Editors), *Agrarian Transformations: Local Processes and the State in Southeast Asia*, Berkeley: University of California Press.

Hutasoit, M.(1954), 'Compulsory Education in Indonesia', *Studies in Compulsory Education XV*, Paris: UNESCO.

Ikhsan, M. (2005), 'Rice Price Adjustment and Its Impact to the Poor', *Economics and Finance in Indonesia*, Vol 53 (1), 61–98.

International Monetary Fund (2003), *The IMF and Recent Capital Account Crises: Indonesia, Korea, Brazil*, Washington: Independent Evaluation Office, International Monetary Fund.

James, William E. and Sherry M. Stephenson (2002), 'The Evolution of Economic Policy Reform: Determinants, Sequencing and Reasons for Success', in Farrukh Iqbal and William E. James (Editors), *Deregulation and Development in Indonesia*, Westport: Praeger, pp. 25–43.

Jones, Gavin W. (1966), 'The Growth and Changing Structure of the Indonesian Labour Force', *Bulletin of Indonesian Economic Studies*, No. 4, pp. 50–74.

Jong, Frida de and Wim Ravesteijn (2008), 'Technology and Administration', in Wim Ravesteijn and Jan Jop (Editors), *For Profit and Prosperity: The Contribution Made by Dutch Engineers to Public Works in Indonesia*, Leiden: KITLV Press.

Kahin, Audrey A. (2012), *Islam, Nationalism and Democracy: A Political Biography of Mohammad Natsir*, Singapore: NUS Press.

Kahin, George McTurnan (1952), *Nationalism and Revolution in Indonesia*, Ithaca: Cornell University Press.

Kahin, George McTurnan (1997), 'Some Recollections from and Reflections on the Indonesian Revolution', in Taufik Abdullah (Editor), *The Heartbeat of Indonesian Revolution*, Jakarta: PT Gramedia Pustaka Utama.

Kaufmann, Daniel, Aart Kraay and M. Mastruzzi (2006), *Governance Matters V; Aggregate and Individual Governance Indicators for 1996–2005*, Washington: World Bank.

Kenward, Lloyd R. (2004), 'Survey of Recent Developments', *Bulletin of Indonesian Economic Studies*, Vol 40 (1), pp. 9–35.

Kim, Nak Nyeon et al (2008), *Economic Growth in Korea 1910–1945* (Japanese translation), Tokyo: University of Tokyo Press.

King, Dwight Y. and Peter D. Weldon (1977), 'Income Distribution and Levels of Living in Java, 1963–1970', *Economic Development and Cultural Change*, Vol 25 (4), July, pp. 699–711.

Klinken, Gerry van (2007), *Communal Violence and Democratization in Indonesia: Small Town Wars*, Abingdon: Routledge.

Kurasawa, Aiko (2010), 'The Education of Pribumi', in Peter Post, William H. Fredericks, Iris Heidebrink and Shigeru Sato (Editors), *The Encyclopedia of Indonesia in the Pacific War*, Leiden: Brill.

Kuroyanagi, M. and Y. Hayakawa (1997), 'Macroeconomic Policy Management and Capital Movements in Four ASEAN Countries: Indonesia, Malaysia, the Philippines and Thailand', *EXIM Review*, Vol 17 (1), pp. 65–120.

Laanen, Jan van (1989), 'Per Capita Income Growth in Indonesia, 1850–1940', in Angus Maddison and Ge Prince (Editors), *Economic Growth in Indonesia, 1820–1940*, Dordrecht: Foris Publications.

Landes, David (1961), 'Some Thoughts on the Nature of Economic Imperialism', *Journal of Economic History*, Vol 21, pp. 496–512.

Landes, David S. (1998), *The Wealth and Poverty of Nations: Why Some Are So Rich and Some So Poor*, New York: W.W. Norton.

Langen, C.D. de (1934), 'The General State of Health of the Inhabitants', in Department of Economic Affairs, *Geld- en Producten-Huishouding, Volksvoeding en –Gezondheid in Koetowinangoen*, Buitenzorg: Archipel Drukkerij.

Lee, J. (2013), 'China's Economic Influence in Thailand: Perception or Reality', *ISEAS Perspective*, No 44, 11 July.

Legge, J.D. (1961), *Central Authority and Regional Autonomy in Indonesia: A Study of Local Administration, 1950–60*, Ithaca: Cornell University Press.

Legge, J.D. (2003), *Sukarno: A Political Biography*, Singapore: Archipelago Press.

Leigh, Andrew and Pierre van der Eng (2009), 'Inequality in Indonesia: What Can We Learn from Top Incomes?', *Journal of Public Economics*, Vol 93, pp. 209–12.

Lev, Dan (1996), 'Between State and Society: Professional Lawyers and Reform in Indonesia', in Daniel S. Lev and Ruth McVey (Editors), *Making Indonesia: Essays on Modern Indonesia in Honour of George McT. Kahin*, Ithaca: Cornell University Southeast Asia Programme.

Lewis, Blane (2014), 'Twelve Years of Fiscal Decentralization: A Balance Sheet', in Hal Hill (Editor), *Regional Dynamics in a Decentralized Indonesia*, Singapore: Institute of Southeast Asian Studies.

Lewis, Blane and Jasmin Chakeri (2004), 'Central Development Spending in the Regions Post-Decentralisation', *Bulletin of Indonesian Economic Studies*, Vol 40 (3), pp. 379–94.

Lewis, W. Arthur (1978), *Growth and Fluctuations 1870–1913*, London: George Allen and Unwin.

Lim, Linda Y.C. and Aaron Stern (2002), 'State Power and Private Profit: The Political Economy of Corruption in Southeast Asia', *Asian-Pacific Economic Literature*, Vol 16(2), pp. 18–52.

Lindblad, J. Thomas (1997), 'Survey of Recent Developments', *Bulletin of Indonesian Economic Studies*, Vol 33 (3), pp. 3–33.

Lindblad, J. Thomas (2002), 'The Outer Islands in the 19th Century: Contest for the Periphery', in Howard Dick, Vincent J.H. Houben, J. Thomas Lindblad and Thee Kian Wie, *The Emergence of a National Economy*, Sydney: Allen and Unwin.

Lindblad, J. Thomas (2008), *Bridges to New Business: The Economic Decolonization of Indonesia*, Leiden: KITLV Press.

Lindblad, J. Thomas (2010), 'Economic Growth and Decolonisation in Indonesia', *Itinerario*, Vol XXXIV (1), pp. 97–111.

Lipsey, Robert E. and Fredrik Sjoholm (2011), 'Foreign Direct Investment and Growth in East Asia: Lessons for Indonesia', *Bulletin of Indonesian Economic Studies*, Vol 47(1), pp. 35–63.

Lipton, Michael (1983), 'Poverty, Undernutrition and Hunger', *World Bank Staff Working Papers, Number 597*, Washington: World Bank.

Mackie, J.A.C. (1970), 'The Report of the Commission of Four on Corruption', *Bulletin of Indonesian Economic Studies*, Vol VI (3), pp. 87–101.

Mackie, J.A.C. (1971), 'The Indonesian Economy, 1950–1963', in Bruce Glassburner (Editor), *The Economy of Indonesia: Selected Readings*, Ithaca: Cornell University Press.

Mackie, J.A.C. (1980), 'Integrating and Centrifugal Factors in Indonesian Politics since 1945', in J.A.C. Mackie (Editor), *Indonesia: The Making of a Nation*, Canberra: Research School of Pacific Studies, Australian National University.

Mackie, Jamie (2005), 'How Many Chinese Indonesians', *Bulletin of Indonesian Economic Studies*, Vol 41 (1), pp. 97–101.

Maddison, Angus (2003), *The World Economy: Historical Statistics*, Paris: OECD Development Centre.

Mancini, Luca (2008), 'Horizontal Inequality and Communal Violence: Evidence from Indonesian Districts', in Frances Stewart (Editor), *Horizontal Inequalities and Conflict: Understanding Group Violence in Multiethnic Societies*, Basingstoke: Palgrave Macmillan, pp. 106–135.

Mangahas, Mahar (1982), 'What Happened to the Poor on the Way to the Next Development Plan?', *Philippine Economic Journal*, Vol XXI (3 and 4), pp. 126–146.

Mangahas, Mahar (1983), 'Measurement of Poverty and Equity: Some ASEAN Social Indicators Experience', *Social Indicators Research* Vol. 13, pp. 253–79.

Manning, Chris (2005), 'Legislating for Labour Protection: Betting on the Weak or the Strong?', *Economics and Finance in Indonesia*, Vol 53 (1), pp. 33–59.

Manning, Chris (2012), 'Indonesia's Turnabout in Employment and Unemployment in the 2000s: Progress or Not', in Anne Booth, Chris Manning and Thee Kian Wie (Editors), *Land Livelihood, the Economy and the Environment in Indonesia*, Jakarta: Yayasan Pustaka Obor Indonesia.

Manning, Chris (2014), 'Labour market regulation and employment during the Yudhoyono years in Indonesia', in Prema-Chandra Athukorala, A.R. Patunru and Budy P. Resosudarmo (Editors), *Trade, Development, and Political Economy in East Asia: Essays in Honour of Hal Hill*, Singapore: Institute of Southeast Asian Studies.

Manning, Chris and Kurnya Roesad (2006), 'Survey of Recent Developments', *Bulletin of Indonesian Economic Studies*, Vol 42 (2), August, pp. 141–70.

Manning, Chris and Kurnya Roesad (2007), 'The Manpower Law of 2003 and Its Implementing Regulations: Genesis, Key Articles and Potential Impact', *Bulletin of Indonesian Economic Studies*, Vol 43 (1), April, 59–86.

Marks, Stephen V. (2004), 'Survey of Recent Developments', *Bulletin of Indonesian Economic Studies*, Vol 40 (2), pp. 151–75.

Marks, Stephen V. (2009), 'Economic Policies of the Habibie Presidency: A Retrospective', *Bulletin of Indonesian Economic Studies*, Vol 45(1), pp. 39–60.

Marks, Stephen V. and Sjamsu Rahardja (2012), 'Effective Rates of Protection Revisited for Indonesia', *Bulletin of Indonesian Economic Studies*, Vol 48(1), pp. 57–84.

Matsumoko, Yasuyuki (2007), *Financial Fragility and Instability in Indonesia*, Abingdon: Routledge.

May, Brian (1978), *The Indonesian Tragedy*, London: Routledge and Kegan Paul.

McCawley, Peter (1978), 'Some Consequences of the Pertamina Crisis in Indonesia', *Journal of Southeast Asian Studies*, Vol IX (1), pp. 1–27.

McCawley, Peter (1980), 'Indonesia's New Balance of Payments Problem: A Surplus to Get Rid Of', *Ekonomi dan Keuangan Indonesia*, Vol 28 (1), pp. 39–58.

McCawley, Peter (1982), 'The Economics of Ekonomi Pancasila', *Bulletin of Indonesian Economic Studies*, Vol XVIII(1), pp. 102–09.

McCawley, Peter (2010a), 'Infrastructure Policy in Asian Developing Countries', *Asian-Pacific Economic Literature*, Vol 24(1), pp. 9–25.

McCawley, Peter (2010b), 'Infrastructure Policy in Indonesia: New Directions', *Journal of Indonesian Economy and Business*, Vol 25 (1), pp. 1–16.

McCawley, Peter (2013), 'The Indonesian Economy during the Soeharto Era: A Review', *Masyarakat Indonesia*, Vol 39 (2), pp. 269–288.

McCawley, Peter (2014), 'Rethinking the Role of the State in ASEAN', in Prema-Chandra Athukorala, A.R. Patunru and Budy P. Resosudarmo (Editors), *Trade, Development, and Political Economy in East Asia: Essays in Honour of Hal Hill*, Singapore: Institute of Southeast Asian Studies.

McCulloch, Neil (2008), 'Rice Prices and Poverty in Indonesia', *Bulletin of Indonesian Economic Studies*, Vol 44 (1), 45–63.

McDonald, Peter (2014), 'The Demography of Indonesia in Comparative Perspective', *Bulletin of Indonesian Economic Studies*, Vol 50 (1), pp. 29–52.

McLeod, Ross (2005), 'Survey of Recent Developments', *Bulletin of Indonesian Economic Studies*, Vol 41 (2), pp. 133–157.

McLeod, Ross (2008a), 'Survey of Recent Developments', *Bulletin of Indonesian Economic Studies*, Vol 44 (2), 183–208.

McLeod, Ross (2008b), 'Inadequate Budgets and Salaries as Instruments for Institutionalizing Public Sector Corruption in Indonesia', *South East Asia Research*, Vol 16 (2), pp. 199–223.

McMillan, Richard (2005), *The British Occupation of Indonesia, 1945–1946*, London: Routledge-Curzon.

McNicoll, Geoffrey and Masri Singarimbun (1983), *Fertility Decline in Indonesia: Analysis and Interpretation*, Washington: National Academy Press.

McVey, Ruth T. (1965), *The Rise of Indonesian Communism*, Ithaca: Cornell University Press.

Mears, Leon A. (1961), *Rice Marketing in the Republic of Indonesia*, Jakarta: Institute for Economic and Social Research, University of Indonesia.

Mears, Leon A. (1984), 'Rice and Food Self-Sufficiency in Indonesia', *Bulletin of Indonesian Economic Studies*, Vol 20 (2), pp. 122–38.

Mertens, Walter (1978), 'Population Census Data on Agricultural Activities in Indonesia', *Majalah Demografi Indonesia*, No 9, pp. 9–53.

Minujin, Alberto and Enrique Delamonica (2003), 'Mind the Gap! Widening Child Mortality Disparities', *Journal of Human Development*, Vol 4 (3), pp. 397–417.

Mortimer, Rex (1973), *Showcase State: The Illusion of Indonesia's Accelerated Development*, Sydney: Angus and Robertson.

Mortimer, Rex (1974), *Indonesian Communism under Soekarno: Ideology and Politics*, Ithaca: Cornell University Press.

Mortimer, Rex (1980), 'The Place of Communism', in J.A.C. Mackie (Editor), *Indonesia: The Making of a Nation*, Canberra: Research School of Pacific Studies, Australian National University.

Mubyarto and Boediono (1981), *Ekonomi Pancasila*, Yogyakarta: Faculty of Economics, Gadjah Mada University.

Mubyarto (2005), *A Development Manifesto: The Resilience of Indonesian Ekonomi Rakyat during the Monetary Crisis*, Jakarta: Penerbit Buku Kompas.

Muhaimin, Yahya A. (1982), *Indonesian Economic Policy, 1950–1980: The Politics of Client Businessmen*, PhD Dissertation, Massachusetts Institute of Technology.

Muzakar, Kahar (1960), 'Down with the New Madjapahitism', as translated and published in Herbert Feith and Lance Castles (Editors), *Indonesian Political Thinking: 1945–65*, Ithaca: Cornell University Press.

MYB (1941), *The Manchoukuo Year Book 1941*, Hsinking: The Manchoukuo Year Book Co.

Myint, Hla (1967), 'The Inward and Outward-looking Countries of Southeast Asia', *Malayan Economic Review*, Vol 12, pp. 1–13.

Napitupulu, B. (1968), 'Hunger in Indonesia', *Bulletin of Indonesian Economic Studies*, No 9, February, pp. 60–70.

National Academy of Sciences (2013), *Reducing Maternal and Neonatal Mortality in Indonesia: Saving Lives, Saving the Future*, Washington: The National Academies Press.

Natsir, Mohammad (1951), 'A Review of Indonesia's Reconstruction', *Indonesian Review*, Vol 1(1), pp. 49–59.

NEDA (1975), *The Philippine Food Balance Sheets, CY 1946 to CY 1974*, Manila: National Economic and Development Authority.

Nehru, Vikram (2013a), 'Survey of Recent Developments', *Bulletin of Indonesian Economic Studies*, Vol 49 (2), pp. 139–66.

Nehru, Vikram (2013b), 'Manufacturing in India and Indonesia: Performance and Policies', *Bulletin of Indonesian Economic Studies*, Vol 49 (1), pp. 35–60.

Niazi, Tariq H. (2012), 'Decentralization', in H. Hill, M.E. Khan and J. Zhuang (Editors), *Diagnosing the Indonesian Economy: Toward Inclusive and Green Growth*, London: Anthem Press for the Asian Development Bank.

Nicol, Bruce M. (1974), *Food and Nutrition in the Agricultural Development Plan for Indonesia*, Jakarta: FAO Planning Team.

Niel, Robert van (1956), *Living Conditions of Plantation Workers in 1939–40: Final Report of the Coolie Budget Commission*, Translation series, Modern Indonesia Project, Ithaca: Cornell University.

Niel, Robert van (1992), *Java under the Cultivation System*, Leiden: KITLV Press.

Nugroho (1967), *Indonesia: Facts and Figures*, Jakarta: Central Bureau of Statistics.

Ochse, J.J. and G.J.A. Terra (1934), 'The Function of Money and Products in Relation to Native Diet and Physical Condition in Koetowinangoen (Java)', in

Department of Economic Affairs, *Geld- en Producten-Huishouding, Volksvoeding en –Gezondheid in Koetowinangoen*, Buitenzorg: Archipel Drukkerij.

O'Malley, W.J. (1979), 'The Bengkalis Hunger Riots of 1935', in F. van Anrooij et al. (Editors), *Between People and Statistics: Essays on Modern Indonesian Economic History presented to P. Creutzberg*, The Hague: Martinus Nijhoff.

Paauw, Douglas S.(1960), *Financing Economic Development: The Indonesian Case*, Glencoe: Free Press.

Paauw, Douglas (1963), 'From Colonial to Guided Economy', in Ruth McVey (Editor), *Indonesia*, New Haven: HRAF Press.

Paauw, Douglas (1978), 'Exchange Rate Policy and Non-extractive Exports', *Ekonomi dan Keuangan Indonesia*, Vol. XXVI (2), pp. 205–20.

Palmer, Ingrid (1972), *Textiles in Indonesia: Problems of Import Substitution*, New York: Praeger.

Palmier, Leslie (1957), 'Occupational Distribution of Parents of Pupils in Certain Educational Institutions', *Indonesie*, vol 10, pp. 320–76.

Pangestu, Mari and Boediono (1986), 'Indonesia: The Structure and Causes of Manufacturing Sector Protection', in Christopher Findlay and Ross Garnaut (Editors), *The Political Economy of Manufacturing Protection: Experiences of ASEAN and Australia*, Sydney: Allen and Unwin.

Panglaykim, J. and H.W. Arndt (1966), 'Survey of Recent Developments', *Bulletin of Indonesian Economic Studies*, no 4, pp. 1–35.

Papanek, Gustav F.(1980), 'The Effects of Economic Growth and Inflation on Workers' Income', in G. Papanek (Editor), *The Indonesia Economy*, New York: Praeger.

Patten, R.H. and J.K. Rosengard (1991), *Progress with Profits: The Development of Rural Banking in Indonesia*, San Francisco: ICS Press for the International Center for Economic Growth.

Pelzer, Karl (1945), *Pioneer Settlement in the Asiatic Tropics*, New York: American Geographical Society.

Penders, C.L.M. (1977) (Editor and Translator), *Indonesia: Selected Documents on Colonialism and Nationalism 1830–1942*, St Lucia: University of Queensland Press.

Penders, C.L.M. (1984), *Bojonegoro 1900–1942: A Story of Endemic Poverty in North-East Java-Indonesia*, Singapore: Gunung Agung.

Penny, David and Masri Singarimbun (1973), '*Population and Poverty in Rural Java: Some Economic Arithmetic from Sriharjo*', *Cornell International Agricultural Development Mimeograph 41*, Ithaca: Department of Agricultural Economics, Cornell University.

Pincus, Jonathan and John Sender (2008), 'Quantifying Poverty in Vietnam: Who Counts?', *Journal of Vietnamese Studies*, Vol 3 (1), 108–150.

Pirard, Romain and Rofikoh Rokhim, (2005), 'Asia Pulp and Paper Indonesia: The Business Rationale That Led to Forest Degradation and Financial Collapse', *Working Paper 31*, Bogor: Center for International Forestry Research.

Pitt, Mark (1991), 'Indonesia', in A. Papageorgiou, M. Michaely and Armeane Choksi (Editors), *Liberalizing Foreign Trade, Volume 5: The Experience of Indonesia, Pakistan and Sri Lanka*, Cambridge: Basil Blackwell.

Pogge, Thomas (2010), 'How Many Poor People Should There Be? A Rejoinder to Ravallion', in Sudhir Anand, Paul Segal and Joseph E. Stiglitz (Editors), *Debates on the Measurement of Global Poverty*, Oxford: Oxford University Press.

Population Reference Bureau (2014), *2014 World Population Data Sheet* (Downloaded from www.prb.org).

Post, Laurens van der (1996), *The Admiral's Baby*, New York: William Morrow and Company.

Pradhan, Menno, Asep Suryahadi, Sudarno Sumarto and Lant Pritchett (2000), 'Measurements of Poverty in Indonesia: 1996, 1999 and Beyond', *Policy Research Working Paper 2438*, Washington: World Bank, September.

Priebe, Jan (2014), 'Official Poverty Trends in Indonesia since 1984: A Methodological Review', *Bulletin of Indonesian Economic Studies*, Vol 50 (2), pp. 185–205.

Pritchett, Lant, Sudarno Sumarto and Asep Suryahadi (2012), 'Targeted Programs in an Economic Crisis: Empirical Findings from Indonesia's Experience in 1998–1999 during the Asian Crisis', in Anne Booth, Chris Manning and Thee Kian Wie (Editors), *Land Livelihood, the Economy and the Environment in Indonesia*, Jakarta: Yayasan Pustaka Obor Indonesia.

Ramstetter, Eric (2000), 'Survey of Recent Developments', *Bulletin of Indonesian Economic Studies*, Vol 36 (3), pp. 3–45.

Ray, Rajat Kanta (1995), 'Asian Capital in the Age of European Domination: The Rise of the Bazaar, 1800–1914', *Modern Asian Studies*, Vol 29 (3), pp. 449–554.

Ravallion, Martin (2009), 'On the Welfarist Rationale for Relative Poverty Lines', in K. Basu and Ravi Kanbur (Editors), *Arguments for a Better World: Essays in Honour of Amartya Sen, Volume 1: Ethics, Welfare and Measurement*, Oxford: Oxford University Press.

Ravallion, Martin (2010), 'A Reply to Reddy and Pogge', in Sudhir Anand, Paul Segal and Joseph E. Stiglitz (Editors), *Debates on the Measurement of Global Poverty*, Oxford: Oxford University Press.

Ravallion, Martin and M. Lokshin (2005), 'Lasting Local Impacts of an Economy-wide Crisis', *World Bank Policy Research Working Paper 3503*, Washington: World Bank.

Reddy, Sanjay G. and Thomas Pogge (2010), 'How Not to Count the Poor', in Sudhir Anand, Paul Segal and Joseph E. Stiglitz (Editors), *Debates on the Measurement of Global Poverty*, Oxford: Oxford University Press.

Reid, Anthony (2010), *Imperial Alchemy: Nationalism and Political Identity in Southeast Asia*, Cambridge: Cambridge University Press.

Repetto, Robert and Malcolm Gillis (1988), *Public Policy and the Misuse of Forest Resources*, Cambridge: Cambridge University Press.

Resosudarmo, Budy P. and Ari Kuncoro (2006), 'The Political Economy of Indonesian Economic Reform: 1983–2000', *Oxford Development Studies*, 34(3), 341–55.

Resosudarmo, Budy P., Ani A. Nawir, Ida Aju P. Resosudarmo and Nina L. Subiman (2012), 'Forest Land Use Dynamics in Indonesia', in Anne Booth, Chris Manning and Thee Kian Wie (Editors), *Land Livelihood, the Economy and the Environment in Indonesia*, Jakarta: Yayasan Pustaka Obor Indonesia.

Ricklefs, Merle (2001), *A History of Modern Indonesia since c.1200*, (Third Edition), Basingstoke: Palgrave.

Rieffel, Lex and Jaleswari Pramodhawardani (2007), *Out of Business and on Budget: The Challenge of Military Financing in Indonesia*, Washington: Brookings Institution Press.

Robequain, Charles (1944), *The Economic Development of French Indochina*, London: Oxford University Press.

Robison, Richard (1986), *Indonesia: The Rise of Capital*, Sydney: Allen and Unwin.

Roepstorff, Torben M. (1985), 'Industrial Development in Indonesia: Performance and Prospects', *Bulletin of Indonesian Economic Studies*, Vol XXI (1), pp. 32–61.

Rokhim, Rofikoh (2005), *Ownership Concentration and Banking Fragility: Evidence from Indonesia 1991–2002*, Doctoral thesis, University of Paris I, Pantheon-Sorbonne.

Rosendale, Phyllis (1975), 'The Indonesian Terms of Trade, 1950–1973', *Bulletin of Indonesian Economic Studies*, Vol XI (3), pp. 57–80.

Rosengard, Jay K., Richard H. Patten, Don E. Johnston Jr. and Widjojo Koesoemo (2007), 'The Promise and Peril of Microfinance Institutions', *Bulletin of Indonesian Economic Studies*, Vol 43 (1), pp. 87–112.

Sadli, Mohamad (2003), 'Recollections of My Career', in Thee Kian Wie (Editor), *Recollections: The Indonesian Economy, 1950s-1990s*, Singapore: Institute of Southeast Asian Studies.

Sajogyo (1975), *Usaha Perbaikan Gizi Keluarga: ANP Evaluation Study 1973*, Bogor: Lembaga Penelitian Sosiologi Pedesaan, Institut Pertanian Bogor.

Sari, Yulia Indrawati and Nurul Widyaningrum (2012), 'Community-driven Development and Empowerment of the Poor in Indonesia', in Anne Booth, Chris Manning and Thee Kian Wie (Editors), *Land Livelihood, the Economy and the Environment in Indonesia*, Jakarta: Yayasan Pustaka Obor Indonesia.

Sato, Masahiro et al. (2008), *Asian Historical Statistics: Taiwan*, Tokyo: Toyo Keizai Inc.

Sato, Shigeru (2010), 'Economic Life in Villages and Towns', in Peter Post, William H. Fredericks, Iris Heidebrink and Shigeru Sato (Editors), *The Encyclopedia of Indonesia in the Pacific War*, Leiden: Brill.

Sato, Yuri (2004), 'Corporate Governance in Indonesia: A Study on Governance of Business Groups', in Y. Shimomura (Editor), *Asian Development Experience Volume 2: The Role of Governance in Asia*, Singapore: Institute of Southeast Asian Studies.

Sato, Yuri (2005), 'Bank Restructuring and Financial Institution Reform in Indonesia', *The Developing Economies*, Vol XLIII (1), pp. 91–120.

Schwarz, Adam (1999), *A Nation in Waiting: Indonesia's Search for Stability*, Sydney: Allen and Unwin.

Schwulst, E.B. (1932), 'Report on the Budget and Financial Policies of French Indochina, Siam, Federated Malay States and the Netherlands East Indies', in Report of the Governor General of the Philippine Islands 1931, Washington: United States Government Printing Office.

Sheng, Andrew (2009), *From Asian to Global Financial Crisis*, Cambridge: Cambridge University Press.

Shepherd, Jack (1941), *Industry in Southeast Asia*, New York: Institute of Pacific Relations.

Silver, Christopher, Iwan Jaya Azis and Larry Schroeder (2001), 'Intergovernmental Transfers and Decentralisation in Indonesia', *Bulletin of Indonesian Economic Studies*, Vol 37 (3), pp. 345–62.

Sivasubramonian, Siva (2002), 'Twentieth Century Economic Performance of India', in Angus Maddison, D.S. Prasada Rao and William F. Shepherd (Editors), *The Asian Economies in the Twentieth Century*, Cheltenham: Edward Elgar.

Sjafruddin Prawiranegara (2003), 'Recollections of My Career', in Thee Kian Wie (Editor), *Recollections: the Indonesian Economy, 1950s-1990s*, Singapore: Institute of Southeast Asian Studies.

Sjoholm, Fredrik (2015), 'Foreign Direct Investment in Southeast Asia', in Ian Coxhead (Editor), *Routledge Handbook of Southeast Asian Economics*, Abingdon: Routledge.

Skoufias, Emmanuel, Asep Suryahadi and Sudarno Sumarto (2000), 'Changes in Household Welfare, Poverty and Inequality during the Crisis', *Bulletin of Indonesian Economic Studies*, Vol. 36(2), pp. 97–114.

Soesastro, Hadi and R. Atje (2005), 'Survey of Recent Developments', *Bulletin of Indonesian Economic Studies*, Vol 41(1), pp. 5–34.

Sompop Manarungsan (1989), *Economic Development of Thailand, 1850–1950*, PhD Dissertation, State University of Groningen.

Strauss, John et al. (2004), *Indonesian Living Standards: Before and after the Financial Crisis*, Singapore: Institute of Southeast Asian Studies.

Studwell, Joe (2007), *Asian Godfathers: Money and Power in Hong Kong and Southeast Asia*, London: Profile Books.

Suehiro, Akira (2001), 'Family Business Gone Wrong? Ownership Patterns and Corporate Performance in Thailand', *ADB Institute Working Paper, 19*, Tokyo: ADB Institute, 2001.

Sugimoto, Ichiro (2011), *Economic Growth of Singapore in the Twentieth Century: Historical GDP Estimates and Empirical Investigations*, Singapore: World Scientific.

Sukarno (1963), 'The Economics of a Nation in Revolution', as translated and published in Herbert Feith and Lance Castles (Editors), *Indonesian Political Thinking: 1945–65*, Ithaca: Cornell University Press.

Suleman, Areef and Zafar Iqbal (2012), 'Infrastructure Development: Challenges and the Way Forward', in H. Hill, M.E. Khan and J. Zhuang (Editors), *Diagnosing the Indonesian Economy: Toward Inclusive and Green Growth*, London: Anthem Press for the Asian Development Bank.

Sumarto, Sudarno, Marc Vothknecht, and Laura Widjaya (2014), 'Explaining Regional Heterogeneity of Poverty: Evidence from a Decentralized Indonesia', in Hal Hill (Editor), *Regional Dynamics in a Decentralized Indonesia*, Singapore: Institute of Southeast Asian Studies.

Sumitro Djojohadikusomo (2003), 'Recollections of My Career', in Thee Kian Wie (Editor), *Recollections: The Indonesian Economy, 1950s-1990s*, Singapore: Institute of Southeast Asian Studies.

Sundrum, R.M. (1973), 'Money Supply and Prices: a Reinterpretation', *Bulletin of Indonesian Economic Studies*, Vol. 9(3), pp. 73–86.

Sundrum, R.M. (1986), 'Indonesia's Rapid Growth, 1968–1981', *Bulletin of Indonesian Economic Studies*, Vol 22 (3), pp. 40–69.

Sundrum, R.M. and Anne Booth (1980), 'Income Distribution in Indonesia: Trends and Determinants', in R.G. Garnaut and P.T. McCawley (Editors), *Indonesia: Dualism, Growth and Poverty*, Canberra: Research School of Pacific Studies, Australian National University.

Suryahadi, Asep, Gracia Hadiwidjaja and Sudarno Sumarto (2012), 'Economic Growth and Poverty Reduction in Indonesia before and after the Asian Financial Crisis', *Bulletin of Indonesian Economic Studies*, Vol 48 (2), pp. 209–27.

Suryahadi, Asep and Sudarno Sumarto (2010), 'Poverty and Vulnerability in Indonesia before and after the Economic Crisis', in Joan Hardjono, Nuning Akhmadi and Sudarno Sumarto (Editors), *Poverty and Social Protection in Indonesia*, Singapore: Institute of Southeast Asian Studies, and Jakarta: SMERU Research Institute.

Suryahadi, Asep, Sudarno Sumarto and Lant Pritchett (2003), 'Evolution of Poverty during the Crisis in Indonesia', *Asian Economic Journal*, Vol 17(3), pp. 221–41.

Suryahadi, Asep, Athia Yumna, Umbu Reku Raya and Deswanto Marbun (2012), 'Poverty Reduction: The Track Record and Way Forward', in H. Hill, M.E. Khan and J. Zhuang (Editors), *Diagnosing the Indonesian Economy: Toward Inclusive and Green Growth*, London: Anthem Press for the Asian Development Bank.

Tadjoeddin, Mohammad Zulfan (2014), *Explaining Collective Violence in Contemporary Indonesia: From Conflict to Cooperation*, Basingstoke: Palgrave Macmillan.

Thee, Kian-Wie (1991), 'The Surge of Asian NIC Investment into Indonesia', *Bulletin of Indonesian Economic Studies*, Vol 27 (3), pp. 55–88.

Thee, Kian-Wie (2010), 'The Debate on Economic Policy in Newly-independent Indonesia between Sjafruddin Prawiranegara and Sumitro Djojohadikusomo', *Itinerario*, Vol XXXIV (1), pp. 35–56.

Thee, Kian-Wie (2012), 'Indonesianization: Economic Aspects of Decolonization in the 1950s', in *Indonesia's Economy since Independence*, Singapore: Institute of Southeast Asian Studies.

Thomas, Martin (2005), *The French Empire between the Wars: Imperialism, Politics and Society*, Manchester: Manchester University Press.

Thomas, Duncan, Kathleen Beegle, Elizabeth Frankenberg, Bondon Koki, John Strauss and Graciela Teruel (2004), 'Education in a Crisis', *Journal of Development Economics*, Vol 74, pp. 53–85.

Thomas, K.D. and Jusuf Panglaykim (1976), 'The Chinese in the South Sumatran Rubber Industry: A Case Study in Economic Nationalism', in J.A.C. Mackie (Editor), *The Chinese in Indonesia: Five Essays*, Hong Kong: Heinemann Educational Books (Asia) Ltd.

Timmer, C. Peter (2015), 'The dynamics of agricultural development and food security in Southeast Asia: historical continuity and rapid change', in Ian Coxhead (Editor), *Routledge Handbook of Southeast Asian Economics*, Abingdon: Routledge.

Twang, Peck Yang (1998), *The Chinese Business Elite in Indonesia and the Transition to Independence, 1940–1950*, Kuala Lumpur: Oxford University Press.

UNCTAD (2013), *World Investment Report: 2013*, New York and Geneva: United Nations Conference on Trade and Development.

UNDP (2003), *Human Development Report 2003*, New York: Oxford University Press.

UNDP (2010), *Human Development Report 2010: The Real Wealth of Nations: Pathways to Human Development*, Basingstoke: Palgrave Macmillan.

Vaidyanathan, A. (1983), 'The Indian Economy since Independence (1947–1970)', in D. Kumar and M. Desai (Editors), *The Cambridge Economic History of India, Vol 2, c. 1750–c1970*, Cambridge: Cambridge University Press.

Veur, Paul van der (1969), 'Education and Social Change in Colonial Indonesia (1)', *Papers in International Studies, Southeast Asia Series No 12*, Athens: Ohio University Center for International Studies.

Vries, E de (1949), 'Problems of Agriculture in Indonesia', *Pacific Affairs*, Vol 22, pp. 130–143.

Vries, Jan de (2008), *The Industrious Revolution: Consumer Behaviour and the Household Economy, 1650 to the Present*. Cambridge: Cambridge University Press.

Wal, S. van der (1961), *Some Information on Education in Indonesia up to 1942*, Amsterdam: Netherlands Universities Foundation for International Cooperation.

Warr, Peter G. (1984), 'Exchange Rate Protection in Indonesia', *Bulletin of Indonesian Economic Studies*, Vol 20 (2), pp. 53–89.

Warr, Peter (1992), 'Exchange Rate Policy, Petroleum Prices, and the Balance of Payments', in Anne Booth (Editor), *The Oil Boom and after: Indonesian Economic Policy and Performance in the Soeharto Era*, Singapore: Oxford University Press.

Weinreb, F. and Madjid Ibrahim (1957), 'Penjelidikan Biaja Hidup di Djakarta', *Ekonomi dan Keuangan di Indonesia*, Vol X, pp. 73–95.

Weinstein, Franklin B. (1976), *Indonesia's Foreign Policy and the Dilemma of Dependence: From Sukarno to Soeharto*, Ithaca: Cornell University Press.

Wells, Louis T. (2007), 'Private Power in Indonesia', *Bulletin of Indonesian Economic Studies*, Vol 43(3), pp. 341–363.

Wells, Louis T. and Rafiq Ahmed (2007), *Making Foreign Investment Safe: Property Rights and National Sovereignity*, New York: Oxford University Press.

Wertheim, W.F. (1956), *Indonesian Society in Transition: A Study of Social Change (Second Edition)*, Bandung: Sumur Bandung.

Wertheim, W.F. (1964), 'Betting on the Strong', in *East-West Parallels: Sociological Approaches to Modern Asia*, The Hague: W. van Hoeve.

White, Ben (1973), 'Demand for Labour and Population Growth in Colonial Java', *Human Ecology*, Vol 1 (3), pp. 217–36.

Wicke, Birka, Richard Sikkema, Veronika Domburg and Andre Faaij (2011), 'Exploring Land Use Changes and the Role of Palm Oil Production in Indonesia and Malaysia', *Land Use Policy*, Vol 28 (1), pp. 193–206.

Wicke, Birka, Richard Sikkema, Veronika Domburg, Martin Junginger and Andre Faaij (2008), *Drivers of Land Use Change and the Role of Palm Oil*

Production in Indonesia and Malaysia: Final Report, Utrecht: Copernicus Institute, Science, Technology and Society Group, Utrecht University.

Widjojo Nitisastro (1955), 'Raising Per Capita Income', as translated and published in Herbert Feith and Lance Castles (Editors), *Indonesian Political Thinking: 1945–1965*, Ithaca: Cornell University Press, pp. 382–85.

Widjojo Nitisastro (Editor) (1956), 'Some Data on the Population of Djabres: A Village in Central Java', *Ekonomi dan Keuangan Indonesia*, Vol IX (12), pp. 759–84.

Widjojo Nitisastro (1970), *Population Trends in Indonesia*, Ithaca: Cornell University Press.

Widyahartono, Bob (1993), 'Konglomerat: Antara Teori dan Realita', in Kwik Kian Gie et al., *Konglomerat Indonesia*, Jakarta: Pustaka Sinar Harapan.

Williams, Lea (1952), 'Chinese Entrepreneurs in Indonesia', *Explorations in Entrepreneurial History*, Vol 5(1), pp. 34–60.

Williamson, Jeffrey G. (2011), *Trade and Poverty: When the Third World Fell Behind*, Cambridge: The MIT Press.

Williamson, John (2004), 'The Years of Emerging Market Crises: A Review of Feldstein', *Journal of Economic Literature*, Vol XLII, September, pp. 822–37.

Wilopo (1955), 'The Principle of the Family Relationship', as translated and published in Herbert Feith and Lance Castles (Editors), *Indonesian Political Thinking: 1945–65*, Ithaca: Cornell University Press, pp. 379–81.

Winters, Jeffrey A. (1996), *Power in Motion: Capital Mobility and the Indonesian State*, Ithaca: Cornell University Press.

World Bank (1980), *Indonesia: Employment and Income Distribution in Indonesia: A World Bank Country Study*, Washington: World Bank.

World Bank (1987), *World Tables, 1987: The Fourth Edition*, Washington: The World Bank.

World Bank (1990), *Indonesia: Foundations for Sustained Growth: Report No. 8455-IND*, Washington: World Bank.

World Bank (1993), *The East Asian Miracle*, Washington: World Bank.

World Bank (1997), *Indonesia: Sustaining High Growth with Equity (Report No. 16433-IND)*, Washington: The World Bank, May 30.

World Bank (1998), *Indonesia in Crisis: A Macroeconomic Update*, Washington: The World Bank, July 16.

World Bank (2001), *Indonesia: Environment and Natural Resource Management*, Washington: World Bank.

World Bank (2006), *Making the New Indonesia Work for the Poor*, Washington: World Bank November.

World Bank (2012), *Indonesia Economic Quarterly: Rising to present and future challenges*, Washington: World Bank.

World Bank (2014), *Indonesia: Avoiding the Trap*, Jakarta: World Bank Office.

World Trade Organization (2011), *Trade Patterns and Global Value Chains in East Asia: From Trade in Goods to Trade in Tasks*, Geneva: World Trade Organization Secretariat.

Yoshida, M., I. Akimune, M. Nohara and K. Sato (1994), 'Regional Economic Integration in East Asia: Special Features and Policy Implications', in Vincent Cable and David Henderson (Editors), *Trade Blocs? The Future of Regional Integration*, London: London Royal Institute of International Affairs.

Yudhoyono, Susilo Bambang (2003), *Revitalizing Indonesian Economy: Business, Politics and Good Governance*, Jakarta: Brighten Press.
Yudhoyono, Susilo Bambang (2004), *Indonesia 2004–2009: Vision for Change*, Jakarta: Brighten Press.
Yudhoyono, Susilo Bambang and Harniati (2004), *Pengurangan Kemiskinan di Indonesia*, Jakarta: Brighten Press.
Yusuf, Arief Anshory, Andy Sumner and Irlan Adiyatma Rum (2014), 'Twenty Years of Expenditure Inequality in Indonesia', *Bulletin of Indonesian Economic Studies*, Vol 50 (2), pp. 243–54.
Zanden, Jan Luiten van (2010), 'Colonial State Formation and Patterns of Economic Development in Java, 1800–1913', *Economic History of Developing Regions*, Vol 25 (2), pp. 155–76.
Zanden, Jan Luiten van and Daan Marks (2012), *An Economic History of Indonesia, 1800–2010*, Abingdon: Routledge.
Zanden, Jan Luiten van and Arthur van Riel (2004), *The Strictures of Inheritance: The Dutch Economy in the Nineteenth Century*, Princeton and Oxford: Princeton University Press.

Index